VALLEY OF
THE SPIRITS

VALLEY OF

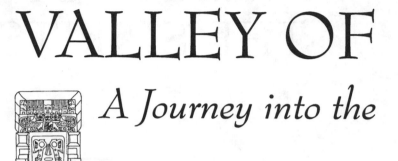

A Journey into the

THE SPIRITS

Lost Realm of the Aymara

Alan L. Kolata

John Wiley & Sons, Inc.
New York • Chichester • Brisbane • Toronto • Singapore

This text is printed on acid-free paper.

Copyright © 1996 by Alan Kolata.
Published by John Wiley & Sons, Inc.

Library of Congress Cataloging-in-Publication Data
Kolata, Alan L.
    Valley of the spirits: a journey into the lost realm of the Aymara /
Alan L. Kolata.
        p.   cm.
    Includes bibliographical references and index.
    ISBN 0-471-57507-0 (cloth : alk. paper)
    1. Aymara Indians.   2. Tiwanaku culture.   3. Aymara Indians—
Religion.   I. Title.
F2230.2.A9K65   1996
984'.004983—dc20   95-20746

Printed in the United States of America

10 9 8 7 6 5 4 3 2 1

For my daughter Justine

I met a traveler from an antique land
Who said: Two vast and trunkless legs of stone
Stand in the desert. Near them, on the sand,
Half sunk, a shattered visage lies, whose frown,
And wrinkled lip, and sneer of cold command,
Tell that its sculptor well those passions read . . .
—*"Ozymandias," Percy Bysshe Shelley (1792–1822)*

Contents

Preface

THIS book is about a people known as the Aymara who live along the shores of Lake Titicaca in Bolivia and Peru. The Aymara are an ancient people with a complex and still imperfectly understood history. They are a people rich in myth, knowledge, and spirituality. For the Aymara, the spectacular, awe-inspiring land that they inhabit is alive with vitalizing energy. Mountains are their ancestors, water is their life's blood, and the land they cultivate is infused with spirits.

Nearly twenty years ago, through a serendipitous twist of fate, I journeyed to the land of the Aymara to recapture the world of their ancestors. The Aymara were the authors of a great but little-known culture of the Americas centered in the ancient city of Tiahuanaco. Between A.D. 400 and 1000, Tiahuanaco was the capital of an empire that spanned great parts of the south-central Andes. Only the Inca empire, some five hundred years later, eclipsed Tiahuanaco in size and social complexity. Although my research began as an effort to explore this ancient world, through time I found myself increasingly enmeshed in the lives of Tiahuanaco's modern descendants. This book tells both parts of that tale: here the Aymara's past and present are interwoven and together they offer us glimpses of their future.

All of the information on the Aymara's past presented in this book is the product of a long-term, interdisciplinary research project—a project that continues as I write these words. Some of the reconstruction of the Aymara past described here will change as the research expands and evolves in new directions. But that is what makes this enterprise of writing the history of a people who have been denied their own history so compelling.

I wish to acknowledge the institutions, agencies, corporations and individuals who underwrote, and continue to underwrite, this multi-institutional research program. In Bolivia, the archaeological and paleoecological research is authorized and conducted under the auspices of the Instituto Nacional de Arqueología de Bolivia (INAR), currently under the Secretaría Nacional de Cultura directed by Minister Alberto Bailey Gutierrez. Over the past eighteen years, my research has been authorized through agreements signed by three separate Directors of INAR: Carlos Ponce Sanjinés, Carlos Urquizo Sossa, and Oswaldo Rivera Sundt. I thank each of them for their personal commitment to the project. Our research has been generously supported by grants from the National Science Foundation (BNS-8607541, BNS-8805490, DEB-9212641); the National Endowment for the Humanities (RO-21806-88, RO-21368-86); the Inter-American Foundation (BO-252, BO-273, BO-374, BO374a); the UNESCO/Man and the Biosphere Program (1753-000566); the National Oceanic and Atmospheric Administration (GC-95-174); the H. John Heinz III Charitable Fund of the Heinz Family Foundation; the Pittsburgh Foundation; the Office of Social Science Research and the Campus Research Board of the University of Illinois at Chicago; the Division of Social Sciences of the University of Chicago; Tesoro Petroleum Corporation, San Antonio, Texas; Compañía Minera del Sur, La Paz, Bolivia; and the Occidental Petroleum Corporation, Los Angeles, California.

Additionally, I wish to acknowledge and specifically thank

several individuals who worked intensively with me to identify and secure funding for the research. These include Ambassador Robert S. Gelbard; Kevin Healy of the Inter-American Foundation; and, in particular, Dr. Robert V. West Jr., former chairman and CEO of Tesoro Petroleum Corporation, who has supported the project financially from its inception in 1978. I wish also to acknowledge the staunch support of Connie Thrasher Jaquith of Louisville, Kentucky, who each year contributes generously to the work of the project.

Over the past two decades of my research career in Peru and Bolivia I have incurred many debts, both personal and professional. I cannot possibly acknowledge all of the individuals and scholars who have contributed to my professional and personal development in distinctive ways: through providing formal academic training, through sharing field experiences, through intense discussions, and, occasionally, through heated debate. They have, in different degrees, enriched my life. In this group, though, I owe a special debt of gratitude to Michael Moseley, my former academic adviser at Harvard University, who provided me my first opportunity to travel to the land of the Aymara.

I wish to specifically acknowledge here my principal collaborators and senior colleagues in the research in Bolivia: Michael Binford, Mark Brenner, Charles Ortloff, and Oswaldo Rivera. Michael Binford has been the coprincipal investigator on the research project since 1986, and he, along with Mark Brenner and Charles Ortloff, have contributed inestimably to the intellectual excitement and personal pleasure of doing scientific research in the Lake Titicaca basin and beyond. After sharing a decade of intense, difficult, and rewarding work, we continue to conduct research as a team. I owe a special and continuing debt of gratitude to Oswaldo Rivera, currently Director of the National Institute of Archaeology, La Paz, Bolivia. Oswaldo is the codirector of the project and has collaborated closely with me in conceptualizing and organizing the research efforts in Bolivia since I first arrived in 1978. Oswaldo is both my research collaborator and my *compadre:* I value both roles highly, but the latter is the most important to me. Many other scholars in Bolivia and the United States, including a remarkable cohort of current and former graduate students at the University of Chicago, have participated in the project. I acknowledge and thank them collectively for their key contributions to the conduct of fieldwork on the project.

Speaking on behalf of all the participants in our research project, our most profound social debt is to the many Aymara with whom we have worked. This book is about their history and their culture, and possibly about their future as well. Without their active collaboration and their intense interest in their own cultural heritage, the work which informs this book could never have been accomplished. The number of individuals involved in the work of the project is, quite literally, in the hundreds, and I cannot acknowledge each of them by name here. But the people of the villages of Tiahuanaco, Lukurmata, Chojasivi, Lakaya, Lillimani, Quiripujo, Chokara, Korila, Wacullani, Khonko Wankané, Chambi Grande, Chambi Chico, Wankollo, Huaraya, Achuta Grande, Kasa Achuta, Pillapi, Guaqui, Yanarico, Patarani, Andamarca, Yanamani, Pircuta, Qorpa, Sullcata, Kusijata, and Copajira are involved, to various degrees, in the work and life of the research. I thank them all.

In Tiahuanaco itself, the Associación de Trabajadores en Arqueología de Tiahuanaco provided the highly skilled workers who participated in all aspects of the research. They are truly extraordinary people. While in Tiahuanaco, the supervisor of the ruins of Tiahuanaco, Cesar Callisaya, my closest Aymara friend, collaborator, and *compadre,* opens his house to me and the entire research team. The generosity of his family cannot go unremarked in any book based on the research of the project. Cesar's knowledge of Aymara communities and his exceptional diplomatic skills have permitted the project to complete its ambitious agenda of research even under the most difficult of political circumstances. He, along with Oswaldo Rivera, are the two individuals most responsible for the success of our joint project to recapture and remobilize the knowledge of the ancients for the benefit of their descendants.

Although they did not request anonymity, the names of all Aymara people specifically described in this book have been altered to protect their privacy. There are two exceptions to this: Cesar Callisaya and Cosme Uruchi. True to his heritage as a warrior, Cosme insisted that, if I ever wrote any account that involved him, I would use only his true name. I honor that request here.

With regard to the publication of this book, I want to extend my appreciation first to my agent, Bert Holtje of James Peter Associates. Glancing through the *Los Angeles Times*, Bert noticed a report on my research in Bolivia. He had the vision to imagine this book, and the insistent faith to see it through to reality. At John Wiley & Sons, I want to acknowledge my editor, Emily Loose, who inherited this book, but still embraced it wholeheartedly. Her tough but sensitive editing immensely improved the flow of the manuscript, even if some dearly beloved passages were left behind on the cutting floor. I thank also Lisbeth Cobas, Emily's assistant, and Nana Prior, who managed production.

Chapters 3–5 of this book are based on my previous book, *The Tiwanaku: Portrait of an Andean Civilization* (Oxford, U.K., and Cambridge, Mass.: Basil Blackwell, 1993). Readers desiring more detailed descriptions and interpretations of Tiahuanaco's natural and social worlds may wish to read that book. Similarly, readers, particularly those with technical training and inclinations, interested in the results of the research on which much of this book is based may wish to consult my *Tiwanaku and Its Hinterland: Archaeological and Paleoecological Investigations of an Andean Civilization, Volume 1: Agroecology* (Washington, D.C.: Smithsonian Institution Press, 1996). This is a multiple-authored work of our entire research team that represents the state of the art in our investigations into the Aymara past.

Finally, I want to acknowledge my wife, Anna, and my daughter, Justine, who tolerated endless, difficult separations and, at times, endured the rigors of the Bolivian high plateau while the research described in this book was in progress. Their love sustains me.

Alan L. Kolata
Chicago, October 1995

1

Into the Aymara World

A T dawn on an intensely cold, brilliantly clear day in early October 1992, the Aymara Indians of Bolivia reclaimed their past. I glanced out the window of my adobe house as two snaking lines of Indian men and women began to climb the massive remains of a ceremonial pyramid in the ancient town of Tiahuanaco. Grabbing my down jacket and wool stocking cap, I rushed to the pyramid's base to accompany them as a witness in this ceremony of cultural resistance and revival.

The Indians ascended the seven eroded tiers of the stone-faced temple in pairs, male and female in symmetrical counterpoise. The procession was alive with the chatter of morning greetings among close kinsmen. The men wore bloodred ponchos of fine llama wool adorned with intricately woven, multicolored belts and sashes. Across their belts, images of rampaging, sword-wielding soldiers on horseback rode into silent battle. Underneath this eye-arresting regalia, the men wore simple, cuffless pants of cream-colored wool and rubber sandals cut casually from derelict automobile tires. A cluster of men at the head of the line carried staves of dark, burnished wood cut from the cloud forests on the wild, eastern slopes of the Andes Mountains many generations before. Each staff was capped with ornamental silver finials.

Silver was the prize that inspired unbridled lust in the Europeans who conquered the Andean world in the sixteenth century. The frenzy for veins of silver from the majestic Andes destroyed entire nations of Indians. After decades of warfare, pestilence and famine, the ravaged native populations were subjugated into slave labor in the hellish mines of Potosí in southern Bolivia. Desperate for laborers to work the fabulously rich deposits, Spanish overlords laid claim to the traditional laborers, the *mit'a,* that the Indian nations rendered to their native monarchs. More than one-seventh of the native population between Cuzco in southern Peru and Tarija in southern Bolivia were pressed into service in the mines of Potosí. Conditions in the mines were bestial. Even the Spanish dogs of war were treated with more compassion than the native conscripts who died in unremembered numbers. An eyewitness account conveys the horror with terrible eloquence:

> When the time came for the conscripts to leave for the mines, chained Indians with iron collars around their necks were to be seen everywhere. Women and children accompanied the miserable lines of exiles, with cries and moans, pulling out their hair and singing in their own language songs of death and sad laments. The local chiefs were beaten and tortured if they failed to supply the labor demanded. Once an Indian returned from the mines to find his wife dead and his children abandoned. His chief forced him into a gang leaving for the hell of Potosí. The *curaca* [native chief] answered the wretched man's pleading, saying, "If I do not complete my quota with you, the Spanish will burn me, whip me and drink my blood." Desperate, the man hanged his two children, "so that they may never serve in the mines," and then cut his own throat with a knife.[1]

The miners labored in narrow, twisting, claustrophobic galleries driven deep into the dark heart of Potosí's Cerro Rico, the Rich Mountain. The silver ore was processed with mercury and if a miner managed to survive his turn of service in the mines, he succumbed, in time, to the insidious effects of mercury poisoning. Slowly, fingers, arms, legs, and tongue failed as the body's neurological system shut down.

For decades, the Spanish Crown bankrolled its military adventures in Europe from the seemingly endless stream of silver that flowed from the veins of Cerro Rico. Potosí became the envy of the Spanish colonial world, a shining, white city high in the barren Bolivian plateau. Soaring churches and basilicas appointed with magnificent silver altars and elaborately carved pulpits graced the city. Colonial officials lived in high style behind the massive walls of their palaces. But the transplanted glitter of Spanish style could not obscure vast, desolate encampments of Indian slaves at the edges of the city's opulence.

The Spanish were not the first to covet Cerro Rico's treasure. The native curacas, too, had mined the mountain. Silver and gold were cherished sources of social wealth to the ancients. Fashioned into crowns, fixed in shining plates to sedan chairs and litters, crafted into libation cups and serving platters, these metals served as powerful symbols of the native chieftains' status and authority. The curacas, too, extracted mit'a labor to support their ambitions.

The silver finials on the staves of the Aymara men ascending the great temple that morning in October were symbols of an ancient system of power. The staffs are emblems of authority, symbols of each man's right to represent his community. The men at the head of the line that morning were the *jilakata* of their communities, the supreme political and ritual officers who guide the Aymara both in the rounds of their daily lives and in their relations with outsiders.

The Aymara women were also adorned that day in the

colors of festival—vermilion and green against the sere, yellowed landscapes. Some wore as many as eight *polleras*, traditional skirts of wool, layered one upon the other like swirling tents about their hips. Their richly embroidered satin blouses reflected the bright light with a milky sheen. On their heads they sported black bowler hats, adapted to local Indian tastes from nineteenth-century European fashion. Many of the women carried infants on their backs. The children were swaddled tightly in cloth and wrapped in a colorful blanket called an *awayo*, worn slung over the shoulders and tied at the chest.

When the procession reached the summit, the people formed two huge circles: the men clustered in the middle surrounded by an outer ring of women. All at once, the group fell silent. Then Tito Flores began to speak. Flores was the highest-ranking political leader of the province of Ingavi, which incorporated the Valley of Tiahuanaco and beyond. He had come to the town of Tiahuanaco that morning to help plant the symbol of Aymara liberation and independence on the summit of the ancient temple. He carried a flag, known as the *whipala*, an enormous rectangle of glossy fabric composed of many smaller, blocks of vivid colors: reds, blues, yellows, and greens. The whipala is an emblem of the Aymara's collective identity, a symbol of their political and cultural autonomy from the Europeanized Bolivian society that surrounds them. In October of 1992—the Columbus Quincentenary and a year of remembrance, grief, and collective action for Native Americans throughout the hemisphere—the whipala was everywhere in the high plateaus of Bolivia and Peru.

Flores spoke with great conviction and passion flickering in his eyes. He made no passionate gestures, no demonstrative flourishes. His body remained virtually motionless, hands in perfect repose at his sides. He seemed rooted in place, implacable.

"Mama-naka, tata-naka, hermanos," he began. "You all

know why we are gathered here in Tiahuanaco. You all know what this day signifies. We are here to take back the past and to gaze upon the future. We are here to reclaim our grandfathers, our grandmothers. We are here to plant the whipala in the heart of our nation. Achachila Akapana. All the achachilas surrounding us, protect us, guard us, give us our bread, amen."

Then, among incense burners streaming white smoke, the Aymara's *yatiri,* the shamans, made their offering to the great, ancient earth shrine. Each of the jilakata in turn invoked the spirits of the land and the sky and sprayed libations of cane alcohol to Pachamama, Lady Earth. Spumes of dust and gravel bubbled up in foamy brown welts where the liquid struck the parched earth. The jilakata addressed their words with great deference to Lady Earth and to all the ancestral spirits of their mountain world. The protocol of prayer demanded that they speak behind their hands or with their dusty felt hats obscuring their mouths. They spoke in soft, urgent prayers swept quickly away by a pitiless chilling wind. The prayers they uttered were for fertility, abundance, and good luck. These men and women gathered on the summit of the Akapana, the great ancient temple of their ancestors, to reclaim their history and proclaim a new age of self-determination. But their private prayers that morning were intimate. They were personal attempts to nourish a fragile tissue of spiritual communion with the deities that animated the physical landscape around them.

Like Native Americans throughout the hemisphere, the Aymara are redefining themselves; they are adjusting their lives and culture to the forces of the modern world. In recent years, they have turned themselves into small entrepreneurs in order to adapt to a global economy. But, at the same time, they are increasingly aware of their several-thousand-year history.

Few people even know that the Aymara nation exists. It is not a Native American group with much global visibility. The Aymara do not inhabit vast Amazonian rain forests threatened with imminent destruction. No environmentalists, rock stars, lobbyists, or politicians clamor to speak in defense of their lives and environment. Unlike the rain forests, the Aymara's habitat is hardly under threat. Instead, it appears unapproachable, eternal in its inhuman scale. The world of the Aymara is one infused with rugged mountains. Soaring glaciated peaks and rolling grasslands perched around the shores of Lake Titicaca sharply etch the contours of the land. The Aymara Indians and their ancestors have lived in the seemingly endless high plateaus of southern Peru and northwestern Bolivia for millennia, and they have made this land their own.

To the foreigner's eye, the Andean altiplano is desolate and intractable, unfit for humans. And this perception of the environment has distorted the image of the Aymara people and their culture. Listen to the words of Harry Tschopik, a pioneering anthropologist of the Aymara, writing around the time of the Second World War:

> Perhaps the drabness and monotony of Aymara culture may be explained in part in terms of physical environment as well as its long history of exploitation at the hands of the Whites. The Aymara live in an inhospitable physical environment in which the struggle for survival is an ever-present reality; their chief preoccupation is with food and protection against the elements. Basically an agricultural people, they must contend with poor soil and a limited choice of crops in a region where a harsh climate makes farming precarious. To the Aymara, the land, the crops and the flocks comprise all-absorbing interests. These time-consuming economic activities make for a rigorous and monotonous daily routine, with the result that Aymara culture impresses the outsider as being extremely "utilitarian." Recreational activities are few and infrequent, and the material aspects of the culture have been emphasized at the expense of its esthetic and ceremonial manifestations. Although markets and trading

expeditions have their entertainment value, emotional release from the daily routine finds its chief expression in orgiastic drinking bouts occasioned by weddings, funerals, and fiestas. . . . The basic preoccupation of the Aymara with the economic aspects of life colors the whole fabric of their culture. Owing in part, perhaps, to the uncertainty of existence on the altiplano, they seek omens in nearly all manifestations of nature and possess an elaborate series of techniques for divining the future; indeed the total culture of the Aymara might best be characterized as "apprehensive." The great bulk of Aymara magic is oriented toward controlling natural phenomena in order to assure economic security. Most public and private ceremonials are designed to produce general prosperity, better crops, larger crops, or more fish.[2]

Other observers of the Aymara have come to even more startling conclusions about the links between their natural environment and the apparent poverty of their culture. Writing around the same time as Tschopik, Arthur Posnansky, an expatriate German entrepreneur and amateur archaeologist, commented that the Aymara "are completely devoid of culture at the present time; they scarcely know how to scratch the soil to provide themselves with their miserable daily bread. They weave coarse cloth to protect their bodies against the inclemency of the weather and they lead a wretched existence in clay huts which seem, rather than human dwellings, the caves of troglodytes."[3]

These images of the Aymara as evolutionary throwbacks, a latter-day band of cavemen living in a hostile natural world beyond their control, reverberates through countless "scholarly" descriptions of their culture. A litany of shallow psychological assessments have been used to portray the essence of Aymara character. They have been called "avaricious," "bellicose," "dull," "hostile," "ill-humored," "pessimistic," "suspicious," "torpid," "treacherous," "unimaginative," and "violent."[4]

But these are not the Aymara that I know. Contrary to the received wisdom of observers unfamiliar with their resilience and resourcefulness, the Aymara are not passive victims of their environment. They shape the natural world around them with both their hands and their minds. This book will reveal something of the ancient Aymara vision of the world, a vision at once radically different from our own and powerfully resonant for other Native Americans in the hemisphere. On the high plateau, spiritual insight flows from hard living on the land, from the yearly cycle of planting, irrigating, weeding, and harvesting. Ritual is grounded in reality, and reality becomes ritual. Through their spiritual life, the Aymara seek health, abundance, and fertility, not a vague sense of harmony with Mother Earth. They are, in a real sense, mystics, but not of the esoteric kind enshrined in our common imagination. Here the spiritual dimension is found in the ordinary acts and objects of everyday life: in the sound of water surging from a mountain's seam, in the smell of eucalyptus burning in the hearth, in the rich, smoky flavor of a new potato baked in a clay oven carved from the earth.

And yet, even as the Aymara respect tradition, they are receptive to change and alive to new opportunities. Though firmly rooted in a distant past, rich with tradition and profoundly meaningful, they eagerly gaze to the future. The Aymara world is populated by ancient gods and spirits of nature and by the forces of modernity. The Aymara accept and seek to accommodate themselves to all these forces. For most of us, the chasm between "premodern" and "modern" ways of thinking is too great to bridge. Yet the Aymara I know live simultaneously in these apparently contradictory worlds. They are not governed by analytical distinctions between the logic of cause and effect and their own deeply embedded, animistic notions of causation. They acutely recognize and believe in both simultaneously. Their way of thinking cannot be summarily dismissed as hopelessly addled. Rather, for the Aymara, there is a deep subtlety to the world,

8

a reality that reaches to textures below the visible surface. Where many see mere cause and effect, they see necessary relationships.

Take the simple case of rain. For us, when atmospheric conditions are right, with the proper mix of cold and warm air masses, rain will fall. The Aymara, too, recognize the physical conditions that will cause rain to fall. But they have a more complex perception of rain, grounded in the special nature of their environment. During the rainy season, almost every day, huge banks of black, swollen clouds well up in the deep ravines and basins of their mountain world. Sudden, ominous thunderstorms sweep the slopes with torrential rains, driving hail, and violent claps of thunder and lightning. Water rapidly pools in the saddles along the summits of the mountain peaks which the Aymara hold sacred, and then begins to flow down to the valley floors where they live. But the flow is not direct. Surface water quickly disappears into subterranean streams that periodically reemerge downslope, gushing and pooling onto natural terraces, only to tumble down inside the mountain again. Water mysteriously appears and disappears with a capricious will of its own. Eventually, gravity gets its due. Runoff from the rains finally surges from the foot of the mountains in rivers, streams, springs, and seeps that are the sources of the Aymara farmers' irrigation and drinking water. The altiplano rainy season is also the growing season, and the success of their farms is tied to this critical period of rainfall.

At the most primal level, as an everyday reality, rain is the source of life for the Aymara. But rain emerges first on the mountains and courses through them before reaching the fields below. Rain and mountains are indissolubly linked, imbued with animating spirit, sacred because they are together the source of nourishment for their fields. The mountain peaks become *wakas,* shrines to the personified forces of nature that dramatically affect and alter human destiny. The Aymara vision of rain is shot through with psycho-

9

logical nuance. Ineluctably, logic, memory, and emotions intermingle as the Aymara sacrifice and wait for the rains to fertilize their fields.

Many of us who live in the industrialized world yearn for this kind of intimate linkage with natural forces. We have become distanced from the earth and the sky. Many of us have never seen a food crop grow, except, perhaps, in the accelerated, special-effects world of time-lapse photography in a nature program on public television. Unseen in its raw state, our food is transformed for us into convenient shapes and predictable tastes. No longer working the land ourselves, we are unaware of the process. Instead, we are buffered by endless layers of food-industry intermediaries. If the wheat crop fails in Nebraska, Canada or Brazil will pick up the slack. We do not feel at risk. Our landscapes have become depersonalized icons of nature, static backdrops for human action. We admire mountain thunderstorms and turbulent streams for their resplendent beauty, perhaps even with great emotion and a kind of keening spirituality, but we do not truly worship and fear them. For us, the protean forces of the natural world are no longer animate. The spirits inhabiting our land have gone undercover. We find it hard to touch them. The vitalizing forces of nature linger on the edge of our consciousness, less palpable, more abstract. They are losing their capacity for impact. They no longer seem to shape our destiny.

By contrast, the relationship of the Aymara with the land is strong and intimate. The shapes and forces of nature *are* their kin. When the Aymara gaze up to the mountains that enclose their world, they see their remote ancestors silhouetted against the sky, turned to stone all around them, infused into the landscape. They see the history of their lineage, their communities, their people writ large on the very structure of the world. Before they sacrifice for the rains, the yatiri recite a long litany, which recalls the names of the ancestral spirits, the *achachilas* and *mallkus,* in strict sequence. These magical names, voiced in a community of worship, create an almost hypnotic protocol of remembrance. When the Aymara go on pilgrimage to the mountain shrines and invoke the achachilas, they address them directly as if they were living grandparents. They beseech and cajole the achachilas to bring the rains and to protect their growing crops from frost and hail. And, like any family, the Aymara argue among themselves and with the achachilas. They hurl insults at, curse, and threaten the achachilas if they do not respond to their pleas for help. After all, from the perspective of the Aymara, the achachilas, as ancestors of the family, owe them loyalty and aid in times of need. To the Aymara, the geography of the world is a projection of the family, and time is a dialogue with the dead. Through the act of remembering their ancestors and incorporating them into their daily lives, the Aymara project themselves, their sense of identity, on the physical reality around them. By doing so, they transform it. I knew little of this when I began my odyssey to the land of the Aymara over seventeen years ago. Even now the strangeness and audacity of this truly ethnocentric take on the world is difficult to comprehend. But I have come to see this insight as an essential step toward understanding and appreciating the Aymara's and their ancestors' special vision of the world.

Place, time, and memory, and the tangled cognitive associations among them, are essential elements of the Aymara worldview. From their perspective, space and time are inseparable and, in some sense, indistinguishable. They have a single word for this space–time convergence: *pacha.*

Pacha is the "thing," the essence, that imparts structure to the Aymara cosmos. It is the root metaphor that gives the Aymara their conceptual purchase on the fundamental nature of the universe. If there is one notion that can be said to shape Aymara philosophy, it is not God, or Being, or Sensation, but Pacha. Pacha itself has multiple aspects, myriad meanings. Situating humankind in space, the contemporary Aymara believe there are three pachas: *Alaxpacha,* the pacha of above and of luminosity; *Manqhapacha,* the pacha of below and of darkness; and *Akapacha,* the pacha of in-between, the here and now, the place and time where creatures, including humans, exist in life. Each of these pachas is populated by particular spirits and animate beings, demons and deities.

For us, the past is usually imagined and described as something behind us: events that have come, gone, and now recede from our consciousness. The future metaphorically stretches out in front of us. But for the Aymara, the place of time is inverted. It is the past that is in front of us, visible, knowable, graven in the physical world and in memory. The Aymara word for eyes, *nayra,* is the same as the word for ancient: what is ancient, what is past, can be seen with one's eyes. The past and the present merge in the Aymara mind. The future, on the other hand, lies behind, invisible and knowable only through ritual specialists trained in the arts of prognostication.

If we think about it, this Aymara sense of time is an eminently logical, modern proposition. We know from scientific cosmology that when we look into the night sky we are looking deep into the past, back to the time when the universe was born. Our expanding universe and its ancient past are, in fact, visible in front of us. But unlike us, the Aymara apply this breathtaking insight to their personal, concrete experiences and not merely to an abstract notion of the physical universe. To the Aymara, events, both ancient and personal, are encoded in the landscape to which they orient themselves. The achachilas infused in the steep scarps and tortuous folds of the mountains remind them daily that they are part of a living, eternal history.

For this reason, the past, the *nayrapacha,* is a profound source for understanding who the contemporary Aymara are, how they came to be, and what they may yet become. But why should we care about Aymara history and culture? Why does it matter what a million Aymara speakers think and say and do in the world? To anyone fascinated by the total experience of humans, to anyone who wishes to go beyond the familiar

12

world, to anyone wanting to push the envelope of their own perceptions, a sojourn into the mind and history of the Aymara is disturbing, exhilarating, and ultimately unforgettable.

The world and its ways have changed much since the remote ancestors of the Aymara first migrated into the high plateaus of the Andes. But the daunting challenges these people faced, the solutions they devised for living in a forbidding environment, and the view of the world they developed over the course of millennia, all speak to us of the possibilities of human creativity and endurance. Like the ancients, we too are faced with the challenge of living in ever-shifting natural and social environments. Increasingly, we feel our world slipping beyond our control. We seek to repair the damage to our global environment caused by the engines of modernity. We are in search of ways to sustain our economic well-being without irrevocably compromising the ecological grounds of our wealth. There are many lessons to be learned from the indigenous worlds both past and present. The rich pharmacopoeia of the Amazon rain forest is but one highly publicized instance of the potential that lays barely tapped in the minds and environments of these disappearing worlds. In these ancient worlds, there are alternative views, different philosophies about the relationships between humans and their environment.

This book is an account of the life and history of the Aymara Indians and of their vision of the world. Perhaps more accurately, it is an intimate portrait of the Aymara as I have come to know them. What I see and report is not so much Aymara reality, as my own perception of Aymara reality, past and present. Those who go out to live among the Aymara return with a multitude of impressions, many of them contradictory. This should not be surprising. Like humans anywhere, the Aymara are a people of contradictions. They confound the expectations of every outsider, even those who have lived and worked among them for many years. Despite impressions to the contrary, the Aymara defy easy characterization. There is no single Aymara reality. There are not even many Aymara realities that can be encapsulated conveniently within fixed boundaries. Their world, like ours, is constantly shifting and they are always redefining the terms of engagement. Their communities are not some archetype of closed, inward-directed "tribes" sealed off from communication with the out-side world. They are not the stuff of anthropological romance: the last, pristine, uncontacted aboriginals living in a harmonious, secluded world. The Aymara are thoroughly contaminated by modern society and they want more of it.

Of the many contradictions in their culture, one of the most striking is that although their ancient beliefs are strong, their grasp on the story of their own history is tenuous, as fragmented as the ruins they live among. Since 1978, I have lived the modern realities of the Aymara, in their ancient city of Tiahuanaco. I walk the dusty back roads. I talk and work and eat in the fields alongside these descendants of a great cultural tradition; a tradition long obscured by historical trauma, forgetfulness, and the changing values of modern life. Many Aymara have little consciousness of their past glories, their rich lineage. What history of their people they do absorb is a poor thing patched together from shreds and tatters, and at its worst, a fragile tissue of distortions and half-truths: the source of a bitter and false consciousness of their role and contributions to world history.

These are truly a people possessed of a glorious past, but at the same time, a people without a history. This contrast was so acute, so intriguing, that I resolved to become a chronicler of that history. I wanted to seam the Aymara's severed past back to their present and future. To help bring history back to these people who had been so thoroughly shorn of it.

Of course, there are no means of reconstructing the full textures of the historical events that shaped this past. No contemporary accounts of Tiahuanaco exist to aid us toward that unreachable goal. As far as we know, the ancient city and its society were preliterate and its own memories were preserved in the mind and transmitted through the generations in the oral histories of its inhabitants. We have only distant echoes of these histories in the myths, legends, and historical accounts transcribed to writings by the Spanish invaders upon their encounter with and subsequent destruction and appropriation of the native Andean world after 1532.

What I have tried to reconstruct in telling the history of the Aymara in this book is not a chronological narrative of ancient events that transpired in Tiahuanaco's world. I seek something rather different: a historical understanding of that world and its transformations and something of the meaning that these held for its creators. Following the lead of the eighteenth-century Italian philosopher Giambattista Vico, such a historical understanding derives from "an imaginative reconstruction" of the lives and actions of people in other milieus.[5] Empiricist critics of Vico's doctrine deride this notion of historical understanding "as some kind of transtemporal telepathy, empathy, or clairvoyance—as though the historian had retrospectively to reexperience the sensations and feelings, imagery and agitations of the men whose story he is reconstructing."[6] But as the eminent philosopher Stephen Toulmin notes, such criticisms misconstrue the point: "The possibility of understanding the actions, customs, and beliefs of men in other milieus rests on our sharing, not common sensations or mental images, but rather common human needs and problems. . . . the cultural patterns and forms of life of other peoples are then open to our understanding, in just those respects and to just the extent that they represent alternative ways of attacking shared human problems and meeting shared human needs."[7]

Just so, I wondered how the people of ancient Tiahuanaco solved the everyday tasks of making a living in their social world. What meaning did they invest in their cities? How did they conceive of themselves, the world, and their place in it? How do their solutions to these perennial human problems compare with those of their cultural descendants, the Aymara, and for that matter, with our own? To answer these questions, I found myself constructing a kind of transcultural, transtemporal dialogue; a dialogue between past and present, us and them, fragmentary and incomplete though such an enterprise was.

If place and time merge ineluctably in the Aymara mind, they will as well in this book. As I recount my journey through Aymara history and culture, I will move freely from present to past and back again. When describing the present, I will focus on the story of several Aymara communities and individuals who live around the southern shores of Lake Titicaca in Bolivia. In describing the past, I will tell the story of an ancient society that flourished in this same locale well over one thousand years ago. The story of this society pivots around the sacred site of Tiahuanaco which, in its time, was the capital of a resplendent empire fully eight hundred years before the Inca emerged to dominate the Andean world. Although the name and achievements of the Inca empire are well known, the people of Tiahuanaco and their Aymara cultural descendents remain veiled in obscurity. This book seeks to restore, in some measure, the distinctive identity of a people to whom history has been denied.

I will begin my account with the story of an extraordinary pilgrimage to a mountain shrine. I made this pilgrimage in the company of several Aymara Indians who became my guides through the endless round of rituals and spiritual practices, as well as in the everyday acts, that make up and give meaning to their lives. That pilgrimage offered my most penetrating view into the character of these people. If, as the Aymara believe, the history of the world is graven in the landscape, if the past is visible before us and we choose to see it, then it is possible to comprehend and to evoke a true sense of distant times and distant places. And this sense of the past, the past of a culture seemingly alien to us, promises to enrich our appreciation of our place in the world as well.

2

The Trembler on
the Mountain

O N a desolate mountain peak rising high above the ancient ruins of Tiahuanaco, Chrisostomos Choque trembled for the last time. From deep within the mountain, a spring surged through a crack in the granite outcrop against which we leaned. The light of the waning sun shimmered on water pooling in the pitted surface at our feet. The wind swirled off the lake, through the quebradas that cleaved the mountain. Earth and gravel sucked into towering funnels of dust gave the wind a gritty texture. Clouds of sediment, whipped into twisting frenzies, coated the alpaca shawl draped over Chrisostomos's head. His body quivered as he stared into a pool of water formed in the hollow of a rock. He gazed through the water, eyes milky with age and glazed by drink.

Chrisostomos Choque trembled in a trance. Hours before in the fragile, dawn light, Chrisostomos had assembled the *muxsa misas,* the ritual offerings to *Pachamama,* Lady Earth. Chrisostomos was a *taliri,* a trembler, a shaker, a shaman of the Aymara, and I was a witness to his final ceremony.

As Chrisostomos tells it, he didn't intend to become a shaman. He simply had no choice. When he was seventeen years old, sometime around 1919, he was struck by lightning while tending his family's sheep out in the marshy lands under the mountains. Hours later, Chrisostomos's uncle Donato found him face down in the field, writhing in pain and unable to speak. The following evening a well-known *curandero*, a healer, from a neighboring village came to Chrisostomos's house. He applied poultices of herbs to soothe the wounds, infused the silent patient with smoke from copal incense, and prayed to the native spirits of the land and the sky and to the Christian saints. Chrisostomos recovered, but he was never the same. He was deaf in one ear and the left side of his face was scored with angry scars.

But more than his appearance had changed. A *rayo*, a lightning bolt, had fallen upon him. In the Aymara's oral traditions, lightning is an animate being brought to life during the rainy season. They believe that lightning, like humans, moves about with a purpose. The lightning bolt that changed his life sought him out. He had been touched by the ineffable power of the sacred, and survived—forever marked as an earthly receptacle and transmitter of supernatural power.

Now that the rayo had confirmed him a shaman, there only remained years of learning how to behave like one. First he became a *partero*, a midwife, who specialized in the most difficult pregnancies. He learned to manipulate fetuses in the womb, to engage them properly for birth. Chrisostomos could ease babies through the birth canal with virtuosity. Countless mothers who would have died hemorrhaging on dirt floors survived because of his practiced hands. Later he became a curandero, apprenticing himself to a local healer renowned for his success with medicinal plants. Chrisostomos keenly absorbed the many subtleties of the healing trade, and gained knowledge of an enormous pharmacopoeia. He began to make arduous journeys through the mountains to collect plants and minerals, at first accompanied by his mentor, but increasingly setting off by himself. From the time he reached his mid thirties, Chrisostomos kept a tightly wrapped textile bundle of medicinal plants around him.

In time, he came to foretell the future. He became a diviner, casting coca and reading fate in the shapes, colors, and dispositions of leaves as they fell on the earth. He took auguries from animals, splitting open the breasts of guinea pigs and llamas to extract their livers and hearts. He looked for discolorations, intricate veining, and strange adhesions on the warm, bloody surface of the organs. He gauged the thickness of their body fat. With these tools of prescience, he then predicted luck and misfortune, windfalls and disasters, for all who sought him out.

Payment for his services came in the form of quail's eggs and bread, cooking oil, flour, chickens and guinea pigs, crackers, beef, potatoes and oca, oranges, quinoa, and beer. Sometimes he accepted money, but more often he preferred help with thatching a roof or plowing a new field. He was always on call, and most of his cures and auguries began at twilight and continued through the night until dawn. Entire families came to his house to be cured, or to have their futures divined. His stamina was legendary and his capacity for nonstop drinking astounding. He became one of the most highly respected practitioners of the ritual arts among the Aymara living around the southern rim of Lake Titicaca. Natives came to him, especially in August.

August in the land of the Aymara is the cruelest month. It is the height of the dry season, when nights are bitterly cold and constant winds turn the high plateau into a choking bowl of dust. It is a barren time between seasons, when luck and prosperity hang tenuously in the balance. The days are filled with a gnawing anxiety. On the cusp of a new season, the Aymara reflect on the successes and failures of the past year. They think about the harvests at the end of one season and look ahead to planting and the beginning of another.

August is a dangerous month. The time when new fields

are plowed and prepared to accept the seed. The earth is cut open and the forces of nature surge up anxious, restless, demanding attention. As Chrisostomos once told me, "In August, Pachamama and the achachilas are hungry. They have their mouths wide open. They are demanding. They must be satiated." For the Aymara, Pachamama is the spirit of the uncultivated earth, and the achachilas are the ancestral mountain spirits, personifications of natural forces that directly affect human destiny. These achachilas are male and female. They can bring good luck or disaster. If they are not fed and feted, they will walk across the land destroying fields and canals, pastures and animals. In the dead time between harvest and planting, Lady Earth rests, depleted from the effort of giving forth her fruits. But in August, along with the ancestral spirits of the mountains, she must be roused again from her slumber. She must feed at the dawn of a new agricultural cycle.

Throughout the centuries, it has always been this way in the high Andes. In the time of the Inca, the kings of the empire sponsored two great festivals, one in August and September during the time of planting and the other from January through February, when virgin earth was plowed for the first time to prepare it for planting in the following season.

During these festivals, the participants drank staggering quantities of alcohol, offering abundant libations to Lady Earth. Women would spend days brewing *chicha,* the native corn beer that fueled these rituals. The celebrants drank to such outrageous excess that one Spanish witness described the Indians at the peak of the festivities holding "in one hand the cup from which they were drinking, and in the other the member with which they urinated." This image of exuberant drunkenness, perhaps comical and puzzling to us, appalled the Spanish clerics charged with propagating Christian morality in the New World. They were particularly incensed because the flow of beer during these festivals was accompanied by unrestrained sexual intercourse among the celebrants.

During the long days and nights of ritual drinking, dancing, and singing, men and women pursued sexual liaisons that were normally forbidden, avidly seeking out the secret subjects of their desire without fear of retribution from the community. In the process, the Inca slaked Lady Earth's thirst, stanched her hunger, and fertilized her sterile earth. Corn beer, semen, and urine were all recycled in a communal ritual. These festivals were held at precisely the time in the yearly agricultural cycle when Lady Earth was perceived to be open to direct communion with humans, susceptible to outside influence. These were the two times of the year when Pachamama was prepared to receive water, seed, prayers, and ritual offerings.

For the Inca, farming was like warfare (a sentiment many American family farmers might readily appreciate). During the time of planting, the Inca referred to the impeccably cultivated agricultural fields as if they had been "conquered." They compared the farmer's conquest of his fields with the sexual and martial domination of subject peoples by their warriors. The native chronicler Waman Poma, who was of mixed Spanish and Inca ancestry, recounts that during the planting in August the Inca would celebrate by singing the *haylli,* their battle song of rejoicing and triumph. The domestication of virgin earth, the planting of crops in previously sterile fields, was seen as a victory wrested from the earth on equal footing with the great battles won by the imperial armies, and to celebrate they sang the same joyous song of triumph.[1]

Festivals of unrestrained drunkenness and uninhibited sex continue to this day in some rural communities of the Andes. August and February remain months when ritual drinking is expected and when normal sexual constraints are loosened. The February first-plowing ceremonies are now assimilated into the transcultural festival of Carnival. But the licentiousness and drinking of Carnival retains an essence of native meaning. Drinking and sex are considered essential human pathways to the revitalization of life-giving earth. Pachamama and her avatars are demanding and ravenous. To awaken and satisfy Lady Earth, body, field, and spirit must merge in ritual offering.

August is a month for purifying the soul, and for cleansing the community of its grief and sins. Throughout the month, the Aymara go on pilgrimage to their sacred mountains. They climb in a predetermined path to strategic points with unobstructed views of the glittering peaks above and their farmlands below, often gathering near springs gushing from seams in the mountain's face or around a distinctive, jutting rock. The mountains are the precious sources of irrigation water for the parched fields. Like a supernatural umbilical cord, sweet waters emerging from caverns or from subterranean seeps connect the mountain spirits to the farmers' fields in the most intimate way. At a glance, the local farmers can trace these glimmering ribbons of life from the fields back to their sources high in the mist-shrouded mountains. Fields and spirits connect and become one.

The Aymara on pilgrimage ascend to the sacred shrines of the springs and rocks bearing with them ritual offerings to feed the achachilas. The offerings they carry seem bizarre to the outsider: a nightmarish witches' brew of llama fat; shriveled, preserved pig and llama fetuses; pieces of skins from wild cats; lumps of resinous incense; coca leaves; ground minerals; colored rock candies; dried fruit; oddly shaped potatoes; exotic, aromatic plants; tobacco; balls of raw sheep's wool; fraying sections of dyed woolen yarn spun with a twist to the left; and *misterios,* confectioner's sweets molded in the images of animals, the moon, the sun, the stars, symbols of the zodiac, and of the Christian saints. All of these elements are brought together in the ritual *misa,* an altar of power. Each object is placed precisely on sheets of cheap paper spread on the ground. The Aymara call the ritual offering the muxsa misa, or sweet misa. By ceremony's end, the muxsa misa will be consumed in a bonfire fueled with llama dung and eucalyptus branches soaked in alcohol. All that will remain to mark the place of offering is the lingering smell of copal incense and a charred mass, bubbling with melted, multicolored sugar, streaming white smoke into the sky.

The objects assembled on the muxsa misa are sensual touchstones for the Aymara, stirring their collective memory of an unbroken chain of offerings that bind their communities to the mountain spirits. When they press grainy, caramel-colored chunks of llama fat into the hollow eyes of potatoes, they sense that they are infusing a raw energy into the plant that is central to their lives. The acrid smell of a blackened, mummified llama fetus, the pungent sting of incense in the nostrils, the sight of brilliant, emerald green coca leaves all evoke a visceral sense of the procreative forces of nature unleashed. The misa, once assembled, creates a map, a sacred landscape of the imagination in microcosm. Each coca leaf mimics a potato field in full bloom. Each pure rock candy or mineral crystal on the misa assumes the spiritual aura of one of the great snowcapped peaks, the most powerful of the achachilas that enclose the Aymara world. Each seed potato smeared with llama fat, festooned with flowers and sprinkled with alcohol, becomes a guide, an avatar, and a protector for its counterparts to be planted in the fields. All elements combined express a communal prayer for abundance and fertility, a fervent plea for life, health, and good luck.

The act of shaping the power-laden geography of the muxsa misa demands experienced hands. All members of the community on pilgrimage to the mountain shrines participate in assembling the misa in a collective spirit of desire and intent. But only ritual practitioners of some skill can construct a truly impeccable offering. They guide the hands of the worshipers to place the coca leaves just so in the proper quadrant of the misa. They insure that all elements of the misa are present and in the proper proportion. They know the prayers that must be recited to call out the ancestral spirits: "Come down here, come here, take your offering, eat it, be satisfied so that we too can eat and be satisfied."

In return for the offering of the muxsa misa, the spirits of the earth, the sky, and the water ward off frosts, cause hail to fall on other lands, protect and care for the fields to be planted in the new season. The Aymara's relationship to the land is subtle, but not at all ambiguous. They say: "We feed the mountains, and the mountains feed us."

In August, the achachilas clamor for food, demand it from humans. But in March and April, just before harvest, the roles are reversed. Humans demand their due from the earth: an abundant harvest. Land and man in the world of the Aymara are equally implacable; each tries to force their desires on the other. It is a yearly contest of wills and the outcome determines the health and fertility of humanity.

So it was that one day late in August of 1989 I rose at 4:00 in the morning, to embark on one of the most profound experiences of my life. The stars still glittered in the black sky. It would be another hour before the first light began to diffuse slowly across the mountains. The early morning was intensely cold, and a heavy crust of frost lay upon the ground.

I was going to Chrisostomos Choque's house in the small community of Qorpa. From there we would set off on a pilgrimage to a mountain shrine to make an offering on behalf of his community. I was accompanied by the man who had become my primary guide to the world of the Aymara: Cesar Callisaya. Cesar had lived and worked in Tiahuanaco all his life as the supervisor in charge of guarding the ruins, a position he inherited from his father. I met him in 1978 when I first came to Bolivia. Over the years we became friends and then, most important of all, *compadres*: I was godfather to his son Ronald, and he became godfather to my daughter Justine. By sharing that intimate bond, we became, as Cesar called it, "spiritual kin." When I venture out among his people, Cesar insists on accompanying me. He knows well the dangers an outsider—even an outsider who has been in the land of the Aymara for many years—can fall into unawares in the isolated, rural countryside that I explore. We were to gather at dawn with Chrisostomos and his family, three other shamans, and a group of community leaders who were sponsoring the pilgrimage. After assembling several of the muxsa misa offerings, we would make our way to the shrine high in the mountains where we would invoke the mountain spirits, calling them down to bless the new fields that were to be planted later that week.

The offering to the achachilas was not just for Chrisostomos's family, but for the entire community. Other families, who did not know me, were also going on the pilgrimage. I was worried that they would take one look at me and demand I leave. This was one of the most critical ceremonies of the planting season, and some of the community members might believe that the presence of an outsider would antagonize the achachilas. Whites were known to cause droughts and bring pestilence. There were rumors all around the local Aymara communities of white-faced supernatural beings who mercilessly slaughtered Indians, then drank their blood and mutilated their corpses. The belief in these creatures is so common that the Aymara have a special name for them: *kharisiri*. The kharisiri take many forms. One of the most prevalent versions I heard was that the kharisiri looked like gringos: extraordinarily tall, pale, gangly figures who wear dark leather boots and jackets and a wide-brimmed hat. The kharisiri prey on Indians foolish enough to walk deserted mountain paths alone. They frequently ambush their victims under bridges or at desolate crossroads in the dead of night, and dispatch them in a spectacular, bloody ritual of slaughter. The kharisiri pounces on his unlucky victim with a powerful slash of an enormous knife or machete that kills in an instant, severing the jugular vein or even striking off the head in a single blow. The kharisiri then drags the body to a nearby cave or abandoned mine to disembowel the corpse "like a goat completely slit down the chest,"[2] and suspends the carcass over a bonfire to render body fat from the remains.

Depending on the teller of the tale, the human fat extracted from the victims is sold for fantastic prices to unscrupulous merchants who export it for use as lubricants in machinery, or as an ingredient in exotic pharmaceuticals. Other versions of this dark tale recount stories of kharisiri who steal unwary Indian children and force them into slavery, or, worse yet, decapitate them and suck the blood out of their tender bodies. Such brutal tales of foreign bloodsuckers and body snatchers are rife throughout the rural reaches of the Andean highlands. In Quechua-speaking regions, the kharisiri are called *pistacos* or *ñak'aqs*, but all of these creatures share certain attributes. They are foreign, and they move with impunity through the perilous landscapes of the night to slaughter and mutilate Indians.

These stories speak volumes about the conflictive, tension-filled relationships between Indians and outsiders and about Aymara cultural realities. The motives of outsiders who come to the Aymara communities are always suspect, and not without reason. An endless parade of foreigners, government officials, technicians from development agencies, missionaries, anthropologists, adventurers, charlatans, and fools troop through Aymara villages bearing promises that are rarely kept. The Aymara have seen little benefit from outsiders, even the most well-intentioned.

I was aware of all of these suspicions of outsiders. By taking part in the pilgrimage, I didn't want to cause these people or myself problems by being the unwelcome stranger at such a pivotal moment in their year. I also didn't want to provoke a scene of ugly recriminations when I showed up that morning. As we set out that morning, I expressed these worries to Cesar, and his response was disconcerting: He said that he too had been troubled about what might happen when we arrived, and he explained that the week before he had gone to Qorpa to discuss the matter with Chrisostomos. They decided to cast coca leaves to determine if my participation was auspicious, or ill-advised. Receiving a positive outcome from the divination, they arranged a meeting with the sponsors of the pilgrimage. At this meeting, they vouched for my character and explained my motivations. Even though Cesar is a natural diplomat and Chrisostomos was one of the most respected men in the community, their arguments did not sway a handful who were bitterly opposed to my taking part in the pilgrimage. They felt an outsider might defile the sacred springs and destroy the power of the offerings. Cesar and Chrisostomos argued on into the night, pressing my case until, finally, they extracted a concession. On the day of the pilgrimage, the shamans would cast coca leaves. If the coca *sorteo* was positive, I would be permitted to participate. If the outcome was negative, I would leave at once without witnessing even the first act of the ritual: the assembly of the muxsa misas. I was told that the casting of the coca leaves would take place inside Chrisostomos's house on a specially prepared "altar" of woven textiles arranged on the earthen floor. Cesar's revelation of all of this that morning made me only more nervous and served as an acute reminder that after all of the time I had spent among the Aymara, I was limited in the degree to which I could partake of their lives.

When we arrived at Chrisostomos's house, the other shamans—who were walking from their villages across the potato fields and pastures through the early morning frosts—were not yet there. We sat down with Chrisostomos, his wife, Eusebia, and his nephew, Lucas, to wait for their arrival. Lucas served up beer all around, the first of many we were to drink that day. Alcohol was to play an important role in the day's events. Suddenly Chrisostomos uttered a prayer in a strange, transformed voice that I had never heard before, some in Spanish, some in Aymara. This is most of what he said:

"Padre nuestro que estas en los cielos danos hoy el pan de cada dia, no nos dejes caer en tentación y en pecado, libranos y protegenos del mal, amen."

"Jesus, Maria, Jose . . . creo en la Santa Maria Virgen, en Cristo que murío en la cruz y que resucitó al tercer día, ascendío a los cielos y ahora está a la diestra del Padre. Creo en los santos católicos y en el perdón de los pecados. Amen . . . Jesus, Maria, Jesus mío.

"Asimismo Pachamama te rogamos y te ch'allamos que nos protejas, nos puedas dar vida plena de felicidad, sin que nos falta nada, Madre Tierra mía. Asimismo, Madre Tierra, Kuntur Mamani tu nos cuidas, nos protejes, nos amparas y por eso te quedamos agradecidos con estas ch'allas, asi te imploramos en esta tarde. Amen, Jesus, Maria, Jesus mío."

This prayer was a compressed version of the Catholic "Our Father" and "Credo," followed by an Aymara invocation to Lord Sky and Lady Earth to protect and guard the community. After uttering the last "amen," Chrisostomos cast his beer into the air with a dramatic, sweep of his arm and passed the cup to us to do the same. Then we each poured generous libations, called *ch'allas* in Aymara, onto the ground, toasting and invoking Pachamama. Toasts of this kind were to be a recurring motif throughout the day. While we waited for the shamans to arrive, Cesar engaged Chrisostomos in a fascinating conversation about how he practiced the ancient arts of the shaman. That conversation reveals much about these little-known practices.

Cesar started by asking: "Tell me, Tata Chrisostomos, what are the signs you look for before you plant? How do you prognosticate the weather?" Since this day was the first of many ritual activities that began the season of planting, his question seemed especially appropriate.

"Well, *hermano*, Doctor, this is what I know. This is what we do here in Qorpa. First we break up the earth, which is called *qhulliña*. This operation we do two times. Later we have to break up the clods of earth so that it stays good for planting. Then we have to move the guano or fertilizer to the location of the planting. We plant about the time of All Saints' [November 1–2]. It may be a little before, or a little

28

after. At times we have to observe certain signs that give us guidelines for the planting of potatoes."

"What are these signs, Tata Chrisostomos?"

"Well, for example, when the *sank'ayu*, [a type of cactus] blossoms, we know that it is a good time to plant. Likewise, when the fish in the river rise or approach the banks as they try to spawn in the sand they make peculiar movements we call *tiwi*. If they auger deeply into the sand, it will be a year of drought, and if they penetrate shallow, it will be a rainy year. Sometimes the fish have the habit of extracting large pebbles as they burrow in. This is a sign that there will be good production. And if they extract very tiny pebbles, the production will also be smaller. This is how we know these things."

"Are there other signs?"

"Yes, yes, Doctor, there are many signs in the sky, in the earth. In the mountains, the *tiwula* [fox] howls. When the fox's howl is clear, sharp, this is a sign that there will be a bad harvest. But if the howl is harsh sounding, muffled and difficult to distinguish, as if the fox had something in his mouth, this is a sign that the year will have a good harvest."

"At which times of the year do you observe these signs?"

"In the month of August, I start to observe the signs for the planting, if we have to plant early or late. Also we observe these signs in the period of Corpus Christi [the end of May]. For example, there are in the mountains some shrubs called *waychapanqara*. If they flower early, we plant early; if they flower late, we plant late. All this knowledge was transmitted to me by an uncle of mine called Donato.

"Another shrub called *t'ola,* according to whether it gives fruits in more or less good proportion, if large or small, is also a sign for planting. But more than that, if the t'ola holds much fruit and is well laden, that is a sign that there will be a good harvest, and if not, the harvest will be minimal. Sometimes the fruit of the t'ola sustains damage because of the frost. This also tells us that we should plant late. Just like this we used to observe everything."

29

"Tata Chrisostomos, you don't take notice of these signs anymore?"

"Ah, not so much anymore. Yes, now it is not as it once was. The new generation ignores these forces that are enveloped in Lady Earth. They only hope that the rain falls. This is not how it should be. Before, this had been our culture. This is no more. It is the beginning of times of drought and scarcity."

"Tata Chrisostomos, what are the signs for this year?"

"I heard some howling the other day in San Miguel. The fox must be on the mountain now. This predicts an early planting. For an early planting, the fox does its howling almost in the last days of August. For a late planting, you do not hear the fox until October. Right now, still, they are not doing it a lot. I heard these howls in San Miguel. They were sharp, clear, almost like a dog. I heard them coming on a wind from a great distance. These are disturbing signs; a change is coming."

At this point, Chrisostomos's nephew Lucas walked into the reception to prod his uncle into talking about the reading of the stars. For untold generations the Aymara have looked to the stars for signs to guide their actions and to foretell the future. They seek out particularly brilliant stars or their visual opposites, the dark cloud constellations (those deep, black shadows of interstellar dust stitched in crazy-quilt patches over the fabric of the celestial sky), to predict the success or failure of crops in the new agricultural year. The Aymara conceptually synchronize the appearance and disappearance, the waxing and waning, of celestial phenomena with the agricultural cycle of the seasons. Like the howling of the fox, the clarity or obscurity of the stars predicts the quality and abundance of the harvest. Like the fox, the time of appearance of *Qutu,* which in Aymara means "handful" or "group," is a guide to when the fields should be planted. Qutu, or *las siete cabrillas* (the "seven little goats") as they are also called in Spanish, is nothing other than the star cluster that Western astronomers call the Pleiades in the constellation Taurus.

"Tio," Lucas asked Chrisostomos, "what have you seen in the stars? What about Qutu, what did you tell me you saw, Tio?"

"What, Lucas, Qutu?"

"Yes, yes, Qutu. Tell them what you told me about Qutu, in the time of Corpus. Don't you remember, Padre-tio?"

"Qutu tells us many things. This year, Qutu was bright, so brilliant in the sky. It shone in splendor. I saw it on the day of Santa Cruz [May 3rd]. This is really early to see Qutu, so we must plant early this year, no ve [don't you see]? Well, let me tell you. If Qutu is divided early, we must plant early. If Qutu is divided late, we must plant late. Isn't this perfectly clear?"

I was thoroughly confused.

What was Chrisostomos saying? What did he mean by "divided?" How can a cluster of stars be divided early or late? What is *that* supposed to mean? Cesar didn't quite grasp what Chrisostomos was saying either. He turned to Chrisostomos and spoke with him at breakneck speed in Aymara trying to clarify. After a few moments of rapid-fire conversation punctuated by intense hand gestures and a final, satisfied, guttural grunt, Cesar explained what the old man meant.

"You see, Doctor, when we see Qutu, sometimes one of the stars appears brighter, clearer than the others. We say that Qutu looks divided. One side is brighter; the other side is obscure. But this changes every year. The bright star moves. Now, when the star in the front of Qutu is bright, we say that Qutu is divided early, and we should plant early. But if the star at the rear of Qutu is bright, we say that Qutu is divided late and we should plant late."

Like everything else that has been explained to me about Aymara modes of perception, this seemed obvious in retrospect. I must constantly remind myself when I am with the Aymara that categories of space and time that Westerners keep distinct merge and interpenetrate in Aymara thought. This was the global concept of pacha in action: space and time converged in a single reality. Front is early, back is late, the past is visible as the stars arc across the sky. And always look to the contrasts to extract meaning from the world: the most brilliant counterpoised against the most obscure. It is at the seam, the point of juxtaposition where differences touch, that we find meaning. All the faculties of perception (sight, sound, smell, touch, thought, divination) gain their acuity and make sense of the world only by means of sharp contrast. It is as if the Aymara constantly calibrate their senses against the sharpest contrasts (male-female, hot-cold, wet-dry, back-front, black-white) to truly perceive and understand the world. Knowledge and understanding seep through the seams of difference. After Cesar explained about the division of Qutu, Lucas continued his questioning of Chrisostomos.

"You say Qutu shone brilliantly, Tio? But this means we will have frosts early too, no?"

"Lucas is right. *Sajjra wiphina* will descend from Qutu early this year. The old man will come down dragging his long, white hair over the earth. He will come furiously with his sack of frozen lightning bolts. He will whip us with frost."

"Who is Sajjra wiphina?" I asked Chrisostomos.

"Sajjra wiphina is the spirit of the frost, Doctor. When he comes early, in June, we make *ch'uño* [freeze-dried potatoes]. He helps us then. But if he comes late, when the plants are small and just beginning to sprout . . . ay, then he is a killer. He torments the fields. He wounds the plants with his icy bolts. Then we must pray, we must lament, crying out, 'Go away, pass on to somebody else's lands.'"

"So how do you protect the plants, the potatoes, from the frost and the hailstorms, Tata Chrisostomos? You don't just wait for Sajjra wiphina to afflict you, do you? You must have some means of protecting your crops?"

"For us hail comes from Qaqajaqi Mountain. To Qaqajaqi we give our ch'allas and offerings with the understanding that he will not destroy our seedlings. We also offer the muxsa misa to try to satisfy the desires of the achachilla Qaqajaqi so that he will go over to other places. We believe that the hail comes to places where there were buried innocents or children who were not baptized, or who didn't have names. We tell Qaqajaqi that we are compensating him with these offerings called *chiwchi misa,* prepared with tiny elements that are like the innocents who died without names."

"And for the time of the frost, what do you do?" Cesar continued.

"For the frost we implore the divine Sajama, offering him *khuchi sullu* [a pig fetus], saying: 'You, San Antonio, do not permit the frost to come to us. For this we offer you a little pig with which you will be content and will go to other sides, sombody else's land.' Reverent, like this, we ask these achachilas."

"Apart from Sajama, to which other divinities or gods in the mountains do you offer ch'allas for the frost?"

"Oh, for the frost we also entreat Qimsachata, Qimsacholita, Chilla achachilla, asking them not to permit the frost to pass over to us from their dominions. We implore San Antonio to hold the frost bound up in the mountains and not send it toward us, because, well, it will damage our potato seedlings, and so we present our offerings and requests.

"And against the hail, to which spirits apart from Qaqajaqi do you offer your ch'allas?"

"Also, in remembrance of the mountains Jachaqhawsaya, Jiskaqhawsaya, Wayllaqullu, Chuntaqullu, and also Qopallika, Akapana achachilla [this is the pyramid-temple of Akapana in Tiahuanaco which is readily visible throughout this part of the valley] and Qinachita, telling them this:

"'Do not receive the hail, but instead let it pass without stopping to other regions far distant, and in the same way do not send us thunder or lightning.'"

"Some knowledgeable people cry out and pray against hail, and do you not know of the practice of these chants and cries?"

"Since old times we always implore, entreat, and invite him saying: 'pass, pass achachilla, do not come by here, go somewhere else. We already have offered you dowries and heirlooms that correspond to this place. Go to other sides, go elsewhere and take your little grandchildren [frost and hail] to other regions.'

"For when there is a night of hard frost, what do you do to protect the crops? Perhaps you know of some practice?"

"Well, we go out at night, lighting bonfires on the mountains with animal dung. All along the mountains we light up the sky with fires and with smoke. I then go to the newly planted fields and there I cry out: 'San Antonio, do not turn on your pigs, on your *wilakhuchis* [sacrificial pigs]; *Khuchiwa, khuchiwa juti*, San Antonio.' Like so we are accustomed to cry out."

At this point, I turned to Cesar. I had a particular question that I had always wanted to pose to Chrisostomos. The year before I had heard that Chrisostomos was sought after by local villagers not only because of his skills as a fortune-teller, diviner, and caster of coca leaf, but also because he was a rainmaker. In the arid, unpredictable lands of the altiplano, effective rainmakers are like manna from heaven. Rain in the right quantity and, equally important, at the right time during the growing season is essential for survival. For centuries, death-dealing droughts have scarred the psyche of humans who have dared to live on the altiplano. Starvation and the prospect of dust-bowl conditions are never far from the minds of the small farmers who cling to their fields on the very margin of human possibility.

The white magician who can ward off frosts and attract the rains is honored and highly sought after. But the flip side of white magic is sorcery, and sometimes the boundary between one and the other shifts and blurs. It is always difficult, and often dangerous, to discuss magic with Aymara magicians. They fear accusations of sorcery. Sorcerers walk the altiplano at night. The unwary can have their souls sucked from their bodies if they are so unlucky to encounter a black magician along a dark mountain path. Sorcerers are the scourge of the community. If their sinister labors are revealed, the reward may be exile, or even death.

Apart from divination, which seemed to him the most natural of all his powers, Chrisostomos was always reluctant to reveal the more active dimensions of his magic. But now we were in an easy rhythm. And we were focused on a theme of great moment to all Aymara living on the land: the subtleties of the relationships among man, plants, and the numinous forces of nature. It seemed fitting at that moment, at the beginning of a new planting season, with a pilgrimage to the mountain shrines imminent, that I ask Chrisostomos how he made rain.

Chrisostomos was a rainmaker in a world tied to the land, to the plants that give sustenance and joy. The rainmaking shaman connects with the most primal of nature's Janus-faced powers: life-giving, death-dealing rain. Too much rain, the torrential, driving rain of tropical latitudes, and seedlings wash away, disappearing into a maelstrom of rivulets snaking relentlessly over bare fields; roots newly established putrefy, blacken and rot to structureless, lifeless mush; and the soil wastes away in vast sheets of water suffused with rich grains of silt or simply, and all at once, collapses in clayey masses into streams and rivers. Too little rain and the struggling, emergent crops succumb, dessicated to a point beyond revival; vegetation, natural and cultivated, withers and lapses back to the cracked earth; and the wind, barren of moisture, assaults the earth, whipping the soil into masses of clouds gritty with the dried texture of a planting season gone disastrously wrong.

Seaming the Janus face of nature, keeping the wild forces balanced, that is what the shaman does. In times of drought, as tension rises, emotions run raw and exaggerated. All eyes turn to the shaman to restore the balance of nature, to bring on the rains that the spirits of the earth and the sky have locked up in the mountains. What secret offense has been committed? What sacrifice has been neglected? How can we persuade the achachilas to take pity on us? These are the questions the community desperately asks of its rainmakers.

"Tata Chrisostomos," I began, "they say that you know how to call the rains. Is this true? Can you tell me how you do this?"

Chrisostomos didn't hesitate for a moment. "Yes, I have called the rains many times, Doctor. There are ways to do this, in stages. I will tell you mine.

"If the rains don't come in November and the earth stays dry and inhospitable, I make my preparations. First I collect the ingredients for a special misa that I will take to the hill Qopallika. I gather *juyraqowa* [an aromatic herb], *untu* [chunks of llama fat], *dulces blancos* [white, crystalline candies], coca, and copal [incense]. Then I prepare a *ch'uwa* of quinoa."

Ch'uwas are sweet liquids made from grains steeped in water and sugar. Ch'uwas come in different forms, colors, and textures, depending on the kind of ingredient. Quinoa, barley, and maize each make ch'uwas with distinct flavors and ritual efficacy.

"Then I go *en comisión* to the top of a certain mountain. [By *en comisión* Chrisostomos meant that he is part of a group of ritual practitioners and their lieutenants charged by the community with conducting the *ch'uwa khiwxata,* or calling of the rains ritual]. We go to Qopallika. But I have gone to Sehuencoma hill too. On Qopallika and on Sehuencoma there are each three springs. These springs are very special. One of the springs is water from the hail. Another is water from the ice [snow and glacial melt]. And the third is water of the rains. These are different kinds of water mixed on these two hills.

"We climb to the summit of Qopallika and we offer the misa to *qarpa achachila* [the guardian spirit of irrigation waters]. We cry out, we call the rains saying, 'Qarpa achachila come here, take pity on us, pour your waters, our land is drying up, water us.' Saying so, crying out altogether we pour the ch'uwa onto the earth and gaze downward as the liquid seeps into Pachamama. Then we burn up our offering of juyraqowa, untu, dulces, coca, and incense of copal. We watch the smoke ascend to Lord Sky. We keep calling on Qopallika until the rains come. Oh, it is hard work."

Cesar interjected, "But Tata Chrisostomos, what if the rains don't come right away? Is there anything else you do to call the rains?"

"Yes, yes, Hermano, you see sometimes our cries alone are not enough; not nearly enough to release the waters. Then we must take other measures. What I do is this.

"I take my bicycle to a place called Pulpira where much water always gushes from the soil. I collect the sweet water in a new jar made just for this purpose, and then I find three toads and put them into the jar. I carry this jar, this little house of the toads, to Qopallika and leave it there on top of the peak. When the sun beats down upon the toads, the water in their little house disappears and they begin to croak. The toads croak in the hot sun.

"They cry tears, you see? Qarpa achachila takes pity on them, and soon the clouds form over Qopallika. Then the rains come without fail and carry the toads back to their place of origin, underground, back to the marshes of Pulpira."

Chrisostomos's tale of the rainmaking toads recycled from the marshes to the mountains and back again is a common one among the Aymara of Lake Titicaca. Long after our conversation on that day, I sought out other references to rainmaking toads among the Aymara. I discovered that during the 1940s Harry Tschopik recorded a fascinating version of this belief among the Aymara on the northern, Peruvian side of the lake:

Of the public weather-controlling rites performed by the white magician (*paqo*), the rain ceremony held at times of drought in Chucuito is perhaps the most elaborate. The community engages a paqo through the agency of "public spirited men" (*p'queña*). The white magician then goes out into Lake Titicaca in a balsa and collects basins of water, frogs, and water plants from certain deep pools where he deposits offerings. He is accompanied by men in other balsas with panpipes and drums. After returning to shore, the magician, the orchestra and the spectators climb the mountain named Atoja, and proceed to the shrine called Father Atoja to deposit the water, plants, and frogs in two basins of the altar which are exposed to the sun. The magician places the offerings in the "mouth" of the altar, asking the mountain spirit to send rain. Everyone sings the frog song accompanied by panpipes, and drinks and chews coca. As the water evaporates, the frogs begin to cry out, whereupon the spirits pity them and send rain.[3]

Toads in Aymara are called normally *jamp'atu,* but they sometimes carry other names with clear ritual significance as well: *pachawawa,* which can mean "twins" or "children of the earth–children of the lightning," and, perhaps even more significantly, *pachakuti,* which means to overturn the earth.[4] The latter name relates to the toads' curious behavioral habits keyed to the cycle of the seasons. During the dry, cold periods of the altiplano year, toads burrow into the earth, into the inner, spirit realm of Lady Earth and the Manqhapacha. But with the onset of the rainy season, as temperatures warm and the dry earth begins to swell with water, the toads reemerge onto the surface, to the Akapacha, the world of humans. The reemergence of the toads signals the rebirth of the earth, the reawakening of Pachamama to fertility and the time for humans to plant their life-giving crops. The toads are signs of the pachakuti, the world turned around, the beginning of a new cycle. They are markers of time as they migrate upward in space from the spirit world of the earth to the active, surface world of humans. They are emblems of cyclical change in time and space. But more than mere signs, this uncanny capacity to travel between the spirit world of the

under earth and the surface world of man made toads mediators between man and spirit. By capturing the toads and making them croak in the sun, the white magicians of the Aymara
use them as vehicles of communication with Lady Earth and
Lord Sky. The toads become, in some sense, portals to the
spirit world which is the ground of all animate life.

Toads become visible to humans just as the life-giving
rains sweep the land that was parched and frozen during the
bitter dry season. Not surprisingly then, to the Aymara, and
to their distant ancestors, toads became powerful symbols of
fertility. Today, in many Aymara communities, farmers still
place small stone images of toads in newly planted fields.
From time to time, the farmers sprinkle alcohol, especially
red wine, on the stomach of these stone toads and then
across the planted fields so that the toads and the fields will
"lay their eggs" (potatoes and other food crops).[5] Images of
toads and serpents, which seem to play a symbolic role similar
to that of toads, are abundant in the archaeological record of
the Lake Titicaca basin, including at the great ancestral sites
of Tiahuanaco. There seems little reason to doubt that these
images were linked to a cult of water and fertility in the past,
just as they are today.

There is not a simple, single side to the symbolism of the
toads. These creatures appear as harbingers of change. As
with any marker of change, the Aymara, like all humans, feel
a certain ambivalence and anxiety about them. Change can be
both positive and negative. The toads may signal a positive
change as the dormant, sterile earth awakens to productivity
again. But what if the toads don't reappear? What if they
refuse to migrate from the belly of the earth to its surface?
The Aymara begin to ask themselves: "Is this a sign of coming drought, of famine?" And, of course, with the close of the
rainy season, the toads inevitably burrow down into the earth
again; their disappearance is a sign of the coming hard times
of the dry season. Toads are signs of the positive-negative
cycle of life incarnate.

The Aymara combat their sense of anxiety before the capriciousness of the elements by manipulating multiple techniques for controlling the weather, for calling the rains. Rainmaking toads are one, but there are many others as well. So it was with Chrisostomos. After describing the rainmaking toads stranded croaking on the slopes of Qopallika, Chrisostomos revealed to us another ancient technique.

"Sometimes I also take water from Pulpira, and mix it with the water from the springs of Qopallika. I join the waters, like two people in a wedding.

"You see, I make the streams from the marshes and the streams from the mountain cross. Then I carry these waters all mixed together in a pot down to our fields and pour them over the newly planted crops. This, too, will bring the rain."

As the conversation ended, we were joined by the shamans we had been waiting for: Ignacio Huanca, Policarpio Flores, and Gregorio Coriza. I knew Ignacio and Gregorio fairly well because they worked with me in my archaeological excavations at Tiahuanaco, but I was surprised to see them this morning. Their role as shamans was something we never talked about while working at Tiahuanaco, and only now was I seeing perhaps the most important spiritual dimension of their lives. Policarpio came from a more distant community and this was the first time I met him.

The time to assemble the muxsa misa had finally come. The moment of truth had arrived. The shamans would peer into the shapes and colors of coca leaves in my presence to see if I was to accompany them to the mountain shrine. But to my great surprise, the casting of the leaves had happened without me. The other shamans had arrived somewhat earlier, while Chrisostomos was sharing the secrets of his art, and they had dispensed with the task on their own. I would be welcome on the pilgrimage. It turned out that casting of the coca leaves was neither elaborate nor particularly ritualized. Nor did it seem terribly important to anyone but me. It was done, and I had nothing to do with it. This was one instance of many in my time with the Aymara that my expectations served as a sharp reminder of how complicated and seemingly paradoxical their worldview is.

We moved into the small adobe hut where the misas were to be assembled. Crude blankets were laid on the packed earth floor. Votive candles were lit and we took our places at the edges of the blankets, kneeling.

Chrisostomos began to assemble the first misa with an invocation to Lady Earth.

"Pachamama, we implore you, we entreat you, we entrust ourselves to you so that you will rapidly return to flower in the radiant colors of white and blue. You, Pachamama, we entrust ourselves to you to protect us against the frost, against the hail, and to you we entrust ourselves. Pachamama, do not permit the frost to come. You will protect us. Likewise, oh, Pachamama, take your sweet offerings, take your red pigs, be content. Amen."

He was begging Lady Earth to put on the lush garments of growing crops, the white and purple colors of potato blossoms. He was asking her to energize the fields that were to be planted this year. And he was imploring her to divert the capricious hail that levels crops in unpredictable swaths, and, worse still, the bitter frosts that stunt and kill indiscriminately. In return for Lady Earth's abundance and protection, Chrisostomos, on behalf of the community, was offering her the sacrifice of sweets and blood.

At this point, Ignacio began his own eloquent oration, a powerful prayer that conveyed the emotional depth of the relationship between the Aymara and their earth, as well as the subtle intermingling of Christian and indigenous beliefs that marks their religious experience.

"Great is your love, Holy Mother Earth, you give us all your products for our sustenance and for our flocks. With your blessings all the animals live for us. You are the food for our cattle, and us, your children, you sustain from your fruits. But at times our brethren are not in accord, and at times this is a great grief for us. Oh, Pachamama! How long we have forgotten you. Forgive us, Holy Virgin Earth. In this way, you are Holy Virgin Earth."

Chrisostomos then pulled small skeins of multicolored yarn from his pouch and began to frame the edges of the paper on which the muxsa misa would be assembled. Ignacio acted as a kind of second in command, handing the ingredients of the offering to Chrisostomos when he asked for them. Throughout the pilgrimage, Chrisostomos, the eldest of the four shamans, called the others his "lieutenants."

Chrisostomos then grabbed a handful of coca and began to select the greenest and most perfectly shaped leaves. Ignacio did likewise. When they were satisfied with the impeccable quality and beauty of their leaves, they cast them down randomly across the paper. Later they were to select other coca leaves to place in specific locations in the sacred geography of the misa.

At this point, Chrisostomos paused and asked for a bottle of red wine and a tin of cane alcohol. He held out a particularly beautiful coca leaf, perfectly formed with neither spots nor dried, curling edges, and dipped it first into the wine. He then shook the wine-wetted leaf over the emerging offering, spraying the coca leaves with alcohol. He repeated this with the pure cane alcohol, praying the entire time. It was almost impossible to understand his prayers since they were murmured, quietly slurred as if Chrisostomos was addressing his words to Lady Earth alone. But I caught the Spanish words *permiso* and *licencia* several times, and I understood that Chrisostomos was asking Lady Earth's permission to make this offering. In the mind of the Aymara, when the community makes an offering to Pachamama, she incurs a debt; she is obligated to respond to their offering with her own first fruits. Chrisostomos was initiating the ritual cycle of reciprocal offerings and prayers that bound the Aymara with their spirit-haunted world. Any time the Aymara farmer harrows the soil, or mixes fertilizer into his fields, or plants a seed, he first asks permission of Lady Earth, and accompanies his petition with a libation of alcohol. The power of Aymara belief is reflected perfectly in the symmetrical beauty of these reciprocal links between themselves and the spirits of the land and sky: Give and you shall receive; receive and you shall give.

All four shamans now rolled chunks of llama fat in their hands. They shaped the sticky substance into images of llamas, gradually working portions of juyraqowa, an intensely aromatic plant, into their little creations. A few sprigs of juyraqowa served to represent the ears and feet of the llamas. When the images of fat were completed, the shamans wrapped them in undyed llama wool, giving them a startling, lifelike appearance. Ignacio even slipped a tiny piece of colored yarn onto the ears of his llama images, just as llama herders do to identify their living animals.

The shamans were moving rapidly now as they distributed the llama fat effigies across the emerging landscape of the misa. Each shaman reached into his pouch and sprinkled ground juyraqowa and copal incense over the llamas. Chrisostomos then reached for two substances I had never seen before. He placed these in four separate locations on the misa. Later, Cesar told me that one of these was *titi*, the skin of a mountain cat, and the other was *mullu*, a special alabasterlike mineral collected in the mountains along the eastern shores of Lake Titicaca. This was followed by tobacco in the form of cigarettes. Chrisostomos then scattered the powder of a whitish-yellow mineral over the misa, and repeated the libation with the coca leaf dipped in wine and cane alcohol. By now, dots of red wine and clear cane alcohol were pooling on the concave surfaces of coca leaves, and seeping into the grease-stained paper below. The sacred landscape of the misa was becoming increasingly complicated.

Chrisostomos and Policarpio then picked up small wax-paper envelopes filled with tiny tin and lead figurines bought in the witches' markets in La Paz. These figurines were schematic representations of people, houses, plants, trees, animals, tools, plates, cups, forks, and spoons; a jumbled domestic tableau in miniature. They opened the envelopes, which the Aymara call *chiwchi,* and distributed the tiny effigies across the surface of the *misa.* Next they unwrapped packets of paper-thin metal foil. Some were colored gold and others silver. They carefully unfolded the metal foil, which seemed to glisten impossibly bright in the low light, and placed several laminas over the tin effigies. The visual effect of the foil was astonishing. The rich, gleaming gold and silver colors of the foil contrasted sharply with the dark browns, grays, and caramel-colored hues of the other ingredients in the offering, all placed against an emerald green ground of coca leaves. Wine and cane alcohol were again flicked over the surface of the misa, which was now nearing completion.

All the shamans, and nearly everyone else, paused to smoke cigarettes. Smoke filled the crowded room rapidly, billowing in perceptible clouds. Chrisostomos, Ignacio, and Gregorio then began to inspect the final elements of the muxsa misa: bags of misterios, those hard, tablet-shaped sweets, and a whole range of rock candies in various shapes, sizes, and colors. The crystalline white misterios, with their embossed images of saints, virgins, and angels, planets, suns, moon, and stars, were especially important. Some days later, I asked Cesar the meaning of these curious images. He told me that each of the misterios has a special significance, but placed together they "called down the power and abundance of the sky." In other words, they were magical amulets invoking celestial fertility. The misterios were to be placed on top of the ingredients of the misa emblematic of earth's fertility: the coca leaves and llama fat, the mullu, titi, and chiwchi. The spirit worlds of earth and sky were being joined on the misa that day in a ritual that would channel their fertilizing powers on behalf of the community.

Chrisostomos placed the first misterio, an image of the

sun with a human face, in the upper right corner of the misa. Then, to my surprise, he handed me the image of a six-pointed star spewing off what looked like bright sparks of illumination. He guided my hand to place the star in the center, near the top of the misa's colored yarn frame. Then Policarpio placed the image of the moon in the upper left corner. With these stars and the moon set in the firmament, Ignacio and Gregorio began to place other images throughout the ritually charged, microcosmic landscape. One by one, Cesar and the members of the community placed misterios and various pieces of rock candy across the surface of the misa, at times with the guidance of the shamans, at other times seemingly at random.

What had been a dark-hued ritual offering began to change character. The chalky misterios and pastel-colored rock candies in pink, rose, yellow, and pale green now cast a subtle luminescence across the surface of the misa, magnified, it seemed, by reflection in the silver-and- gold sheets of metal foil. Chrisostomos heightened the effect of a chameleonlike color change by throwing a heaping handful of confetti over the surface. The confetti seemed to fall like so much multicolored snow across the rock candy mountains. He and the other shamans followed this with several handfuls of pungent copal incense. The misa was finally assembled. There remained only to activate it by offering ch'allas, libations of alchohol, and then burning it quickly in a proper fire of intense heat. We would carry the misa on our pilgrimage to the earth shrine and burn it high on the mountain. But we would consecrate it first with our libations. After assembling the first misa, the shamans and we pilgrims collaborated quickly to produce three more; each slightly different in the quantity and disposition of the elements, but each essentially the same. All four would be our sweet offering to the ravenous, immortal Lady Earth.

The ritual assembly of the four misas took over three hours. The adding of each new ingredient was followed by lengthy invocations and earnest prayers to the achachilas that protect the community and to Pachamama, and each prayer was accompanied by a libation or ch'allas. We were now ready for the final ch'allas. Chrisostomos raised his voice in a long, and, to me, totally incomprehensible invocation. I caught only the names of wakas near Qorpa, and then those of the majestic, soaring peaks that surround all the Aymara villages along the southern shores of Lake Titicaca: Illimani, Mururata, Qaqajaqi (Huayna Potosi on Western maps), Illampu, Sajama. Chrisostomos was calling each peak by name; each spring; each sacred place venerated by the villagers. He begged the wakas to take pity on them, to protect them, to ward off the frosts and hail.

The other shamans soon joined in the litany, calling on the native spirits of the earth and the sky, the Christian saints, the Virgin Mary. In the midst of his invocation, Chrisostomos seized a cup of cane alcohol and almost violently spattered it over the carefully composed misas, wetting them with his expelled prayer. Ignacio, Policarpio, and Gregorio, too, made their libations with excited voices, now suddenly loud, intense, urgent with prayer. Chrisostomos filled the cup and thrust it in my hand, pushing my elbow, physically forcing me to do my own ch'alla. I muttered under my breath the name of Pachamama, Illimani, and Mallku Akapana, hoping this would serve, but Chrisostomos filled my cup again and cried out: "No, no, Doctor, you must make the ch'alla properly. Speak the names, and cast the liquor just so. In this way you must do it. Right now you must do it." As he said this he mimicked me throwing the alcohol with a clockwise sweep of my arm; he then showed me that the proper way was in the counterclockwise direction. This was the proper path for the ch'alla. I made another attempt, crouching over the misa, pouring small quantities of alcohol over the various ingredients, all the while invoking as many names of the achachilas as I could recall and in some semblance of the sequence others had uttered. I made certain that I rotated my libations

through the entire frame of the offering in the proper counterclockwise direction. Then I straightened up and threw the
remaining alcohol over the whole muxsa misa. Chrisostomos
seemed satisfied with this performance.

Eusebia and two other women I didn't recognize began
to wrap the muxsa misas in the dark, striped textiles to form
bundles in which they would be carried to the earth shrine. It
didn't matter now that the misas' painstaking architecture, its
carefully planned landscape of ritual objects, was hopelessly
jumbled as the women rapidly and casually wrapped them in
the worn, earth-stained blankets. It occurred to me that
sacred order, once invoked and consecrated, cannot easily be
altered or destroyed. The peculiar organization of ritual elements on the misas orchestrated by Chrisostomos and the
other shamans was witnessed by all the pilgrims and dedicated
to Lady Earth and the guardian spirits of the community. This
was enough. Sacred order, the order infused in the mind and
the spirit, was what counted; that the physical objects were
now mixed chaotically in the textile bundles was irrelevant.

Eusebia and her kinswomen had prepared an *aptapi*, a
communal meal, in the central courtyard of the compound. A
long line of worn but once-elegant blankets was lain out on
the ground. All the members of the community contributed
to the country feast with potatoes of various sizes and flavors,
chuño, oca, broad beans, eggs, cheese, fried bananas, and
platters of roast pig and lamb. They heaped the food on top
of the textiles; earth's table was set. We ate with our hands
amid a whirl of barking dogs, clucking hens, a magnificent,
strutting rooster, and the laughter and tears of small children.
Today the women of the community sat on one side of the
"table" and the men on the other, facing each other as we
talked and ate. The shamans began offering libations to Lady
Earth and to the achachilas that surrounded the community,
thanking them for their bounty and imploring them to protect the new fields.

Finally, Chrisostomos turned south, toward the jagged

peaks of the Qimsachata mountain range that enclosed the valley. I heard him utter prayers to the achachilas of the mountains and then to the spirits of the crops. He was beseeching the spirits of the plants to come down to Qorpa, to animate the plants, to infuse vigor and life into their seeds. His prayers were soft, but strangely urgent. He was facing the earth shrine, the object of our pilgrimage, hidden in the deep shadows of the mountain peak. Then, in a single, seamless motion, he rolled his poncho off his right arm, grabbed a cup of cane alchohol that Policarpio handed him, and whirled the liquid off into the air, to his left. He then made a quarter turn to the east and offered a second libation. He repeated this gesture twice more, each time rotating his body a quarter turn to the left, each time invoking the names of distinct wakas, different holy places. By the time he completed his circle of prayer, he had invoked and offered libations to all the community's mountain deities. He turned again toward the earth shrine in the southern mountains and addressed a final prayer to Pachamama.

At this point, I expected we would set off on a long walk to the ancient path worn into the bedrock of the mountains by countless other pilgrims ascending to the shrine. I had mentally prepared for a long trek: the summit to which we were heading was over seven miles from Chrisostomos's house. I was only partly right. The ascent to the shrine would be an arduous climb, but we would not travel all the way by foot. Instead, the group piled into my jeep to drive from Chrisostomos's house to the base of the mountain, known as Qimsachata (Three Peaks), to the very end of a rutted narrow road leading into the world of the achachilas. Once again, I had allowed a false assumption to color my understanding of Aymara ways. I had gotten it into my head that this pilgrimage, any pilgrimage, was something done on foot. My expectations were unconsciously shaped by romantic images of a North American Indian–style vision quest, accomplished by physical ordeal, captured only through mortification of the flesh. But as in so many other ways, here again the Aymara seamlessly mix the modern with the ancient in one of their most sacred rituals.

As we drove to the base of the mountain, I could see steep, andesite scarps looming above us, and, in the distance, higher up the slopes, wisps of the sublimating snow on the summit. A few twisted *q'iswara* trees clung tenaciously to the sides of quebradas that cut deep scars into the lower mountain slopes. On this last leg of our journey, we left behind the cultivated landscapes of man and entered a treacherous world of barren rock and swirling, searing winds.

There were fourteen of us. Cesar and I, the four shamans, and eight others from Qorpa: four women and four men. The women each carried one of the textile bundles in which Eusebia had wrapped the muxsa misas. As we started out on foot, we headed up a path skirting a deep ravine, walking in single file. Within half an hour, the terrain changed. We arrived at a huge talus slope, treacherous with gravel and broken rock. The path cut across the slope in almost continuous switchbacks and we had difficulty finding our footing. Gravel frequently slid out from beneath our feet, slowing progress to a painful crawl. I found myself picking my way crabwise with great care. At the crest of the slope, we paused for a moment. We had ascended far enough so that the entire valley opened out before us. But what riveted my attention was not the bucolic scene below. It was instead the privileged view we had of the two greatest wakas of the Aymara world: Lake Titicaca and the soaring, glacier encrusted peaks of the Cordillera Real. A few cirrus clouds, reflecting lake light on their undersides, took on a mottled, yellow-orange glow. The glaciated peaks on the distant horizon reflected a purer, more transparent light: a bright, white mantle of new snow astride ancient layers of opaque ice. These were the primordial mountain gods to which all Aymara communities oriented themselves. They were the spirit-infested, mystical sources of fertility and calamity. They gave gifts of rain and melting sweet water for the fields, but they also sent hail, frost, and winds across the lands of the entire Aymara world. Many different communities went on pilgrimage to the shrines of these gods far above us and just below the snow line.

But the object of our pilgrimage was an earth shrine of more modest scope, and of more local significance. Although conscious of the importance of the mountain gods residing in the Cordillera Real, each village acknowledged first their own community's shrines. The shaman's litany of sacred names and memories of the holy places began with the intimate earth shrines of the community and gradually spiraled out to the great, ice-clad achachilas of the Cordillera. Most of the hard work of ritual sacrifice occurred in familiar community shrines, not on the distant slopes on the horizon.

As we continued up the mountain, we encountered again a series of tortuous switchbacks across a steep slope littered with broken rock and gravel. We saw no one. We were even above the reach of the most determined (or desperate) shepherds. We had passed beyond the habitat of man. The path abruptly ended in a field of andesite. Here, the living rock was completely exposed to the elements. At this altitude, soil never developed; under the constant assault of wind and water, pulverized bedrock moved relentlessly down the slope. Our dirt path was transformed into a path of pure stone.

Suddenly, I heard the sound of flowing water, although I saw no source and I could not distinguish the direction from which the sound was coming. The wind was swirling, playing acoustical tricks on our ears. Chrisostomos murmured to Cesar that we were nearing the earth shrine and it struck me that this sound of water was a warning to the people of Qorpa. We were approaching their waka, a dangerous, holy place of transition and transformation, and the flowing water was the voice of the spirit of the earth. The earth shrine was a fixed point of mediation between god and man. A place where god and man touched and communicated their desires to each other in the shared language of nature.

The shamans walked with renewed energy now across the bedrock, following a path that was invisible to me but clearly familiar to them. From time to time, the sound of the rushing water wafted away in the wind, and I thought we must be headed elsewhere, away from the source. But each time we turned a corner through the field of boulders, I heard the rush of water ever more acutely. I thought we would arrive at the spot imminently. But Chrisostomos kept leading us further and further through complicated rock formations, across quebradas, past small springs and pools each of which I was convinced at first were the source of the flowing water, but never were.

My perception of time and distance on this trek was completely different from that of my companions. When Chrisostomos whispered that we were near the shrine, I assumed it was merely a matter of moments before we would arrive. To Chrisostomos, the proximity of the shrine had nothing whatsoever to do with linear distances or estimated times of arrival. To him, the nearness of the shrine was a function of sacred geography. I realize now that Chrisostomos had remarked that the earth shrine was near precisely at the point where we entered the vast, chaotic field of boulders, and the sound of flowing water suddenly became obvious. I wonder if the four shamans experienced a heightened state of awareness at this point of transition from the dirt track to the stony path. Did the visual and aural cues of the impressive stone formations and the sudden sound of water transport them into a liminal state, a state of sacred preparedness from which they could properly offer the muxsa misas to the earth shrine? I imagine this must have been the case. I know that at this point of transition I felt distinctly strange, possessed of an exquisite, yet disturbing, hypersensitivity. My senses seemed abnormally acute. I could focus with great clarity on individual sounds and sights, but my overall perceptions of people and landscapes seemed indistinct. Even now I remember small details of objects, of places, of scenes with extraordinary precision,

51

while my impression of the whole experience is inchoate. It was as if I was viewing the world through a magnifying glass in which elements that normally lie beneath the threshold of visibility suddenly loom large, while the structure itself blurs at the edges. If this stage of the pilgrimage was evoking these emotional states in me, what was happening to the mind and sensibilities of my Aymara companions, and especially to the shamans, our mediators with the spirits of the earth and sky?

Finally we came to a massive outcrop of smooth, reddish sandstone, beyond which a rugged ridge-and-saddle formation of rock extruded from the mountain. There, on the far side of the ridge, water was gushing as if pressurized from a deep, black fissure in the heart of the earth. This was the source of water we sought, the earth shrine of Qorpa.

The company of pilgrims stopped in front of the outcropping. Chrisostomos and the other shamans invoked Lady Earth, Lord Sky, and the sacred names of the earth shrine. They led us in libations as we faced east, in the direction of the spring. Now they urged us on to make the final climb to the earth shrine. We moved rapidly past the smooth, tabular outcrop of sandstone. I saw with surprise and the delighted heart of an archaeologist that there were petroglyphs pecked into the surface of the stone. A phalanx of llamas with bundles on their backs sauntered across this miniature sandstone world guarded by stick-figure humans. Pumas lurked among cactus along one side. Spirals, circles, rectangles, diamonds, rhomboids, and what looked like hieroglyphic renderings of portals and staircases were engraved everywhere in the soft surface of the stone. Small images of footprints eternally followed circuitous paths that seemed to lead nowhere. In another corner, a warrior wearing the snarling mask of a puma held a fearsome ax in one hand and the doleful, decapitated head of his vanquished opponent in the other. This was unmistakably an image carved over one thousand years ago in the time of the Tiahuanaco empire. So, the earth shrine was not simply Qorpa's. It belonged to the past, to the world of the ancestors as well. The gushing spring of this mountain shrine must have spoken with the voice of the earth's spirit to countless others. This pilgrimage was a continuing act of collective memory and worship, an age-old tradition that linked us directly to the mind and the spirit of the ancients.

The signs of other pilgrimages more recent than those of the ancients were engraved in the sandstone blocks. Ashes, broken green-glass bottles, and the cold, charred remains of burnt offerings still lingered in the smoke-stained niches on the rockface next to the spring.

The four women of Qorpa untied the bundles with our muxsa misas and laid them out on the ground. Then the tempo of the shamans' actions quickened dramatically. Ignacio and Gregorio rapidly heaped up four large piles of eucalyptus branches that the men had carried with them. Policarpio pulled out a bottle of alcohol and doused the woodpiles which were placed in a vaguely rectangular array in shallow rock hollows. He then bent down and lit fires from a book of matches. The wind on the ridge created a tremendous draft and the dry wood began to burn fiercely. From time to time, Policarpio flung alchohol onto the piles to stoke the fire into a fury.

Each of the four couples from Qorpa picked up a muxsa misa and laid it down next to one of the burning woodpiles. The shamans began to pray with their heads tilted back upward to the sky. The light was nearly horizontal with twilight rapidly descending. In the east, the summits of the Cordillera Real were brightly illuminated by the setting sun. The lake was pure silver, suffused with the dying light. These two great wakas of the Aymara world were the only elements of the landscape that were luminous now, still animated by the sun. The four shamans raised their arms in supplication to the Christianized spirits of the land. Again I could hear the word *licencia,* the prayer for permission, followed by prayers of purification. Each of the shamans completed a ch'alla over the misas, sprinkling red wine and alcohol over them, as we had done that morning in Qorpa. They turned to Cesar and me and to the couples from Qorpa, inviting us to make our libations. Then, with heartrending invocations to Lady Earth to take pity on the community, each of the four couples picked up a muxsa misa and gently lowered it onto the fire.

Instantly, four plumes of thick, aromatic smoke streamed skyward. Chrisostomos, Policarpio, Ignacio, and Gregorio, kneeling on the ground next to the pyres, stared intently as the smoke twisted in the air. A sudden gust of wind deformed the columns of smoke, nearly doubling them over and blowing them in our faces. Some gravitational pull of the spirit seemed to want to draw the smoke down into the fissures of the mountain. Then, all at once, the plumes surged skyward again. The smoke from the burnt offerings swirled in a wild, erratic dance.

The yatiris continued to offer libations over the burning sacrifices, fanning the flames anew with each stream of alcohol. Then Chrisostomos stood up with a bottle of red wine in his right hand, rolled back the drape of his poncho, and began to circle counterclockwise around the four pyres. As he circled, he uttered a continuous stream of prayers and sprayed the burning misas with alcohol.

Finally, the fires began to die down. The eucalyptus branches were completely consumed. The scent of alcohol, wood, and copal was replaced by the desolate smell of ash. Wisps of smoke still escaped from the charred misas, and the wind began to scatter the ashes. Chrisostomos's three "lieutenants" quickly began to gather up the remains of our burnt offerings, which they then placed in niches in the rocks beside the spring. They remain there today, one more link in an ancient chain of sacrifice extending back into the remote past.

With the ritual completed, I assumed we would quickly descend the mountain to avoid a dangerous climb down in the dark; but that was not to be the case. The smoke's erratic behavior was a bad omen. The augury was not good. The smoke should have streamed skyward without hesitation, directly from earth to sky. The smoke was a vaporized prayer of communication to the supernatural forces we were invoking, and the erratic pattern of the smoke meant that our prayers had been distorted. Lady Earth might accept these offerings, but the strange, vacillating comportment of the smoke weakened the force of our petition for health, fertility, and abundance. This is why I witnessed Chrisostomos Choque tremble that day, in the performance of a wrenching ritual that sought to read the fortune foretold by the behavior of that errant smoke.

Chrisostomos had the ability to put himself into a trance, through which he looked into the future. As Chrisostomos prepared, Policarpio drew a folded, black shawl of alpaca fiber from Chrisostomos's bundle and reverently laid it over Chrisostomos's head, adjusting its drape with extreme care. It was as if, with this black shawl, Policarpio was isolating Chrisostomos from the natural world around us, wrapping him in the trappings of another reality. Chrisostomos was concentrating his vision inward, away from the luminous, expansive landscapes of nature, toward the obscured, telluric world of the earth spirits. Kneeling on the textiles that had once held our *muxsa misas*, he was preparing to call the spirit of the earth. I asked Cesar what would happen. He said simply that in his trance Chrisostomos would determine if this would be a good year or a bad one.

"He will see if we will have an abundance or not. He will talk with the *ispallas.*"

"What are ispallas?"

"Ispallas are the spirits of the plants. Chrisostomos will concentrate on the ispallas and call them down. He will ask their benediction so that the plants will grow, and the harvest will be abundant."

"But how will he prognosticate? How will he tell the future?"

"He will concentrate on the ispallas. He will communicate with them. They will reveal if the community will have good luck or bad luck this year."

Chrisostomos looked in excruciating pain. He constantly shifted the weight on his knees, as if his body were growing heavier every minute, pressing into the earth. The thin wad of blankets beneath his knees did little to protect or comfort him from the stony ground.

Policarpio, Ignacio, and Gregorio kneeled to one side of Chrisostomos; the rest of us crouched on the other side against the earth shrine's rock pediment. The three shamans poured Chrisostomos many small shots of cane alcohol that he drank in staccato bursts while half singing, half chanting in a strangely muffled voice. They kept pace with him and passed glasses filled with the clear liquor to Cesar and me and the other pilgrims from Qorpa. To seek the vision, all the company of pilgrims would have to drink. Chrisostomos cried out repeatedly, "Ispall mama, *jawilla,* [welcome] *jawilla,* come from wherever you are."

The earth shrine was submerged in shadow now. I heard Chrisostomos moan. Alarmed, I glanced at him to find that he had been wrenched into a trance. His entire body quaked, wracked with spasms, as if he were in the throes of an epileptic seizure. I saw now what a taliri was, and I knew at once that this was not a path anyone would consciously choose.

In an act ages old, Chrisostomos trembled on the mountain beside the surging, turbulent stream, seeking a vision of what was to come. His village, his people, depended upon his knowledge of the earth and the sky, of the subtle tricks Lady Earth and Lord Sky play. By peering deeply into the shifting face of nature, he predicted the future. Calling the ispallas, Chrisostomos seized his vision, and what he saw was drought and scarcity. He saw early rains followed by a dry spell that would last through the year. He saw potato fields withered and blackened from frost and the pale stalks of quinoa gone leprous. He saw the harvest fail. He saw these signs in the swirling, capricious winds, in the nests of birds perched low on the water of the lake, in the sharp, desolate howl of the fox on the mountain. When Chrisostomos emerged from his trance, after perhaps minutes, he told us bluntly, almost without pity, of the scarcity and want he had seen. A heavy melancholy came over us, but there was nothing left to do but begin our tortuous descent. The wind on the mountain was piercing. Above us the Milky Way was spectacular, as if on fire, trailing dense clouds of stellar smoke. The moon was lamp-lit, nearly full, with only a sliver floating obscured against the night sky. With the sun in full retreat beneath the horizon, our path now was illuminated by the moon and the stars. We spoke hardly a word on the walk down. If not for the occasional scuff of sandals against the ground triggering shimmering cascades of pebbles down the black mountain, I would have thought the silence surrounding us was complete. If not for Chrisostomos's dire prediction of drought and frost I might have paused, as I have done many times before, to admire the crystalline beauty of the southern skies. Instead, I shivered and stared toward the ground to follow the rugged, broken contours of the land down to the distant plain before us.

As word of the bad omen spread later, I feared the worst of what the community would think of me. Was *I* the cause of the calamitous predictions? Did my presence at the earth shrine influence the achachilas to reject the muxsa misas? Did my unskilled performance of the libations to Lady Earth and Lord Sky break the authentic flow of sacrifice? I discovered later that my fears were justified, although the reaction was not as grave as I had imagined. My participation in the pilgrimage caused a minor schism in the community, not bitter, as it happened, or of great duration, but real nonetheless and one that is still recalled after nearly a decade.

But when I described my fears about the community's opinion of my role to Chrisostomos he merely shrugged. I kept probing; asking, I suppose now, for some absolution for my imagined complicity in Chrisostomos's dire prediction. A taut, perceptible trace of irritation inflected Chrisostomos's response. "Look, Doctor," he said, "you walked with us to the shrine, you made libations, you offered the muxsa misa with us. It is as it is. That's all. There's nothing more." Chrisostomos was telling me that his vision on the mountain did not really concern me. The results of the pilgrimage and of Chrisostomos's vision would not have the same grave effects on me as they would have on the villagers of Qorpa. They would suffer the effects of a bad harvest, and I would simply observe them. I was consciously seeking comfort, psychological reassurance that Chrisostomos's prediction was not my fault, and Chrisostomos was telling me that my participation and my personal concerns were irrelevant. I could never "cause" a prediction to fall one way or another in the minds of the Aymara. My pilgrimage, finally, was over.

Chrisostomos Choque died early in the following year. From time to time, his nephew Lucas offers ch'allas to his Padre-tio, and when I am in Qorpa, I am sometimes invited to join in, to remember Chrisostomos. Lucas now leads the pilgrimages to the earth shrine high on the mountain, although, in recent years, these have not been as frequent.

The words and knowledge of Chrisostomos Choque were fed by centuries of native experience. This knowledge, this experience was like a thick bed of sediment on the ocean floor, accumulated over the ages grain by grain to become the ground of the Aymara's unique vision. The cumulative experience of a people forms a knotty skein, impossible to untangle, difficult to perceive as a whole. But from these jumbled strands sometimes emerges a coherent worldview, a practical philosophy that guides everyday life. This is what the Aymara and their ancestors achieved.

Of course, the worldview of the Aymara's distant ancestors was not identical with that of their contemporary descendants. Too many acts of conflict, conquest, brutality, and colonization have transpired, too many connections to foreign cultures, religions, and economies have been established, for this ancestral, pre-Columbian vision of the world to survive unmediated into the present. To remain vital, responding to the needs and realities of its bearers, this vision changed and adapted under the influence of each new social and historical encounter.

Still, the roots of the Aymara worldview reach deeply into the space and time of the ancient past. The shapes and dimensions of the Aymara's imagined cosmos emerged from, and partake of, an ancient understanding of the world and the place of humans in it. To truly grasp their worldview in all its subtlety and nuance, we must make a journey back to the nayrapacha, to the time and place of the Aymara's genesis.

3

Andean Genesis

To truly understand the Aymara of today and their vision of the world, one must appreciate the ancient taproots of ethnic identity that nourish them. Before the coming of Columbus to the New World, the Aymara had no written language and no books to record their own history. Everything we know about them before the sixteenth century and the Spanish conquest is conjecture; reasoned conjecture based on substantial archaeological evidence, but conjecture nonetheless. There are no cuneiform tablets or papyrus libraries of the Aymara. We have no Dead Sea Scrolls or Rosetta stones. We are forced to glimpse the precolonial Aymara world through the ambiguous lenses of myth, legend, oral tradition and the physical remains they left behind. Recent archaeological discoveries are touchstones for grasping the power of the ancestors in the contemporary Aymara imagination.

For the Aymara with whom I live and work, archaeology is not a wanton search for treasure, or less still an arid academic discipline seeking generalizations about the evolution of the Andean peoples. Nor is it even a means for recapturing their own lost history (although some of the more politically motivated among them, attuned to the power of an imagined past as effective propaganda, have begun to appreciate the ideological possibilities of an "Aymara history"). For most, archaeology, apart from being an occasional source of employment, is a means of reestablishing contact with the ancestors. When a particularly fine or unusual object comes out of the ground in the course of excavation, work comes to a grinding halt. Excitement spreads through the work gangs. The foremen of the crews call for coca leaf and cane alcohol. Prayers and libations follow. They have a special relationship to these monuments from their past. They invest ancient sculptures with supernatural powers: the power to walk at night, the power to inflict illness or restore good health, the power to attract the rains. Like the mountains behind the ruins, these objects partake of the sacred and offer a connective thread to the ancestors and the spirits of the natural world.

For the Aymara, ancestors and remembrance are at the core of spirituality. In a sense, their ancestors never die. They play a central role in the fortunes of the living well after they have passed into another reality's realm. Each Aymara house today maintains a shrine to the *abuelos*, the grandparents, the founders of the lineage. Frequent sacrifices and offerings of coca, alcohol, and food at these shrines remind the family that the ancestors remain an active part of the community. The Aymara also extend the concept of ancestry from the private, intimate setting of the household into the encompassing social, moral, and natural worlds. The great mountain peaks and their shrines become achachilas (ancestors) and mallkus (ancestral lords). Achachilas and mallkus evoke an overwhelming, organic essence of the procreative power of the ancestors. Their names impart a sense of origin, of belonging, of ethnic and family roots. Certain visually impressive or unusual archaeological sites, like the great pyramids of Tiahuanaco, also carry the honorific achachila and mallku. Objects associated with these sites are themselves wakas, essences of the sacred, supernatural members of the family.

For the past eighteen years, I have worked as a professional archaeologist, side by side with the Aymara, in the heart of their ancient glory, the once majestic capital of Tiahuanaco, seat of a vast empire over one thousand years ago. Massive pyramids and eroding monoliths of granite, graven with the portraits of dead kings, loom outside my window. In ancient halls where royalty clad in the glittering emblems of their unassailable authority once commanded torrents of tribute, shepherds now graze their mangy flocks. In this surreal setting, the sense of what once was seeps unbidden into you. You cannot escape the shreds and patches of an unwritten history that everywhere pokes up at you through the sediment of ages.

I remember with almost preternatural clarity one evening, just before sunset, walking along a moldering lane in Tiahuanaco. As I took a turn down to the river, a shaft of cylindrical light, shimmering with the dust of the dry season, suddenly shot through a hole broken in the adobe wall of an old corral. The shaft, like an arc light on an old vaudeville stage, brightly illuminated a precise spot on a wall on the opposite side of the street. There, perfectly framed in the middle of the spot, was a ruddy, imperious face of ancient Tiahuanaco. During construction of the adobe wall some twenty years before, a piece of shattered vase modeled with the portrait of a nobleman was mixed randomly into the mortar. By chance, the face, staring outward, became embedded in the wall like a prehistoric insect trapped in crystalline amber. I froze, transfixed by this apparition from the past. The face of the nobleman was no bigger than a fist, but it possessed a grave air of authority, of sublime arrogance. His nose was prominent, aquiline. And his eyes were those of a shark—cruel and glossy black. The mouth was drawn tight and a cobalt blue labret was inserted under his lower lip. Patience, humility, compassion, none of this reflected from that ancient face. Who was he? Was he a hero? A priest? A warrior? A king?

Tiahuanaco does that to you. You wander dusty, forlorn

paths and the past envelops you. Constantly you imagine what it must have been like here one thousand years ago. The past is somehow too present. It is easy to be seduced by the mystical qualities of the place. Nearly five hundred years ago, the first man to bring Tiahuanaco into written history, the Spanish conquistador Pedro de Cieza de León, was afflicted with puzzlement and melancholy upon gazing on Tiahuanaco for the first time:

> Tiahuanaco . . . is famous for its great buildings which, without question, are a remarkable thing to behold. Near the main dwellings is a man-made hill, built on great stone foundations. Beyond this hill there are two stone idols of human size and shape, with the features beautifully carved, so much so that they seem the work of great artists or masters. They are so large that they seem small giants, and they are wearing long robes, different from the attire of the natives of these provinces . . .
>
> Some of the stones are very worn and wasted, and there are others so large that one wonders how human hands could have brought them to where they now stand . . . When one considers the work, I cannot understand or fathom what kind of instruments or tools were used to work them . . . I asked the natives in the presence of Juan Vargas (who holds an encomienda over them) if these buildings had been built in the time of the Incas, and they laughed at the question . . . However, they had heard from their forefathers that all that are there appeared overnight. Because of this and because they also say that bearded men were seen on the island of Titicaca . . . I say that it might have been that before the Incas ruled, there were people of parts in these kingdoms, come from no one knows where, who did these things, and who, being few and the natives many, perished in the wars.[1]

The Inca emperors, shrewd politicians that they were, eagerly appropriated the mystique of Tiahuanaco by claiming direct descent from its more ancient royal dynasties. The peculiar source of Tiahuanaco's sacredness stemmed from its legendary role as a place of genesis in the native Andean world. The story of the Aymara begins over ten thousand years ago when the first natives migrated into the Andes from North America.

The story of this genesis as told by the Incas, the last native lords of the Andes, is redolent with miracles. As the story goes, Viracocha, the great creator god, rose from the deep, cold waters of the mystical inland sea stranded high in the Andes. He strode with purpose from Lake Titicaca to the sacred precincts of Tiahuanaco, where he undertook the primordial act of human creation.

> Leaving the island on Lake Titicaca, Viracocha passed by the lake to the mainland taking with him two servants . . . He went to a place now called Tiahuanaco in the province of Collasuyu, and in this place he sculptured and designed on a great piece of stone all the nations that he intended to create. This done, he ordered his two servants to charge their memories with the names of all the tribes that he had depicted, and of the valleys and provinces where they were to come forth, which were those of the whole land.
>
> He ordered that each one should go by a different road, naming the tribes, and compelling them all to go forth and people the country. His servants, obeying the command of Viracocha, set out on their journey and work. One went by the mountain range which they call the heights over the plains on the South Sea. The other went by the highlands which overlook the mountain ranges that we call the Andes, situated to the east of the said sea. By these roads they went, saying with a loud voice, "Oh you tribes and nations, hear and obey the order of Tici Viracocha Pachayachachic, which commands you to go forth and multiply and settle the land." Viracocha himself did the same along the road between those taken by his two servants, naming all the tribes and places by which he passed. At the sound of his voice

every place obeyed, and people came forth, some from lakes, others from springs, valleys, caves, trees, rocks and hills, spreading over the land and multiplying to form the nations which are today Peru.[2]

For the Inca, recounting their myth of genesis, Tiahuanaco was the *pacarina:* the holy place of human emergence.

The Creator of the Andean world was an imagemaker; he skillfully sculptured the many nations of humankind in stone at Tiahuanaco, and then called them to life from the heart of the earth. Even today in that ancient place of origins, tourists wander through the shattered, graven images of creation scattered across the ground. Unaware of what lies beneath their feet, they tread upon the Creator's cosmic handiwork. Viracocha himself still stares implacably over the land and the people he created at the dawn of time. His imperious face is enshrined on the "Gateway of the Sun," the native Andean world's most perfect image of divinity. Viracocha gazes eternally to the east, to the rising sun, from Tiahuanaco's Temple of the Kings, the monumental structure known in Aymara as *Kalasasaya,* the Place of Standing Stones. His vision seems fixed on the distant horizon emphatically marked by the saw-toothed, shimmering white peaks of Mount Illimani. Arrayed in splendor, the Creator still presides over the abandoned halls of Tiahuanaco's kings. He wears a resplendent crown, fashioned from the very rays of the sun. He poses regally on a sacred, triple-terraced pyramid, holding a lightning bolt in his right hand, and an *atlatl,* the Native American spear thrower, in his left hand. Within the pyramid, we see the characteristic U shape of a cave, opening upward. We realize then that Viracocha's dramatic stage is not a simple, man-made temple, but rather a supernatural pyramid. The Creator stands on the sacred mountain-pyramid from which the waters of all life flow.

In exquisite irony, the original text of Andean Genesis lies unrecognized, obscured under the lichen-encrusted faces of the granite statues that haunt the ruins of Tiahuanaco. What we have left to speak to us about the original beliefs of the ancient Andean peoples are written texts created by the Spanish; texts which purport to faithfully record the beliefs of the ancients, but remain little more than distorted simulacra. These Spanish versions of native Andean oral literature caricature native beliefs and twist them with more than a little Christian morality and cosmological outlook.

Tici Viracocha Pachayachachic was more than an aesthete, a carver and shaper of humanity. He was a god of action, a creator and destroyer of many worlds: the Shiva of the Andes. Before successfully creating the world of humans, Viracocha annihilated two prehuman worlds; first by fire and then again by flood. But the Creator, at last, established permanent cosmological order in Tiahuanaco. He carved the images of nations. Then, with the help of two faithful subjects, he called forth humanity from the natural world. Viracocha commanded the various tribes of man to emerge from the sacred landscape of "springs, valleys, caves, trees, rocks and hills," finally bestowing on each its natural name. Even at the dawn of time, Andean identity was inextricably bound to sacred places and to sacred names. Like Chrisostomos Choque and the yatiris of the contemporary Aymara world who call the achachilas by name, Viracocha subdues the wild, natural world with his voice, with the generative power of naming. Viracocha, the first shaman of the Andean world, expertly manipulates the tools of the seers' trade. He creates the universe with his voice and with his memory.

In true Andean fashion, humanity emerged not from a utopian Garden of Eden, but from the hard, living rock and water of the natural world. In this great tale of Andean Genesis, Viracocha shapes and reshapes humanity in the forge of trial and tribulation. In the latter half of the sixteenth century, Antonio de la Calancha preserved another version of the genesis story. This myth again recounts the sequential destruction of two prehuman worlds, first by fire and then again by flood, by the creator, here called only Pachayachachic, the "Invisible

Lord." Pachayachachic unleashed his fury upon the inhabitants of these worlds when they directly began to worship the forces of nature—water and springs, mountains and rocks—rather than the Creator himself. Only a few who had not given themselves over to the ecstatic worship of natural forces escaped Pachayachachic's wrath by retreating to protected redoubts on the highest mountain peaks. After the waters receded, these survivors were charged with repopulating the land. In time, these too lapsed into animistic worship and the Creator responded by turning them into stone. Finally, according to Calancha's version of the myth, "it is said that until now Pachayachachic had not created the sun, nor the moon, nor the stars but that he made them now in Tiahuanaco and in the Lake of Titicaca."[3]

After abortive attempts subverted by the infidelity of his subjects, the Creator at last establishes permanent cosmological order in Tiahuanaco. From chaos and rebellion, the natural and social orders are reintegrated. The sun, moon, and constellations are created at the place of origins and the era of mankind begins. The passage of these celestial bodies through the heavens creates Time itself. Their regular movement through the night sky becomes the astronomical guide by which humans mark the annual cycle of the seasons. Stars and man become synchronized. By observing the stars, the planets, the sun, and the moon, humans now possess the knowledge to interpret and intercept the flow of natural forces for their own benefit.

Still other versions of Andean Genesis at Tiahuanaco were recorded by Juan de Betanzos (1551), and Crístobal de Molina (1553). In the priceless, early version of Andean Genesis preserved by Betanzos, the world creator, here named Contiti Viracocha, emerges from Lake Titicaca and creates "the sun and the day, and the moon and the stars" at Tiahuanaco. Viracocha orders "the sun to move in its path"—and so the time of mankind begins. After calling out people from caves, rivers, and springs scattered through the mythical landscape of creation time, Contiti Viracocha furiously turns some into stone for sacrilegious behavior. Then, beginning the act of creation again, the Creator fashions a new race of people to populate the earth. He created "a certain number of people and a Lord to govern over them and many pregnant women . . . and the children that they had in cradles, all of whom were made from stone." Contiti Viracocha dispatches these people of stone to the distant corners of the Andean world. "In this fashion," the Creator made "all the people of Perú and its provinces there in Tiahuanaco."

Viracocha keeps with him in Tiahuanaco only two faithful companions who become his sacred messengers and his divine memory. He charges his messengers to remember the names of all the people he created, as well as the precise location ("the springs and rivers and caves and mountains in the provinces") from which they will emerge after their creation in Tiahuanaco. Then he sends his divine messengers in opposite directions out into the newly created world to call forth the new race of humans: "One he sent to the part and province of Condesuyu, that is, to the left hand side standing in Tihuanacu with one's back to where the sun rises . . . the other he sent to the part and province of Andesuyo, that is, to the right hand side standing in the manner indicated, with the back to where the sun rises."[4]

In Crístobal de Molina's version of the same myth, these two culture heroes are the Andean Adam and Eve: the primeval male-female pair and the children of Viracocha.[5] Like the other variants on the theme of genesis, the events of the myth begin after a universal flood: ". . . all the created things perished through him [Viracocha] except for a man and a woman, who remained in a box, and when the waters receded, the wind carried them to tierra Guanaco [Tiahuanaco] . . ." Viracocha orders the pair to remain in Tiahuanaco, and gives them, as surrogates of the Creator, dominion over the people they are charged with calling forth from the sacred landscape. The female of the original couple, called the *ymay mama vira-*

cocha, is given domain over the mountainous lands, while the male, the *tocapa viracocha,* receives the mandate over the peoples of the plains and lowlands. Viracocha first creates the natural world, and then organizes it into complementary halves: the people of the mountains and the people of the plains.

The variations of the genesis myth recorded by Betanzos and Molina not only identify Tiahuanaco as the pacarina, the sacred place of origin for the physical universe, but also as the central point of partition of the social universe. The concept of duality, the world and all things in it divided into two parts, was deeply embedded in the worldview of ancient Andean peoples. Notions of duality still shape the mind of the native Andean peoples. In these myths, recorded during the death throes of the Inca empire, Tiahuanaco represents a kind of boundary marker, the point of cleavage between two archetypal social groups. To the ancients, Tiahuanaco was the revered center where complementary, but potentially competitive, social groups merged in a shared cultural identity. But who were these social groups? Where did they come from?

In his classic treatise on the natives of the New World, the Spanish cleric Bernabé Cobo informs us that before the Lake Titicaca region was conquered by the Inca during the mid-fifteenth century, the original name for Tiahuanaco was Taypi Kala. As Cobo explains it, Taypi Kala meant "the stone in the center"; the natives ascribed this name to the site because they considered the city to be in "the center of the world, and that from there the world was repopulated after the flood."[6] According to our earliest dictionary of the Aymara language, compiled by the Italian Jesuit Ludovico Bertonio in 1612, *taypi* refers to something situated in the middle.[7] But the term taypi does not merely denote a central location in space or time. Within the more subtle textures of meaning, taypi refers to a place, a zone, or a quality where two distinct things converge. For instance, Aymara Indians living today on the eastern side of the Bolivian Andes use the term taypi to refer specifically to the area on the mountain slopes where corn and potato farming converge. This is an important zone of agricultural production defined by the altitude at which both corn and potato farming is viable. This altitude, ranging from about 1800 to 3000 meters above sea level, incorporates the richest and most fertile regions of the Andean world.[8] Here the concept of taypi emphasizes the quality of the melding of opposites (corn versus potato; grain versus tuber) to form a productive whole.

During the sixteenth century, we know that the Aymara Indians organized their social and physical landscape in a sacred geography redolent with symbolic associations. According to Aymara ways of thinking, their entire world was divided into two halves: Urcosuyu and Umasuyu. Urcosuyu referred to the mountain peaks and to the high, arid, rolling lands to the west of Lake Titicaca. Umasuyu, on the other hand, was the fertile valleys to the east of Lake Titicaca, from the lake edge into the Cordillera Real and beyond to the spectacular incised gorges and lush subtropical landscapes of the Amazonian watershed. In Aymara, *urco* conveys the sense of maleness and solidity. The people of the Urcosuyu were constantly in motion, nomadic pastoralists tending vast herds of llamas and alpacas. They moved freely across the roof of the Andean world in pursuit of fresh pasture and watering holes for their animals. In the mind of the Aymara, the inhabitants of the Urcosuyu were associated supernaturally with the celestial sphere—with lightning, with thunder, with the spirit world of the sky. Dwellers in Urcosuyu were thought to possess the masculine qualities of virility, aggressiveness, and stoicism. They were a people as hard as the stones of their mountain world. The people of the Umasuyu, on the other hand, practiced a sedentary, agricultural lifestyle, and enjoyed fishing and hunting along the shores of Lake Titicaca. *Uma* itself means water in the Aymara language, and the inhabitants of Umasuyu were truly people of the lake. They were associated supernaturally with the underworld, with the watery domain of the spirits in the heart of the earth. Uma conveyed notions of passivity and domesticity and evoked the organic fertility of females. Between these two ecological and conceptual poles, between Urcosuyu and Umasuyu, between the People of the Mountains and the People of the Lake, was the taypi, the essential zone of convergence. The taypi that connected these two distinct social and physical halves of the Aymara world was Lake Titicaca itself. As Thérèse Bouysse-Cassagne, a French student of Aymara culture, perceptively remarked:

> As an element of Aymara thought, Lake Titicaca is not merely a specific geographical location: It is at once a centrifugal force that permits the differentiation of the two terms *[Urcosuyu* and *Umasuyu]* in opposition and a centripetal force that ensures their mediation. In the symbolic architecture, the *taypi,* place of convergence, is crucial to the equilibrium of the system . . . In fact, Titicaca is located in a fairly temperate climatic zone where crops from the puna [the highlands] and from the warm lands can both be grown. The microclimatic features of its shores and islands permit the cultivation of certain varieties of potatoes . . . as well as the tiny sacred maize.[9]

So, for the Aymara, Lake Titicaca was not simply an inanimate place, a physical point on the map. The lake was an active, living force emblematic of the union of a world cleaved in two. It was the sacred seam where Urcosuyu and Umasuyu merged. It was the place where the conflicting forces of nature were brought into balance.

Many of the rich symbolic associations of urco, uma, and taypi are expressed in compressed, almost telegraphic fashion in the origin myths collected in the sixteenth century by the Spanish. The twin culture heroes, ymay mama viracocha and tocapa viracocha, are the primeval female-male couple. They are associated with west and east, with mountains and plains. In the act of creation, they journey along diametrically opposed paths (east versus west) defined by the axis of the sun's daily points of rising and setting. The divine force of creation, Viracocha, walks the intermediate path, the taypi. All three, the origin twins and Viracocha himself, set out from Tiahuanaco, the essential point of origin, partition, and convergence.

In this scheme, if Lake Titicaca was perceived as the taypi, the city of Tiahuanaco was Taypi Kala, the sacred center at the center of the world. The great, ancestral city of the Aymara nation and the lake beside which it was founded were imbued with a symbolism that crosscut and unified entire religious, social, economic, and political traditions. This special vision of a world divided into two parts even bridged the chasm of linguistic and ethnic divisions. The same concepts were held by the native Aymara populations of the Lake Titicaca basin and by their Quechua-speaking Inca overlords on the eve of their own conquest by European invaders in 1532. Long after its disastrous decline and fall in the eleventh century of our era, Tiahuanaco retained its capacity to strike awe in the minds of the pilgrims who journeyed there to gaze upon its monumental, broken ramparts. This most sacred center at the center of the Andean world continues to emanate a mysterious, commanding aura of spiritual power. Tiahuanaco figures prominently in the protocols of religious memory. Aymara shamans still invoke the holy names of its ruined temples. And natives still climb the staircase of Akapana, the sacred pyramid-mountain, to plant symbols of their independence and cultural identity.

But if a dualistic worldview was broadly shared by native Andeans in the centuries just prior to the Spanish conquest of the New World, when did such notions emerge? What was their genesis? Why do such concepts persist even today in the mind of the Aymara?

A people's perception of the world is deeply embedded in their psyche, an ancient product of common experience. The long chain of ancestors disappearing beyond the horizon of memory links us directly to our history, to the ultimate ground of our culture. A vision of the world, a philosophy of life, persists stubbornly in the mind. Such fundamental beliefs and emotional attachments to the world around us are not quickly formed or lightly abandoned. If they change, they change incrementally, almost imperceptibly. Only rarely will people radically transform their view of the world. If they do so, it is usually because of some catastrophe so profound, so incomprehensible that the world truly is not the same. The Black Death; the Spanish conquest of America; the world wars of the twentieth century; Hiroshima: all these made people question the stability and ultimate meaning of their worlds. To the Andean mind, such devastating events were thought to happen cyclically, although their precise form and time of occurrence could not be predicted with precision. They were what the ancient Andeans called Pachakuti: the "World Turned Round." Mercifully rare, social tragedies of such immense scope crack the cultural consensus. When they do occur, people desperately seek new meanings, new ways to explain and to understand a world turned inside out.

In searching for the roots of the Aymara's view of the world, we will catch glimpses of Pachakuti, ancient events that radically transformed their ancestors' lives. But we will also see millennia of shared experience in a seemingly eternal world. Both the ordinary acts of countless lives lived out on the high plateau and the episodic, earthshaking events of Pachakuti shaped the Aymara's vision of themselves and the world around them. The substance of their vision is the product of a constant struggle to make a living in one of the most forbidding human environments on the globe. But more than merely feeding themselves and their children, the Aymara Indians and their ancestors sought to imbue their lives and their world with meaning. Trembling on the mountain, Chrisostomos resonated to the same forces of nature as the first taliri who ascended to the earth shrines on the Qimsachata Range thousands of years ago. Both strove mightily to feed Lady Earth and to supplicate the capricious mountain deities who give life and deal death with equal indifference. Both shared a philosophy of spirituality exquisitely sensitive to the rhythms and nuances of the natural world.

To understand this subtle philosophy, this breathtaking vision of man and nature, we must transport ourselves well into the past, back beyond the Inca, the first native Andeans to enter into written history—a history written tragically by their Spanish conquerors. Our sojourn into the nayrapacha, the time and place of the Aymara's genesis, takes us back over four thousand years, to the cultural predecessors of the Tiahuanaco empire. It is then that we see monuments and objects crafted by the distant ancestors of the Aymara Indians which offer the first tangible clues to how and when this philosophy came into being.

But, in some sense, the first steps of our journey really begin over fifteen thousand years ago when the first humans laid eyes on the vast, high plateaus around Lake Titicaca. These Andean pioneers were descendants of the earliest migrants to the New World who had passed over the Bering Strait from northeast Asia many generations before. As best we can reconstruct from the fragmentary evidence available to us, these early Native Americans organized themselves in small, highly mobile bands. They ranged widely over the landscape, hunting and foraging to earn their livelihood. Our desire to know who these earliest colonizers of the high Andes were and how they conceived of the world around them is frustrated by our sketchy evidence. These pioneers left few material traces of their passage through the Andes. Many of the landscapes in which they originally lived are inaccessible to us now, deeply buried under tons of alluvium, river sediments washed down from the mountains over the millennia. The clothes they wore to ward off the bitter cold of the night, the plants they collected to cure their sick, the objects they carved in wood and bone to express their relationship with the spirit world—all are decayed now, indistinguishable parts of the altiplano's earth. Only a few archaeological sites in the high plateau preserve remnants of their ancient actions: a small campsite here, a station for butchering game there, perhaps the remains of a quarry, or a stone-tool manufacturing site. Without richer archaeological clues than a few stone flakes and the smeared charcoal of an ancient campfire to guide us, we cannot hope to develop a complex portrait of their lives. They remain little more than disembodied spirits, wraithlike creatures from the ancient world who inhabit only the most obscure corners of our imaginations.

But one stunning discovery in the cool, pine forests of southern Chile has changed our image of these earliest natives of the Andes forever. In 1976, woodcutters working the humid forests of Chile's southern extremities accidentally stumbled across some strange, fossilized teeth protruding from the eroded, sandy banks of Chinchihuapi Creek. They reported their discovery to a local student of archaeology who, in turn, alerted Tom Dillehay, a North American archaeologist living and teaching in Chile at the time. Instantly, Dillehay realized the importance of the find.

The woodcutters' unusual fossils were the molars of mastodons, distant American cousins of modern elephants. Dillehay knew that mastodons disappeared at the end of the Pleistocene, some ten to twelve thousand years ago, possibly hunted into extinction by the original colonizers of the Americas. He began to suspect that at some time in the remote past humans stalked these huge animals along Chinchihuapi Creek. He hoped to find evidence of a kill site somewhere in the vicinity. If he could reconstruct what happened on the banks of Chinchihuapi Creek, he would fill an enormous gap in our understanding of the migratory paths and lifestyles of the earliest Americans.

Were the mastodon remains protruding from the soil the remnants of an ancient feast celebrated by some lucky hunters? Or were they merely the forlorn markers of an extinct elephant graveyard, unassociated with humans at all?

To confirm his suspicions that humans were preying on the hapless mastodons, Dillehay organized a campaign of excavations with scientists from Austral University in Valdivia, Chile. What Dillehay and his Chilean colleagues discovered over the course of their excavations between 1978 and 1981 at the site they called Monte Verde astounded the archaeological world.[10]

Pursuing any evidence of human activity associated with the mastodon teeth, they unexpectedly uncovered an entire community of ancient hunters and gatherers who roamed across the bogs and rain forests of southern Chile thirteen thousand years ago. What was so astonishing about the find was the great diversity and almost perfect state of preservation of the archaeological remains. Instead of a few chipped stone flakes strewn anonymously across the ground, Dillehay uncovered the most intimate details of the lives of these earliest Andeans. Perhaps the most remarkable discovery of all at Monte Verde was a series of rectangular huts built on foundations of logs and rough-hewn hardwood planks staked to the ground. The walls of these dwellings were fashioned from animal hides stretched over a wickerwork of slender saplings. Dillehay's team excavated a series of rooms, each ten to fifteen feet on a side, arranged to form two parallel rows.

An amazing array of stone, wood and bone tools, plants, animal bones, and clay-lined hearths were miraculously preserved inside these ancient huts. Isolated from the rectangular huts, the ancient community of hunters erected a special wishbone-shaped building on the western side of Monte Verde. The building opened out toward a plaza pockmarked by small, clay-lined pits that served as braziers. Scattered about the open plaza in a dense constellation of debris, Dillehay patiently recovered the remains of animal hides, woodworking tools, butchered mastodon bones, mollusks, burned seeds, cuds of chewed medicinal plants, and hearths. Everywhere his team discovered thirteen-thousand-year-old plants of all types: wild potatoes, seeds, berries, nuts, fruits, leafy vegetables, edible algae. Many of these plants thrived in completely different ecological settings than the sandy banks of Chinchihuapi Creek. Some came from the Pacific coast, others from mountainous highlands, still others from river plains. These plants were specially sought out by the people of Monte Verde as they foraged widely across the lush, spectacular landscapes of their ancient world. They carried these exotic plants and other unusual substances such as rock minerals and pitch back to their permanent home on Chinchihuapi Creek.

By chance, after this small community abandoned their dwellings, perhaps moving on to better hunting grounds, Chinchihuapi Creek changed course, stagnated, and eventually sealed the fragile settlement with a layer of peat. Like the lava and ash from Mount Vesuvius that entombed Pompeii, the peat perfectly conserved the evanescent traces of these ancient lives. Although no human remains were ever found at the site on the banks of Chinchihuapi Creek, the evidence of complex human activity is unambiguous.

With this rich, fortuitously perserved collection of artifacts as our inspiration, we can readily imagine what life was like for these earliest inhabitants of the Andes. They lived in the intimate social world of a band in which food was shared and eaten together as a community around common hearths. Apparently the aptapi, the communal meal, was an extremely ancient institution, one of the cornerstones of social life that may have come into the New World with the original migrants from Asia. The people of Monte Verde also shared the dangers of the hunt. Six huge mastodons were taken down and butchered in a single ambuscade not far from the huts along Chinchihuapi Creek. We can envision these hunters at first pelting the enraged mastodons with smooth, egg-shaped sling stones from a safe distance. Then, fearlessly, they closed for the kill. The hunters speared the mastodons again and again with sharp stone lances, jumping back nimbly from the confused, swirling mass of the dying animals. Finally, the beasts, exhausted from fear and pain, collapsed ponderously to the earth, mortally wounded, their life's blood flowing into the creek. Immediately they were set upon and gleefully butchered by the hunters. Later the band would feast together on the fatty meat and marrow of the mastodons in the flickering light of the braziers set into Monte Verde's plaza.

But something more than communal eating went on in this plaza. The enormous quantity and variety of medicinal plants, herbs, and exotic minerals recovered by Dillehay's research team reflects a more esoteric world, a world of belief and of shared ritual action. It is not hard to imagine that the isolated, wishbone-shaped structure on the plaza was the community's shrine. Within its hide-covered walls, shamans chanted through the night, peered into the future, cured the sick with special plants gathered in pilgrimages to the foothills of the Andes far from Monte Verde. Perhaps, too, the people of Monte Verde sought visions in the shadowed recess of their shrine; some of the plants they consumed had hallucinogenic properties.

The discoveries at Monte Verde open an unprecedented new window of interpretation for us. Now we can place real flesh on the scattered bones of early human life in the Americas. We can finally put a human face to these earliest inhabitants of the New World. Their actions are no longer merely ciphers spun from the flimsy fabric of enigmatic stones, broken bones, and random stains of charcoal. In the remains along Chinchihuapi Creek, we can envision the social life of a thirteen-thousand-year-old community adapting ingeniously to the rigors of their Andean home. We glimpse, too, something of their understanding of the world around them, and their relationship with the supernatural.

At Monte Verde, we witness, if not quite the birth of belief, at least the earliest display that we have of Andean spirituality. This spirituality bears the distinctive mark of an even more remote past. The ancestral bands of hunters who migrated over the Bering Strait into North America brought their shamans with them. They came with a shared view of the world that evolved slowly as they moved through alien territory to the very tip of the South American continent. Some scholars believe three genetically distinct populations of Asiatic origin crossed the land bridge into North America more than ten thousand years ago. But only one of these original population groups eventually filtered into South America. Over the millennia, these original migrants populated the entire southern continent, colonizing the great Andean highlands and gradually penetrating into the secluded forests of the Amazon. From this breathtaking perspective, the indigenous peoples of South America are truly one. All share the same genetic heritage. With that genetic heritage came a common substrate of beliefs. These beliefs changed and diverged, along with other elements of social life, but they retained a fundamental essence of commonality.

This is the cultural counterpart to the "founder's principle" described by biologists. If an organism is allowed to reproduce over many generations in a closed environment, most of the descendants will carry some original attributes of the first reproducing pair. So a pair of fruit flies with red eyes will pass along that attribute to thousands of their descendants. Random mutations will produce variation, but many original attributes will be retained in the genetic makeup of the population.[11] Although beliefs and religious concepts are not fruit flies, evolving according to Mendelian principles, there is a valuable analogy here. In a real sense, the original migrants into the Americas were the founders of Native American consciousness. When these pioneers crossed the Bering Strait, they carried with them abstract concepts of how the universe was ordered, specific forms of social organization, attitudes about their relationships with nature. All of these original cultural attributes contributed fundamental structural elements to the social and mental makeup of their descendants. I imagine that if they could have bridged the chasm of thirteen thousand years, the shamans of Monte

Verde would have had much in common with Chrisostomos Choque. Plants of power, pilgrimages, trances, the supernatural forces that govern the earth—these would have been their shared language.

Of course, the historical connections between the modern Aymara and their most ancient hunting-and-gathering ancestors are remote. But these original migrants to the Andes developed essential strategies for living in this daunting environment that remained virtually unchanged for millennia. Many of these strategies would not have seemed alien to the more recent ancestors of the Aymara in the rural reaches of the Tiahuanaco empire fifteen hundred years ago.

One economic strategy worked out by these first Andeans was a pattern of seasonal nomadism between highlands and lowlands. From about 8000 B.C. on, the Pacific coastal populations of modern-day Chile and Peru were actively engaged with contemporaneous populations living at high altitudes in the Bolivian altiplano to the east. For several millennia, at regular intervals during the year, populations that lived seasonally on the coast, exploiting the rich biomass of the nearshore environment, would journey into the inter-Andean basins and high grasslands to hunt for vicuña and guanaco, wild cousins to the llama.

At some point before the fourth millennium B.C., this form of exchange, wholesale population migrations up and down the mountains, changed as agriculture and domesticated llamas and alpacas were added to the economic repertoire. With agriculture, both highland and coastal communities established permanent, sedentary settlements. Yet the movement between highland and coast did not cease with the development of these more stable communities. On the contrary, after about 2000 B.C., large pack trains of llamas traveling along these vertical axes between the established villages and towns of the highlands and coasts were a common scene throughout the southern Andes. Over time and space, these llama caravans were organized in different ways. Most often, the Andean caravans were operated by politically independent pastoral societies. These pastoral nomads followed predetermined trade routes, visiting communities on the coast and in the high Andean basins in a fixed seasonal round. The social relationships that bound the nomadic pastoralists with their sedentary trading partners was a form of kinship arrangement. Natives in the Andes rarely operated through impersonal markets linked to the value of commodities alone. Stable, reciprocal kinship bonds were essential to a system that demanded high-risk ventures over the trackless, desertic wastes of the southern Andean altiplano. Caravan traders would not hazard a perilous journey without the assurance of a guaranteed consumer for their products and, just as importantly, family-style hospitality at the end of the trail.

These great southern Andean caravans fueled an extensive interchange of people, products, and, just as importantly, political and religious ideas. The earliest inhabitants of the Andean high plateau pioneered a strategy and established a pattern that preadapted subsequent altiplano populations to extensive social and economic relationships with their lowland-dwelling contemporaries. The form and intensity of these interactions changed in the context of local historical events, but highland-lowland relationships always formed a salient feature of the social landscape in the southern Andes. The people of the Andes were differentiating themselves, settling into particular ecological, social, and economic niches. But, at the same time, they avidly cultivated contacts with others, diversifying and enriching their cultural and economic spheres of action.

At some time early in the second millennium B.C., the Andean high plateau around Lake Titicaca experienced a cultural breakthrough, a rapid movement toward what we might call true civilization. Suddenly, we see in the archaeological record a profusion of increasingly complex human settlements: a vital, interacting network of villages graced with expanding economies. The natural resource endowments of

Lake Titicaca powered these village economies, permitting a stable, abundant food supply. In good Malthusian fashion, native populations on the high plateau exploded.

Each of these villages had access to a rich suite of natural resources that enabled them to diversify production and to reduce their risk of exposure to the catastrophic famines that are common to small-scale, isolated societies in marginal environments. The cornerstone of these villages' economies was the effective merging of three distinct kinds of specialized occupations: farming, fishing, and herding. None of these villages was tied to a stagnant, monolithic economy. Primary production from this rich, diverse economy generated sufficient surplus to stimulate a whole range of secondary, wealth-producing occupations. At this time, we begin to see compelling archaeological evidence for activities such as large-scale manufacture of craft goods, extensive local and long-distance trading, production of public sculptures and luxury items for conspicuous consumption, and many others besides. These Lake Titicaca villages in the time prior to the emergence of the Tiahuanaco empire were behaving like protocities, generating food surpluses and transforming these surpluses into new products and services. They began generating their own wealth by adding new work to old, by layering new divisions of labor onto old ones.[12]

The cornerstone activities of fishing, herding, and farming themselves took place in distinct ecological zones, required different technologies of production, and demanded different work schedules, occupational skills, and labor organization. Work in agricultural fields was heavily seasonal, involving an intense but uneven investment of labor through the year and requiring considerable village cooperation and coordination of labor. As is still the case today, most agricultural work in the high plateau took place in two intensive bursts of activity: field preparation and planting between August and November, and harvest from the end of March through May. For ancient Andean farmers, both land and labor were scarce resources, and resources that required virtually full-time management.

In contrast, fishing and herding were occupations pursued in a more diffuse manner. Unlike agriculture, the natural resources exploited by herders and fishers were not concentrated, but rather distributed widely and relatively evenly over the environment. Locating good pasturage in the high grasslands for llama and alpaca herds, for instance, requires movement across a fairly extensive area. Herding, unlike farming, was never geographically fixed. Similarly, the work of managing herds was not as concentrated and collaborative as that of agriculture. Llama and alpaca herds require constant attention, but this work can be delegated to a relatively few specialists who live among and move with the herds. Still, the relationship between humans and llamas in the Andean high plateau is an ancient and pervasive one, a peculiarly intense form of symbiosis. Although managed by a few, herds of llama and alpaca carry intense emotional significance for all native Andeans. Economic uses of llamas and alpacas speak only superficially to the complementary social, ritual, and psychological roles that these animals play. The llama is an essential source of food and tools, fine wool clothing, and transport. It is an avatar of the supernatural, an animate creature both sacred and profane. Llama sacrifices mark critical episodes of the human life cycle. Like animals in the Zodiac, llamas mark the cyclical passage of time. Andean people see the llama as a constellation in the night sky; to them, the stars we know as Alpha and Beta Centauri are the eyes of the llama. In the old Inca and Tiahuanaco empires, royal priests offered bloody sacrifices of llamas to Lady Earth and Lord Sky to ensure bounteous herds and rich harvests. The propagation of vast llama and alpaca herds was the obligation of the emperors. For these imperious lords of the Andes, the health and size of the royal herds became tangible signs of divine favor and of personal power. Llamas represent the vital, blood-driven life force that courses through all creatures. In some sense, they are themselves divine. We are hard-pressed to exaggerate the importance of these strangely beautiful animals in the minds of the native Andeans, past and present.

Fishing, too, is an ancient and extremely productive mode of food production in the Lake Titicaca basin. Like herding, fishing is diffuse in terms of the environment it exploits and the labor organization that it requires. Simple watercraft, nets, hooks, snares, and atlatls, or dart throwers, were all that was necessary to fish and forage successfully on the lakes and rivers of the high plateau. The work is mobile, constant, and not subject to seasonal variation. Unlike herding and agriculture, which depended on specific management techniques, scheduling of activities, and localized distribution of good pasturelands or potentially arable soils, fishers and aquatic foragers responded to the natural population cycles of the wild resources they harvested. They could not domesticate or maximize the population size of the animals on which they depended, as could herders, nor could they artificially intensify food production, as could agriculturalists.

Before the European conquest of the Andes, Lake Titicaca supported substantial populations of specialized aquatic foragers and fishers. Spanish accounts from the sixteenth and seventeenth centuries describe a special ethnic group that traditionally, if not exclusively, earned their daily subsistence by intensive aquatic foraging. These were the people called the Uru. In the pre-Hispanic past, the Uru were distributed along an eight-hundred-kilometer-long aquatic axis from Lake Azángaro in Peru to Lake Titicaca and down the Desaguadero River to the great saline lakes of Poopó and Coipasa in southern Bolivia. The Uru fished and gathered the wild resources of these lakes and rivers. They exchanged fresh and dried fish, edible algae, waterfowl and eggs, totora reed and other lake products for goods such as llama wool, potatoes, and quinoa with their more terrestrially oriented neighbors. Working with census data from the general inspection ordered by the Spanish viceroy, Francisco de Toledo, between 1573 and 1575, the French anthropologist Nathan Wachtel projected that approximately eighty thousand Uru lived along this aquatic axis in the late sixteenth century, representing about twenty-four percent of the native population.[13]

The Uru's name for themselves is Kot'suñs, or "People of the Lake," clearly reflecting an intense identification with their aquatic home. This name self-consciously sets the Uru apart from those they refer to as the "Dry People," the farmers of the high plateau. The Uru consider themselves to inhabit a separate reality: the aqueous realm, physically and symbolically distinct from the telluric, earth-dependent setting of the agrarian lifestyle. Again, we find embedded in the mind of the indigenous Andean peoples a reflexive mapping of the social world into the deep contours of the physical universe: The Uru define themselves in terms of the the sharp, sensually apparent opposition between the terrestrial and the aquatic, the dry and the wet. Paradoxically, the Uru are the most aggressively insular of Andean ethnic groups and yet simultaneously the people of the high plateau who depend most for their livelihood on established relationships of exchange with their terrestrial neighbors.

Today their population is drastically reduced. Remnant families of Uru still live around Lake Titicaca and along the Desaguadero River, but their numbers continue to dwindle. In contemporary Bolivia, the Uru are a tiny minority embedded in the larger, more powerful native world of their Aymara neighbors. They are doubly dispossessed. Regarded as primitive curiosities by the urbanized populations of Bolivia, they lack the nationally influential political organization of their far more numerous Aymara counterparts. Today, the Uru persist in a reality that becomes increasing marginal to the modern world, a twilight existence tinged with a poignant penumbra of the past. Their language and their ancient culture are in inexorable decline. Their children drift away from the villages of their birth seeking to escape the bitter realities of rural poverty. The Uru have no future as Uru in the twenty-first century. At the turn of the millennium, they will witness the extinction of their special identity. The Kot'suñs were present at the birth of the great Tiahuanaco nation. But soon, only memories of their ancestors' unique contribution to native Andean culture will remain for them. Their world is finally coming to an end. Still, some families linger on, fishing the deep waters of the lake, hunting and gathering among the totora reeds, faithfully reenacting a drama of rural life thousands of years old.

The unique economic niche that the ancestors of the Kot'suñs carved out for themselves played a fundamental role in the emergence of what was to become the Tiahuanaco civilization. By organizing and integrating these three specialized occupations—farming, fishing, and herding—the pre-Tiahuanaco societies around Lake Titicaca created an inherent form of social complexity. This complexity conferred on them competitive and adaptive advantages. They were able to diversify their subsistence portfolios and reduce the risk of catastrophic food crisis. Diversification and stabilization of the village economy stimulated more and different kinds of work and new divisions of labor. In this reciprocal process, new divisions of labor further accelerated village social complexity, creating new occupations, new structures of work, and substantial new wealth. New wealth gradually opened up these societies, moving them outside of their circumscribed, parochial reality into a broader social world. Previously self-sufficient villages became profoundly dependent on other communities to sustain their newfound sources of wealth. With that interdependence came inevitable culture change—in economies, in aspirations, in power relations.

By the latter half of the second millennium B.C., the villages around Lake Titicaca were reaching a critical mass of accelerating social complexity. This new social complexity, marked by diversified economic activities, multiple divisions of labor, and broad regional exchange of goods and services, was the essential touchstone for the emergence of urban life in the early state of Tiahuanaco. But at this time something just as significant as vital, expanding economies emerged in the Lake Titicaca basin: A new religious cult swept through the villages and towns of the high plateau. If we think about it, this should not come as a surprise. It is almost predictable. Once a population threshold had been reached in the high plateau, the rapid emergence of a religious cult that attracted widespread public adherence was inevitable. At the heart of civilized life, we find ideas; fundamental ideas about the proper relationships among humans and between humans and nature. Such ideas might be framed in the secular terms of abstract political theory, or in a philosophy of science. But in the archaic world, the world of ancient civilizations, these core ideas about nature and society were invariably cast in the idiom of religious belief. Proper social order, civilization itself, was a gift of the gods. God and man were inextricably linked in the construction and maintenance of social reality.

As human communities on the high plateau expanded in size, sophistication, and communication, some synthesis of core religious ideas was literally unavoidable. Elements of this shared faith were present in the minds of the ancient Andeans for countless generations, perhaps reaching back as far as the first Asiatic hunters who ventured into the Americas. But the essential crystallization of these religious concepts, or at least the first that we can recognize in the fragmentary annals of prehistory, occurred around 1500 B.C.

Partaking of a tightly interwoven economic world of common resources and trade, the increasingly sophisticated societies on the shores of Lake Titicaca began to share a community of worship. For the first time, they expressed their faith with monumental temples and public works of art: the life's blood of archaeologists seeking an entrée into the conceptual and spiritual world of the ancients. We see the material evidence of this faith centered on animistic worship of nature's essential forces throughout the Lake Titicaca basin.

The shattered remnants of temples and religious sculptures produced by this cult appear with particular intensity on the southern, Bolivian shores of Lake Titicaca, in the vicinity of the old Tiahuanaco homeland.

What was this faith like? What were its core ideas about spirituality? How did its adherents conceive of their relationship to the natural world and to each other? What kinds of religious practices did they engage in? We can extract at least partial answers to these questions from the physical remains of religious experience that they left behind. Just as in and of themselves, the soaring cathedrals and rich, religious iconography of medieval Europe reveal much to us about early Christian spiritual aspirations, the stone sculptures of this pre-Tiahuanaco cult embed essential clues to a spiritual world now lost to us.

Without written records, we cannot reconstruct the original name of this faith which embroiled the Andean high plateau in spiritual fervor nearly 3,500 years ago. But the sculptural style associated with this cult, and the religious tradition itself, have been defined by Karen Mohr Chavez, an archaeologist who has worked around Lake Titicaca for decades.[14] She christened this religious tradition with the name "Yaya-Mama," after the extraordinary style of stone sculpture found associated with pre-Tiahuanaco temples in the Lake Titicaca region. We know that the carved monuments of this style relate to a religion that codified animistic beliefs to express and to celebrate the intimate connections between humans and their life-giving environment. The iconography of these sculptures is exuberant and complicated. They combine densely packed images of stylized humans and animals, serpents, lizards, toads, and plants with strangely abstract geometric figures. One stone stela perfectly captures the essence of the Yaya-Mama style.

The two principal faces of this sculpture represent, on one side of a sandstone pillar, a female with clearly depicted breasts, and on the other side, a male. Both figures place one

Rollout drawing of a Yaya-Mama–style stone stela. (Drawing reproduced courtesy of Karen Chavez and Sergio Chavez.)

hand high on the chest and the other below on the belly. Other Yaya-Mama stelae display similar images of a male-female pair. Flanking these human (or god?) figures on the sides of the stela are two pairs of undulating, double-headed serpents. Each pair of serpents is arrayed in such a way that one serpent is above the waistband of the human and the other below. The humans stand upon gnarled plants or trees. The fruits or seeds of these plants appear to be animal heads. Although symmetrical overall, the details of the principal figures vary noticeably. The two humans, for instance, wear different neck and head ornaments, and they stand on different kinds of plants.

The extreme remoteness in time and cultural tradition of these sculptures obscures the full meaning of these images. What significance did these figures have for the faithful? What kinds of emotions did they feel when they gazed upon one of these sculptures set within the windswept courtyard of a temple open to the sun and the sky? In truth, I can only offer reasonable conjectures about the original meanings mutely encased in these stones. When we project abstract concepts, meanings, and religious experience so distantly backward in time, we stand precariously on intellectual quicksand. Still, if we wish to grasp the deep cultural and historical strata that underlie the emergence of Tiahuanaco and, ultimately, of the Aymara themselves, we have few alternatives.

What is it that strikes us first about these Yaya-Mama sculptures? The images themselves are primitive, but at the same time subtly executed. The sculptors contained raw, almost childlike depictions of humans and animals within elegant, symmetrical frames. Each sculptural element has its counterpart, its twin, on another face of the stela. But this is not the symmetry of a mirror image. The twins are not identical. These sculptors worked with complex notions of duality and not with the idea of mere replication. Expressions of duality fairly burst from the surface of these sculptures. We see duality and complementarity repeatedly in the symmetrical representation of the two stylized humans, one side male, the other female: in the two pairs of serpents; in each serpent itself possessing two heads; in the spatial design of the serpent pairs, with one serpent placed above the horizontal waistband and the other below; and in the pair of plant representations at the feet of the humans. The sculpture conveys an almost obsessive concern for displaying dual, opposed figures, plants, animals, and humans.

Both sexual dichotomy and the complementarity of the human male-female pair are effectively expressed through the convention of carving the images on opposed faces of the sculpture. The images look out in different directions, but they are carved of the same block of stone. The carefully rendered waistband, the only obvious element of clothing on these figures, encircles the entire sculpture, relating one human to the other. So, the male-female pair are simultaneously opposed, yet joined by form and by design. There is both tension and repose here.

Duality and complementarity extend to the plants and animals depicted on the Yaya-Mama–style stelae, hinting that, to the pre-Tiahuanaco peoples who created these images, the organizational principles of the social world of humans extends to the natural world of plants and animals. If nature and society is organized fundamentally in the same way, then to understand human society, one must observe nature, and to understand nature, one has only to look to society. These precious icons of a world long gone encode an encompassing spiritual vision. They tell us that nature and human society are fundamentally one. Both are cleaved in two. Both depend for their reproduction on the biological union of the divided self: the union of the male and female pair.

Although we can arrive at this interpretation by analyzing the objects alone, I am always left with the uneasy feeling that other meanings linger out of our reach just beneath the surface of these sculptures. The original sculptors can no longer tell us what these images meant to them in all their rich, personal significance. Three thousand years interposes an opaque curtain of time between ourselves and the authors of this religious art. These images can truly be understood only by those completely enmeshed in the ancient vision of the world that produced them. Yet, to satisfy my curiosity, I asked my Aymara companions to give me their interpretation of these images. After all, although distanced in time, the contemporary Aymara share much with their ancestors. They live in virtually identical physical landscapes and exploit many of the same natural resources. The Aymara, or at least those who have not migrated to the cities in search of work and a new social identity, live a rural life that in some respects remains timeless. They reside in small communities dispersed across the high plateau in a pattern of settlement that would not have been alien to the eyes of their ancestors. After centuries, they still depend on the rains and the health of their livestock to support themselves and their families. I thought my Aymara friends might have distinct or exotic insights into the meaning of these complicated images.

I showed photographs and drawings of several of these Yaya-Mama–style sculptures to Chrisostomos and Policarpio and later to Ignacio. Somehow I expected them to shrug and make a few general remarks about the photographs. I wasn't sure if they would have any interest in such things. Instead, to my surprise, they became extremely animated and proceeded to spin elaborate, detailed commentaries about the meaning of these images.

Both Chrisostomos and Policarpio immediately said that the male-female pair on the sculptures were meant to represent Lady Earth and Lord Sky. To them, the double-headed serpents were really rainbows that united the earth and the sky. Even more, to Chrisostomos and Policarpio these serpents were "rainbow-rivers." I asked them what they meant.

"What is a 'rainbow-river,' Tata Chrisostomos?"

"Oh," Chrisostomos explained, "there are two different rainbows, you see? The one here [Chrisostomos pointed to the male side of the sculpture] is the rainbow of the sky. This brings the rain. This is the water that falls from the sky."

"And the other one?" I asked, gesturing to the side of Pachamama, Lady Earth.

"That one is the water that flows from the earth."

"Tata Chrisostomos, do you mean that the serpent is like a river?"

"Yes, Doctor, or like a spring. All water from the earth."

"So what does this mean?"

"Well, Doctor," Policarpio interjected, "this is a prayer for water, you see? The ancestors called the rain with this. The water from the sky, and the water from the earth. I suppose they wanted to join the waters, just like Chrisostomos."

Immediately, I recalled Chrisostomos's long description on the morning of my pilgrimage of how he mixed different types of water together to call the rains.

When I showed the same photographs to Ignacio independently, he too saw Pachamama in the stylized image of the female. But he wanted to concentrate on the serpents and toads that appear in profusion in the Yaya-Mama–style sculptures. It was as if for Ignacio the human figures were a given, almost in the background. What really attracted Ignacio's attention were the obsessive representations of serpents and toads, almost to the exclusion of any other animals. He saw in the vibrant, undulating serpents on these sculptures an image of the swirling waters of a river at the height of the rainy season. Ignacio didn't say a word about rainbows, but he was sure that the sculptors were referring to "turbulent water, like water from the mountains" when they carved the double-headed serpents. In fact, rivers in the altiplano go wild in the rainy season, surging dangerously down the mountains from their sources in the high peaks. They carry huge amounts of rock and sediment from the heights and bring life-giving water to the planted fields of the farmers. In the altiplano, the growing season and the rainy season correspond. To Ignacio the jamp'atu, the toads, on these sculptures were also signs of the rainy season. But he commented that the toads were associated with the great pools of stagnant water that quickly form in the lowest-lying grasslands of the altiplano. He compared the toads with water seeping up from the ground; in the rainy season, both migrate to the surface from their dwellings in the heart of the earth.

These sculptures "talked" to Chrisostomos, Policarpio, and Ignacio about the eternal concerns of people who make their living from the earth. Whether they saw rainbows or not, all three described water as the true message of these sculptures. The images engraved on these sculptures were mystical emblems of the fertilizing power of water. These were really prayers for fertility. In this, all of my Aymara friends concurred.

I imagine now that the Yaya-Mama stelae were meant to capture for its human creators the concentrated essence of fertility: the generative power of water and the procreative union of the male-female pair. They were icons worshiped for the purpose of increasing human and natural abundance. This fundamental theme, expressing the interdependence of the human and natural worlds, reoccurs even more graphically in the monumental religious architecture and art created by the people of Tiahuanaco. The roots of Tiahuanaco religious ideology clearly reach back to an ancient concept of spirituality that was exquisitely attuned to the nuances of the natural world. Elements of this spirituality still nourish the Aymara today when they sacrifice to the achachilas, seeking release of the rains.

But all of the pre-Tiahuanaco villages in the Andean altiplano did not subscribe to the same cultural and religious traditions. Even if some fundamental religious beliefs were widely shared, the ways of expressing those beliefs varied enormously. In fact, we can perceive a fascinating cultural fault line in the social history of the high plateau as early as the second millennium B.C.

The people who participated in the Yaya-Mama religious

cult were concentrated geographically around the shores of Lake Titicaca. Their communities are distinguished in the archaeological record by public temples and, of course, by the Yaya-Mama–style sculptures. A cultural complex that has come to be known as Chiripa is emblematic of this tradition. This complex was first defined by one of the North American pioneers of Andean archaeology, Wendell Bennett, who excavated at the site of Chiripa itself on the southern shore of Lake Titicaca.[15] Bennett's excavations revealed that the site was a massive platform mound faced by stone retaining walls on at least three sides. Arranged around the sides of this artificial mound were a series of subterranean houses that faced a centrally located open courtyard. These constructions were substantial undertakings that required the organization of a corporate labor pool and, quite likely, the participation of specialists in stone cutting and carving. According to archaeological evidence, the earliest occupation of Chiripa occurred around 1200 B.C. In the period between 900 and 100 B.C., the mound was enlarged and refurbished many times. This period is associated with the exotic polychrome and modeled pottery characteristic of the Chiripa tradition. At some time between 500 and 100 B.C., the people of Chiripa built a rectangular sunken court on the summit of the mound. Colored floors of red and yellow clay were laid down continuously from the house structures to the interior of the sunken court. Carved stone plaques were set into the walls of this semisubterranean court, and sandstone stelae with serpent, animal, and human motifs were erected in its interior. These large plaques and stelae were clearly intended for public viewing. They were set in unroofed, open-air courtyards within structures that were designed explictly for the display of these religious icons. The Chiripa stelae and carved stone plaques are stylistically similar, if not identical, to the classic Yaya-Mama style of religious art distributed around the circum–Lake Titicaca basin. Chiripa society was clearly highly developed and in constant contact with other communities around Lake Titicaca. These people shared a "great tradition" of religious activities in which ideas, as well as goods, were avidly exchanged. By the end of the second millennium B.C., the lake district had become a single communications network through which technical and conceptual innovations flowed rapidly—a pre-Columbian version of the information highway.

Farther south in the high deserts around Lake Poopó, we enter another world in terms of both environment and cultural tradition. Away from the moderating influence of Lake Titicaca, intensive forms of agricultural production are rare as the landscape gradually becomes more arid and desolate toward the southerly reaches of the Bolivian high plateau. Here enormous barchan sand dunes loom across the horizon, driven forward inexorably by the ferocious windstorms of the altiplano. Saltating sand that rapidly chokes rudimentary canals and increasingly saline soil place nearly intolerable burdens on the farmer. Agriculture in the southern altiplano is a desultory affair. Today, the isolated, chronically poor villages of the region plant little more than quinoa, an Andean grain that is saline tolerant and highly resistant to the brutal, ultraviolet solar radiation characteristic of the high plateau. In certain locales, native inhabitants developed artificial techniques for manipulating river water to enhance agricultural production. In the region of the contemporary Chipaya Indians west of Lake Poopó, for instance, villagers construct small diversion structures and dikes of sod blocks to impound the icy waters of the Lauca River which tumble down from quiescent, snowcapped volcanoes along the nearby Chilean border. With this simple form of irrigation, I have seen the Chipaya coax, with great skill and ingenuity, a single crop of potatoes and quinoa from their salt-encrusted fields. At other times, though, the vagaries of precipitation reduce the depth of the mountain snowpack, the river level falls, and the crops wither. Given these debilitating environmental conditions, the core of the southern altiplano economy was not intensive agriculture, as it was farther to the north around Lake Titicaca.

Here economic livelihood, social and ritual life, and even philosophical conceptions of the indigenous inhabitants revolved around pastoralism. The vast, gently undulating plains of the region were the natural habitat of llama, alpaca, guanaco, and vicuña. Given the hostility of their environment for agricultural production, it is not surprising that llama and alpaca play a pivotal role in Chipaya life. The care and breeding of enormous herds of llama and alpaca was always the linchpin of the southern altiplano way of life.

And so it was in the second millennium B.C. Archaeological research in the region around Lake Poopó revealed the physical remains of a cultural tradition contemporaneous with that of Chiripa, but distinct in many ways. This cultural tradition has been called Wankarani, after the archaeological site at which this tradition was first discovered.[16] Wankarani villages consisted of a cluster of circular adobe houses with thatched roofs. House clusters were often encircled by an adobe wall to create a defendable enclosure. We can reasonably infer from this configuration that houses were occupied by nuclear or extended families, while the larger clusters as a whole reflect some kind of lineage groupings. Unlike Chiripa and other pre-Tiahuanaco villages in the Lake Titicaca region, Wankarani sites lack elaborate temples and cult centers. Religious activities in Wankarani society revolved around interior household shrines, and were not pursued in obvious public forums. But numerous stone llama head effigies have been discovered within ordinary Wankarani houses. These effigies were the focus of personal worship by families and lineages. Although thematically similar in subject matter, each effigy has an idiosyncratic style of representation. Wankarani never promulgated a formal, public art style associated with an organized religious cult. These icons can best be interpreted as tutelary deities focused on the fertility and health of llama herds.

Why did the people of Chiripa emphasize public rituals within impressive temple complexes while the Wankarani peoples' religious expression remain focused inward on household shrines? There were considerable differences in the scale and complexity of social organization between Chiripa and Wankarani that generated this distinction between public and private religious traditions. Chiripa was a society with a greater degree of social integration and an emerging sense of a great tradition focused on a shared ideology that demanded religious proselytism. This distinction between public and private religious traditions stemmed from long-standing ethnic differences. Despite a general similarity in material culture, the ceramic traditions of these two societies are radically different, hinting at significant variations in language, social outlook, and cultural and artistic conceptions. Based on the distribution of native languages in the altiplano during the sixteenth century, we might speculate that Chiripa was ancestral to the Uru-speaking groups documented ethnohistorically for the lake district, while Wankarani reflects a proto-Aymara language group. Of course, we are on rather shaky ground making these kind of correlations between archaeological cultures and historic populations, and in this we can make no definitive claims. Yet the distinct ecological, geographic, and economic orientations of the Chiripa and Wankarani peoples intensifies the striking feeling of ethnic difference that one perceives when confronting the divergent cultural remains they left behind.

Our archaeological evidence suggests a startling conclusion: The "myths" of Andean genesis recounted by the Spanish chroniclers tell tales with more than a kernel of historical truth. Even at the dawn of Andean civilization, the high plateau was divided conceptually into Urcosuyu and Umasuyu. The aggressive pastoralists of Urcosuyu may be none other than the proto-Aymara people of Wankarani. The agriculturalists and fishers of Umasuyu may trace their origins to the people of Chiripa. From history comes myth; from myth, history.

In all this speculation, we are left with an even greater mystery. How did one protocity come to assert its dominance over others in the Lake Titicaca region by the first centuries of the Christian era? What spurred Tiahuanaco on to political preeminence and not, say, Chiripa, or one of any number of similar villages strung out along the lake edge? This question is not easily answered. From the archaeological record, we can piece together the necessary preconditions for the emergence of a preeminent settlement, but we cannot easily specify why a particular settlement assumed that role. There are many instances of great cities and capitals emerging through a complex chain of historical contingencies, chance, or the charisma of individual leaders. The precise geographical and topographical location of an important city may result from widely shared beliefs regarding the meaning and cultural role of cities, rather than from fortuitous pragmatic factors, such as location along a navigable stream or astride a lucrative trading route. For instance, René Berthelot argued that the predominant factor in the location and nature of the Chinese city was a complex of shared ideas and cosmological conceptions which he referred to as "astrobiological principles."[17] These astrobiological principles treat human reality (and the built-city environment) as a function and replication of a celestial archetype. The necessary parallelism between the humanly constructed, animate environment and the physical universe necessitates performance of cyclical rituals in specific, propitious locations to maintain harmony between nature and human society. These principles reached their most formal expression in the geomantic tradition known as *feng-shui*, a distinctive Chinese system of ideas in which certain configurations of the landscape were believed to retain and conserve the life essence. A passage in the *Chou-li*, a text dating most likely to Han-period China, succinctly captures the essence and implications of shared cosmological concepts on the form and location of cities: "Here where Heaven and Earth are in perfect accord, where the four seasons come together, where the winds and rain gather, where the forces of *yin* and *yang* are harmonized, one builds a royal capital."[18]

We can eliminate economic factors in the emergence of

Tiahuanaco as the predominant religious and political capital of the Andean high plateau. Tiahuanaco's location conferred no particular resource advantage on the city. In fact, one could argue on economic grounds alone that an early lakeside settlement such as Chiripa should have held competitive advantage over Tiahuanaco, given the former's direct access to the considerable natural resources of Lake Titicaca. Tiahuanaco was not located near the site of concentrated natural resources, such as a particularly rich obsidian resource, that might have generated extraordinary wealth. Monopolized control and distribution of a precious commodity is one clear path to rapid economic growth that was exploited by many cities throughout the preindustrial world. But the basic natural resources on which a society might build wealth along the southern rim of Lake Titicaca are fairly uniform. There was, in other words, no unique economic advantage to the location of the protocity of Tiahuanaco.

Originally, Tiahuanaco's supremacy may have been the product of aggressive raiding in the territories of other villages and towns. Yet Tiahuanaco's growing power and prestige was most likely not maintained by virtue of aggression alone, but by conversion of the emergent capital into a shared center of moral and cosmological authority, a place of pilgrimage and wonder. The transformation of the early village of Tiahuanaco into a ritual center of supreme importance in the ancient Andean world occurred at some point between A.D. 100 and 300. Given that the villages of the region shared broadly similar cosmological and religious beliefs, once Tiahuanaco started on its path to power, by whatever means, there was probably little local resistance to its emergence as the preeminent center of Lake Titicaca–basin civilization.

Within a few centuries of Tiahuanaco's founding, the sacred precincts of the city glittered with the accumulated wealth of empire. Tiahuanaco's kings raised wondrous temples sheathed in bands of gold to the greater glory of their gods. Palaces of finely wrought andesite blocks decorated in

101

the rich, exotic colors of new wealth became the sumptuous homes of regal courts. Tiahuanaco became the ultimate center of pilgrimage, an Andean Mecca, the first truly cosmopolitan city of the ancient Andean world. Only here could the gods be worshiped impeccably. After all, Tiahuanaco was the place of creation; the vessel of divinity. Only here could pilgrims contemplate the inscrutable faces of their gods, enshrined in the city's imposing stone temples. At its political apogee, Tiahuanaco controlled the southern Andes, sending out first traders and emissaries, and then permanent colonists, to exploit new territories. Enormous caravans of llamas carrying the fruits of military and diplomatic victory funneled vast wealth back to the capital on the shores of Lake Titicaca. Great parts of southern Peru, Bolivia, northern Chile, and northwestern Argentina were drawn into Tiahuanaco's sphere of influence. More than anything else, Tiahuanaco's imperial cults brought unity to the disparate peoples of the southern Andes. The social effects of these cults shaped the subsequent history of the Andes. Even today, despite centuries of calamity, social transformation, and the inevitable loss of cultural memory, distant echos of Tiahuanaco's religion reverberate in the beliefs of the contemporary Aymara Indians. In its inexorable movement toward political and cultural dominance in the Andean high plateau, Tiahuanaco was forever transformed from one parochial village among others into, in Lewis Mumford's memorable words, "a new symbolic world, representing not only a people, but a whole cosmos and its gods."[19]

Even five hundred years after its catastrophic fall from grace in the eleventh century, Tiahuanaco's religious mystique remained intense in the mind of the native Andeans. To the Inca and their Aymara subjects of the early sixteenth century, mankind, or at least civilized man, was created at Tiahuanaco. Here the world and all its people were brought into harmony with the cosmos. In Tiahuanaco, the natives gazed upon the remote past; they experienced the time and place of their own origins. But, for them, this vision must have held both wonder and terror, pride and despair. For, in looking upon their Garden of Eden, they saw colossal wrecks: monumental granite statues of gods and dead kings strewn about carelessly like children's toys, and ancestral temples, once perfectly conceived and masterfully executed, reduced to doleful foundations of shattered stone. By the sixteenth century, this city of the gods had become a windswept, holy ruin, entombed in the sediment of ages.

The new conquerors, the European authors of the last great Pachakuti in the Andes, were equally affected by this abandoned city. Upon gazing for the first time on the ruins of Tiahuanaco, their words evoke the dreamy sense of awestruck tourists. Witness, for instance, the words of Pedro de Mercado de Peñalosa in a letter to the king of Spain, recounting his visit to Tiahuanaco:

> [Tiahuanaco] has enormous buildings and temples. It is a thing of great beauty to see the artfulness, the style and the great size of the stones with which they built those buildings. For this reason the town of Tiahuanaco was memorable, for having . . . in it such grand and sumptuous structures which can count among the wonders of the world. [These structures were] . . . made of huge stones, which were not set with mixtures of mortar, or sand, or mud, and they are so well joined and seated that one can hardly insert the point of a knife between the blocks. The buildings are divided in two parts, one an arcabuz shot from the other. There are building stones thirty-seven feet long by fifteen feet wide and others somewhat smaller, and all so well made that they could not be worked better in Vizcaya . . . In one of the buildings, there are statues of giants of great stature with crowns on their heads and many other stones, rectangular and so well worked that they excite admiration. [These stones] served to enclose the building. And what is even more remarkable is that in all that region, one

cannot find quarries that contain such stones, nor even evidence of the quebrada where these stones might have been quarried. And so, of what the ancient Indians accomplished, because no one has knowledge of their origins, it is said that all this was made in a single night . . . neither the natives or their ancestors know in what time, nor by who, nor under whose orders [these great structures] were founded . . . There is a rumor that a great treasure lies under this building, and because it would be an extremely difficult task to disinter that great quantity of stones, Your Majesty alone would be able to afford the cost. People from many lands come only to witness the greatness of these buildings.[20]

Even in utter ruination, Tiahuanaco evoked intense emotions of admiration and wonder from both Indian and European alike. According to the Spanish chroniclers, the natives of the land did not remember who had raised Tiahuanaco to greatness. Still, they oriented themselves to this antique, spirit-haunted city. Even the Inca, who irrupted in conquest onto the high plateau some eighty years before the Spanish, considered establishing their court at Tiahuanaco. Their king, Pachakuti Inca Yupanqui, perhaps the greatest American Indian conqueror in history, reorganized the dynastic capital of Cuzco according to an architectural model drawn from the ancient ruins. In doing so, Pachakuti was laying claim to Tiahuanaco's ancient political and religious mystique. In constructing mythological associations between Cuzco and Tiahuanaco, the Inca lords were proclaiming their descent from the ancient kings of Tiahuanaco and consciously emulating the physical symbols of power vested in the monumental architecture of that ancient city.

The Spanish chronicler Cieza de León recapitulates a core element of this Inca mythography by reporting that among the ruins of Tiahuanaco "are the lodgings of the Incas and the house where Manco Inca II, son of Huayna Capac [the last independent ruler of the Incas], was born, and near them are two tombs of native lords of this town, as tall as [they are] broad, square-cornered towers, with their doorways to the rising sun."[21] These "broad, square-cornered towers" are nothing other than the great pyramids of Akapana, and its counterpart in the southern part of the ancient city, the ruins today called Pumapunku ("Gateway of the Lion"). Here the Inca claim of dynastic association with Tiahuanaco is made most explicit: an heir to the throne was born at the site of the ancient capital alongside the monumental burial mounds of Tiahuanaco's own kings. In one symbolic master stroke, Manco Inca II, and by extension the Inca imperial household, appropriated the majesty and political legitimacy of a more ancient dynastic line, and established his right to the mandate of empire by fabricating a royal birthright.

But Cieza's passage also subtly implies that the royal mythographers of the Inca attempted to evoke a more deeply nuanced and profoundly meaningful association of their specific dynastic line with Tiahuanaco than by asserting a simple historical fact: the birth of an heir apparent in that sacred city. Cieza casually notes that the sepulchral towers of Tiahuanaco kings possessed doorways that face the rising sun. This seemingly prosaic reference to the spatial orientation of the royal tombs symbolically associates the Tiahuanaco dynasty directly with the forces of nature, specifically with the apparent cyclical passage of the sun through the heavens. Tiahuanaco's kings were truly Sun Kings, invested with the sacred, energizing power of the universe. This symbolism links the human social order of ancient Tiahuanaco with the natural order of the universe. Tiahuanaco's coveted legitimating power resided as much in its perceived status as a principal contact point with the sacred as in its historical role as the seat of a royal dynasty and capital city of a culturally influential empire.

Inca myth and history speaks to us of the ineffable power of the sacred inscribed in Tiahuanaco's cityscape. Once, the fabric of the universe was reflected in this city at the top of the Andean world. If even five hundred years after its demise

105

the decaying ramparts of Tiahuanaco could elicit such emotions, imagine what it must have been like to dwell in this city of the gods at the height of its powers. Public spectacle and religious pageantry, fused with a sense of historical destiny, must have been the order of the day. The kings of Tiahuanaco emulated the very structure of the universe when they designed their capital. They had the vision, the audacity, to construct their own palaces, their ultimate centers of authority, according to the majestic plan of nature itself. In doing so, they transferred the sense of inevitability humans experience in nature. The order of the universe simply is what it is. Humans cannot change cosmic order because we are in it; we are of it. And so, the kings of Tiahuanaco proclaimed with the mimetic design of their capital city that the social order they controlled, too, was necessary and inescapable. In elaborating this seemingly arrogant piece of propaganda, Tiahuanaco's kings had a natural advantage. For Viracocha, the Andean High God, chose to create the world from Tiahuanaco, from Taypi Kala, the Stone in the Center. Tiahuanaco was the Creator's point of purchase from which He set time in motion and called forth the nations of mankind. Tiahuanaco was the birthplace of humanity, and, to paraphrase T. S. Eliot, Tiahuanaco's kings became still points at the center of the turning world.

How could such an illustrious, magical world subside into obscurity? After the original historical accounts of the city recorded in the chronicles of the early Spanish conquistadors, clerics, and explorers, we hear little about the ruins and their significance until the mid-nineteenth century. The wars of conquest waged by the Spanish against the natives of the high plateau, and the later internecine conflict among the Spaniards themselves, wrought havoc in the land. Colonial period censuses preserve the sobering realities of the biological disaster of contact between Old and New Worlds: Some provinces of modern Bolivia near the Tiahuanaco region lost nearly eighty percent of their native population within the first fifty traumatic years of conquest and European domination. Thousands of Indians perished in the wars, countless others succumbed to the silent terror of pandemic diseases like measles and smallpox carried by the Europeans to the New World. Forced labor in the nightmarish silver mines of Potosí exacted an awful toll on tribute-paying natives. Death by starvation, physical exhaustion, mine-shaft collapses, and the insidious effects of mercury poisoning devastated families and entire ethnic groups who were transplanted to Potosí as cheap labor. Before the close of the seventeenth century, enormous tracts of once densely populated lands were reduced to virtual ghost territories whose people had died, been forcibly relocated to the mines, or had fled to wilder lands to escape the tribute assessments which were, in effect, death warrants.

One result of this demographic collapse of unprecedented proportions was an inevitable weakening of social identity as autochthonous and previously self-sufficient communities disappeared suddenly from the landscape. The indigenous memory of the native lords who shaped empires and controlled rich, distant provinces faded rapidly under the yoke of European domination. There were new, equally demanding foreign lords to serve, and fragments of remembered glory gave little comfort. In the wake of the Spanish conquest, the image of historic Tiahuanaco was lost.

But many essential truths about Tiahuanaco remain embedded in derelict ruins under the earth, and in the living communities that still inhabit the altiplano. In a real sense, the people of Tiahuanaco never vanished completely. Their cultural and biological descendants remain on the lands of the ancient realm, tilling the intractable soil of the high plateau, fishing the great lake of Titicaca, and herding their precious animals in secluded mountain pastures. Llama caravans bearing aromatic and hard woods, resinous shrubs, and blocks of pure salt still come down to the shores of the lake as they have for at least one hundred generations, although today they are much attenuated, slowly disappearing before the onslaught of motorized traffic along primitive roads that are penetrating even the most desolate stretches of the high plateau. The yatiri continue to perform complex rituals, performances, prayers, and sacrifices at planting and harvest ceremonies. The health, productivity, and survival of the Aymara communities still depends on a vision of man and nature with roots that reach deeply into the past. To grasp meaning in the Aymara world, we must learn to appreciate their tortuous history. At the ancient core of that history is Tiahuanaco. And it is to the historical Tiahuanaco, not the Tiahuanaco of myth, legend, or the imagination, that our journey of discovery must take us.

4

The Sacred City

I took my first journey to Tiahuanaco in the austral winter of 1978 in the company of Bolivian archaeologists from the National Institute of Archaeology. Several of us squeezed into a small, tanklike Russian jeep and corkscrewed up the steep sides of La Paz's basin onto the high plateau. I gaped at the ice-clad Cordillera Real draped in wreaths of slate-colored clouds. Jagged black peaks emerged suddenly and then, wraithlike, disappeared again. It was cold and it was definitely going to rain. But the bleak weather couldn't veil the grandeur of the land: great, unending plains of treeless fields gently undulated to the horizon.

After an hour and a half's worth of a jarring ride, a low mountain range confronted us: our driver informed me that above us was the pass of Lloko Lloko, from which we could see the Valley of Tiahuanaco. As we wound our way up to the pass, the rain began to fall—the strangest, most dangerous rain I've ever seen. It began conventionally enough. But halfway up the mountain, we were pelted with a slurry of water and earth: thick mud was mixed in with the rain. As we slowly ascended the mountain, the slurry changed character again as it began to freeze. Within minutes the wipers failed as they labored impossibly to scrape the ice-stiffened glaze of mud from the windshield.

I had heard apocryphal tales of toads that had been swept up in the ferocious windstorms of the altiplano later raining back down from the heavens. Now I could believe it. Huge amounts of dust must have been sucked up into the atmosphere, changed into aerosol, and then precipitated back out in the rain. However I explained this strange phenomenon of frozen, muddy rain, I knew we were in trouble. Our driver leaned out of the window with an oil-stained rag trying futilely to clear the glass. Freezing-cold air streamed into the cabin. I began to shudder. We could barely see twenty feet in front of us, and I suggested that we stop to wait out the storm. The driver shook his head: "We can't stop now. There's no room on the mountain. If another truck comes down while we're stopped, we'll never leave here alive. Wait until you see the crosses up at Lloko Lloko, then you'll understand."

I sat rigidly upright gripping the hard, metal edge of the seat, waiting for my destiny. The driver kept up a steady stream of chatter, warding off unwelcome thoughts until we crested the pass and managed to pull into a wide spot next to the roadside shrine of Nuestra Señora de Lloko Lloko.

The Virgin stood in a stucco niche, her feet cemented to a cinder block pedestal. Broken green bottle glass was scattered like jewels before her, the shattered, sparkling residue of long-forgotten prayers. The smoke from melted candles stained her sky blue porcelain robes. The faded paint of her golden hair had turned chalky in the sun. Despite being ravaged by the pitiless elements at the mountain's summit, she wore a cryptic, peaceful smile. The driver was right. Among the shattered glass, there were white wooden crosses sprouting like mushrooms at the feet of the desolate Virgin. I wondered how close I had come to lying underneath one of them.

We waited on the high pass for the foul weather to clear. Sheets of cold rain swept over us. Intense, deafening pulses of hail clattered off the jeep's hood, pitting the thin sheet metal. The furious wind whistled and moaned past our ill-fitting doors, stirring up small cyclones of dust around our feet. During a momentary pause in the storm, I climbed to the shrine to gaze out over the high plateau. Great banks of deep gray clouds moved rapidly on the distant southern horizon. To the northeast, the sun had already broken through the heavy cloud mantle, illuminating the three peaks of Mount Illimani and bathing the basin of La Paz in the waning golden light of late evening. But high on the isolated pass of Lloko Lloko, we remained in the epicenter of the storm. Lightning flashed along the mountains hemming in the Tiahuanaco Valley far below. Peals of thunder echoed in the folds of hills around me. The violent rain had laid the dust; the pungent smell of pulverized dirt and animal dung hung in the air. Patches of glistening hail on the verge of sublimation clung to the yellow, needlelike grass covering the slopes. I drew it all in through my eyes and ears and nose, breathing the sharp, cold air into my lungs. With a deep shiver, I returned to the jeep.

After about an hour stranded on the heights of Lloko Lloko, the worst of the storm had blown far off to the southwest, toward the trackless deserts and extinct volcanoes straddling the border with Chile. Horizontal shafts of sunlight splayed out from beneath the clouds over Lake Tititcaca. Our driver decided we could descend safely to the Valley of Tiahuanaco. The rain still fell in fits and starts, but the temperature had risen and we were no longer pelted by frozen slush. The track down the mountain was gouged by the heavy traffic and slicked with patches of dirty ice. Deep trenches of raw, red earth rutted the roadbed. Our tires slipped treacherously from one trench to the other, spewing up a cascade of muddy gravel behind us. We nearly grazed a few undersprung Indian buses swaying precariously under the weight of their loads. Eventually, we made our way to the valley floor without incident. At the base of the mountains we turned westward, chasing the setting sun, toward Lake Titicaca and Tiahuanaco.

The sun had set by the time we finally drove into the village. We were exhausted, frozen, and famished. Tiahuanaco seemed deserted. All the small shops along the Pan-American Highway were tightly shuttered. A string of roadside lamps suspended by wire swayed rhythmically in the night wind. Against the impenetrable dark, their pale, swirling light first revealed, and then concealed, the barren streetscape. Behind the shadows, I caught glimpses of swirling paper and plastic bags tumbling along dirt lanes, rough-hewn wooden doors, and polished stone thresholds. Halfway through the village along the highway, light streamed from a building that turned out to be a truck stop. There I took the first of many meals in the ancient, sacred city of Tiahuanaco.

When I began work at Tiahuanaco, it was hard to imagine that the dusty, virtually abandoned village of today was once the urban epicenter of the Andean world. Gazing across a decaying landscape of moldering adobe walls and pitted, trash-strewn streets, I could barely conjure a vision of Tiahuanaco as a vibrant city, graced with sumptuous temples, urban gardens, monumental sculptures set in elegant courtyards, and the palatial residences of a wealthy elite. Yet I knew from Spanish documents that Tiahuanaco and the nearby Lake Titicaca were sites of enormous religious prestige. Pilgrims from throughout the southern and central Andes were attracted to this sacred landscape of supernatural power. For centuries, these two preeminent *wakas* of the Andean world were venerated by an enormous population.

Time and the vagaries of social fortune conspire to veil the true face of Tiahuanaco. To the casual eye, Tiahuanaco looks like a city without a plan. A few monumental buildings loom isolated above the surface, dramatic landmarks in an otherwise featureless plain. The eye is drawn to these monuments and tourist paths cut straight toward them. Yet, walking from one structure to another, the ground undulates underfoot, dropping from time to time into large hollows, or suddenly stepping up onto low platforms. On close inspection, ancient public plazas and private courtyards can be discerned in vague tracery. Weathered stone pillars project from the earth, marking the corners of ruined buildings now deeply buried under fine-grained sediment. A few miraculously intact stone sculptures and the shattered remains of others lie about, slowly turning to dust in the pitiless embrace of the elements. The sediment of erosion from ancient adobe structures and from the surrounding mountains, deposited over the centuries, obscure much of what was once the elaborate urban design of Tiahuanaco. The old city is literally entombed.

So much of the city is destroyed or buried that it is difficult to capture its essence. But lines of sight remain along walls and between structures that are perceivable to the eye accustomed to looking for such alignments. This was what intrigued me about the place. I couldn't get out of my mind the underlying sense of mystery that enveloped me. Despite my inauspicious beginning in the teeth of a cold altiplano rain, I lingered on, first one year and then another, exploring the shadowy contours of ancient Tiahuanaco, while sharing in the lives of the great city's descendants. The strange disjunctures of past and present always confronted me. Bits and pieces of a once profoundly sacred place lay all about.

After eighteen years, my research team and I have gained substantial new knowledge of Tiahuanaco's history. Other scholars have taken up the challenge throughout the empire's old dominions. Each year we seem to make discoveries so fast that we can no longer assimilate them easily into our increasingly subtle understandings of Tiahuanaco. The "true" tale of Tiahuanaco and its history is not yet written. In reality, I believe it will never be. Writing the past remains always a work in progress. In the process, new and better understandings undeniably emerge, and these sustain the excitement of the enterprise. But we must never delude ourselves that our history making will ever come to an end. New generations will continue the quest. Rather, we should aspire to the goal of writing history prescribed by the great scholar of Rome, Theodor Mommsen: "[T]o work out by the imagination—which is the author of all history as of all poetry—if not a complete picture, at any rate a substitute for it."[1] What follows is just that: the best and most vivid reconstruction of the Aymara's distant past that I can offer now, at this moment; my substitute for the complete picture until a better one emerges.

At some point in the fifth century, Tiahuanaco emerged as the cultural and spiritual capital of the Andean world. Between A.D. 400 and 1100, the city was transformed into the political heart of an empire that had profound, transformative effects on the geopolitical structure of the Andean world. In terms of politics and religious prestige, Tiahuanaco came to dominate the entire Lake Titicaca basin. But its cultural and political influence reached well beyond the confines of the high plateau.

From A.D. 400 to 600, Tiahuanaco's power was extended throughout the Lake Titicaca basin into the *yungas,* the warm, subtropical regions at lower altitude, and particularly into the agriculturally fertile enclaves to the east of the Bolivian high plateau. But, apart from a few exceptions, the expansion of Tiahuanaco was not the product of a militaristic grand strategy worked out self-consciously by the lords of Tiahuanaco and implemented through force of arms. Tiahuanaco was not Rome. Its empire was not of the same order of magnitude as that of the classical empires of the Old World, or even that of the Inca. Nor was Tiahuanaco's expansion primarily the work of warrior-kings with huge standing armies ready at an instant to conquer, intimidate, and oppress local populations. Military stratagems and conscious efforts to conquer territory played a relatively small role in the movement of Tiahuanaco into foreign territories. Rather, Tiahuanaco's empire was a dynamic mosaic of populations linked, at times imperfectly, by changing strategic policies and political relationships devised by the empire's elite interest groups in an ad hoc fashion. These political stratagems responded to local cultural and political diversity and specific historical circumstances.

Tiahuanaco's elite shrewdly manipulated a variety of economic and political techniques to link themselves with local populations. Among those favored by Tiahuanaco's ruling class were direct conquest and administration of strategic regions, large-scale regional colonization or selective enclaving of populations in foreign territories, administered trade, propagation of state cults, and the establishment of clientage relationships between themselves and local elites. These techniques could be either coercive or consensual, depending upon the specific geographic and political context. As a result, Tiahuanaco's administration of its dependent provinces took a variety of forms; it could be direct or indirect, centralized or decentralized, and it could take strong or weak forms. The ability to incorporate other societies and other ethnic groups into a greater, productive whole required that Tiahuanaco shrewdly balance force and persuasion, coercion and consent.

Tiahuanaco's elites were not loath to apply force against local populations and competing polities whenever necessary. Policies of forceful, direct appropriation of productive lands were implemented in areas that were of prime importance to the economic and political well-being of the state, such as the rich agricultural lands along the shores of Lake Titicaca. Without secure sources of improved agricultural land for surplus crop production and high-quality pasturage for their herds, the power of Tiahuanaco's elite classes to expand into foreign territories would have been tenuous at best. At the same time, it is evident that Tiahuanaco did not rely solely on coercion to pursue its expansionist political and economic ends. State religion and imperial ideology performed much the same work as military conquest, but at significantly lower cost. In areas over which Tiahuanaco held demographic and organizational superiority, the prestige of the state religion and elite beliefs was sufficient to command respect and political subordination. Of course, along with the adoption of state cults, local people, or at least local elites, received the distinct economic advantage of being incorporated into a wider social network controlled by their altiplano patrons.

The relationship between Tiahuanaco as an emerging imperial power and local communities into which it was expanding was not invariably an oppressive, extractive proposition. We should not forget that empires and local communities are often counterpoised in a complex dynamic of mutualism. Although empires exert control over regional economies, and in the process impinge on the traditional prerogatives and autonomy of local communities, they also incorporate these communities into more inclusive social and economic worlds. Empires create dynamic interconnections among diverse communities and, in the process, promote accelerated local economic development. In turn, by identifying themselves as the agents of development, empires derive legitimacy, prestige, and an intensification of their social power.

Given the bewildering diversity in social and physical landscapes which confronted Tiahuanaco, it is not surprising that the empire's elite never established a uniform strategy of administration throughout its realm. The humid, subtropical yungas to the east of Tiahuanaco's high-plateau heartland were radically different from the arid yungas lying to the west. The altiplano around Lake Titicaca was vastly more fertile and suited to intensive agriculture than the higher, drier reaches of the southern Bolivian high plateau, where llama and alpaca pastoralism dominated. Each of these areas differed substantially in natural resources, and in the size and degree of organization of human populations. In the rich but tortuous terrain of the eastern yungas, Tiahuanaco faced agricultural societies subsisting on slash-and-burn agriculture on steep mountain slopes, a form of shifting cultivation still practiced today. Along desolate stretches of the Desaguadero River flowing southward toward Lake Poopó, Tiahuanaco's mobile caravan traders encountered and bartered with small clans of Urus who fished and foraged for food along the river banks and on the lake itself. In the dry, western yungas of the Peruvian and Chilean coasts, local populations were well established in large, densely settled villages. These coastal peoples were well accustomed to trading with highlanders and had done so for centuries. In the Titicaca basin itself, Tiahuanaco shared long-standing cultural ties with neighboring groups, and was simply the most brilliant exemplar of an urban civilization that had deep roots extending back to Chiripa and Wankarani. Here Tiahuanaco was not so much a society different in kind from the others, but different in scale and cultural influence. South of the Titicaca basin, cities never developed, and any sense of urban civilization among local populations was gained from contact with visitors and resident colonists from the lake district. Yet, because of Tiahuanaco's vigorous political expansion from the fifth through eleventh centuries, many people who never saw the great, glittering cities along the shores of Lake Titicaca still participated, however remotely, in Tiahuanaco's urban civilization.

Although the Aymara Indians are direct descendants of Tiahuanaco, we should not assume that they share much in the way of specific political, economic, and social organization. The contemporary Aymara—or, for that matter, the Aymara of the colonial period—cannot be used uncritically as a model for understanding Tiahuanaco. Tiahuanaco was a native empire, one that developed within an entirely indigenous context. It had the capacity to organize populations on a regional scale, and to freely appropriate and exploit natural resources within its territorial boundaries. The Aymara, on the other hand, are a colonized people. They have been subordinated to a foreign power for centuries. From the time of that colonization, they were converted into serfs and submerged in the identity of a peasantry. The Aymara adapted many of their cultural forms and social behaviors to this reality. Even in the arguably most conservative realms of world-view and of their fundamental conceptual frameworks, the Aymara reality of today is indissolubly interpenetrated and syncretized with European modes of thought. Over the past five centuries, the Aymara have become a hybridized culture. Of course, many elements of native belief still inhere in contemporary Aymara thought and action, but the fundamental organizational forms of economy, politics, and civil society are radically different from that of Tiahuanaco.

One dimension of Tiahuanaco's distinctiveness was its unique urban culture. If we reflect carefully on the nature of the social identities, occupations, and activities in Tiahuanaco, we come to an unusual conclusion. Viewed from the perspective of the contemporary Western eye, Tiahuanaco would have been foreign in the extreme, not conforming to standard conceptions of what a city, even a premodern city, "ought" to look like. Unlike other great cities of antiquity in Europe and the Near East, Tiahuanaco's raison d'être had little to do with commercial or mercantile activities. Western perceptions of ancient and medieval cities invariably conjure images of jostling crowds snaking through narrow, cobbled lanes, spilling out of markets and bazaars, churning up clouds of dust in the frenzy to buy, sell, and barter. Bedraggled street vendors hawking cheap trinkets; sharp-eyed, tight-fisted merchants hunkered down over piles of precious rugs, spices, and other exotica newly arrived by caravan; potters and jewelers, leather workers and carpenters, stonemasons and artisans, bakers, butchers, and tallow makers, porters, jugglers, clowns, prostitutes, and thieves plying their trade in workshops, public squares, and back alleys—all are familiar characters in this perception of the archaic city. The heart and soul of this image revolves around trade, commerce, and the daily life of the marketplace. Throughout Western history, the city has been a place of meeting and of melding for many different kinds of people. From this perspective, all "real cities" require a central market, or, better yet, many markets big and small to keep the economic blood flowing. Through trade and exchange, through buying and selling of every imaginable kind, the city was made and remade. People from the countryside migrated to the city to escape the grinding, invariant rhythms of farms and fields, to exploit new economic opportunities, to set up shop, to settle in, to become entrepreneurs.

But this familiar image, so essential to Western conceptions of urban life, does not fit Tiahuanaco. Tiahuanaco had no markets. There was no flourishing merchant class. There were no free artisans and craftsmen organized in guilds who could exert independent pressure and political checks on the decisions of municipal authorities. There were no commercial transactions in the modern sense of disinterested buyers and sellers brought together in a marketplace. There was no broad-based public participation in the political life of the city. Tiahuanaco was not like the West's cherished archetype of urban democracy, the ancient Greek polis. Moral, political, and military authority in Tiahuanaco flowed from the ruling lineages and from their coterie of kin, retainers, and camp followers. Tiahuanaco, to a greater degree than urban centers in other parts of the preindustrial world, was an autocratic city, built for and dominated by a native aristocracy. In this sense, Tiahuanaco was truly a patrician city; a place for symbolically concentrating the political and religious authority of the elites. Although not entirely absent, in comparison with the ancient cities of the Western world, Tiahuanaco boasted little in the way of pluralism and social heterogeneity.

The social map of Tiahuanaco was not a riotous mosaic of many peoples anonymously and independently pursuing their livelihoods, moving into and out of the city as employment opportunities waxed and waned. Rather, in Tiahuanaco, there was a singularity of purpose and a higher degree of social control. The true raison d'être of the city turned on servicing the aristocratic lineages and their entourages. The city was an extension of the elite households, as well as a public expression of their religious and secular authority. Its residents were

119

attached one way or another to the economic, political, and social fortunes of the princely households. Tiahuanaco's public architectural ensembles reflected and sustained that singularity of purpose. If there was a visual and cultural focus to the city, it was not a central market or caravansary, but rather the great temples and religious sculptures of the city, the distilled essences of elite ideology. The religious and political mystique of the elite, wielded in premeditated self-interest, shaped the city, not the invisible hand of the marketplace.

Focused as they were on the needs and politics of the aristocracy, the cities created by the people of Tiahuanaco were small by modern standards. Tiahuanaco itself, despite being the capital of an empire, approached a peak population of perhaps only thirty to forty thousand. The secondary cities it spawned or incorporated into its realm probably never reached ten thousand inhabitants. In contrast, the hinterlands hard by the urban centers were thickly settled by rural commoners, fishers, farmers, and herders. Unlike the preindustrial metropolises of Europe and Asia, which were irrepressible magnets for the surrounding countryfolk, there was little economic or social incentive—or, perhaps more precisely, opportunity—to migrate to Tiahuanaco's cities. Right of residence in Tiahuanaco's regal-ritual cities was tied to some kind of relationship with the patrician lineages, either as kin, fictive kin, or retainers. The inherent structural limitations of this kind of patron-client relationship, which demands a greater measure of face-to-face contact, limited the scale and diversity of social relations in Tiahuanaco's cities. Lacking the natural democracy and entrepreneurial opportunity that comes with a market, Tiahuanaco was essentially a "company town" catering to the twin, interpenetrating businesses of state religion and politics.

Households in Tiahuanaco were organized into distinct barrios, or neighborhoods enclosed behind soaring adobe walls. The residents of these purposely segregated neighborhoods owed personal fealty to Tiahuanaco's nobility, but they also maintained close, and at least partially autonomous, social relationships with distant populations. Although many people immigrated to the great pilgrimage center that had formed near the southern shores of Lake Titicaca, they continued to maintain economic, political, and religious ties with their kinfolk in their original homelands. This flow of immigrants with their own set of "foreign relations" imparted something of a cosmopolitan character to Tiahuanaco. But relative to other premodern cities, social diversity and a multiplicity of independent economic and political actors was not a particular hallmark of Tiahuanaco urban culture.

Urban economic activity and policy, such as it was, was stimulated and controlled by the aristocratic households. Artisans on the periphery of Tiahuanaco were not producing pottery and lapidary work for sale in an urban market. They were not completely free economic actors. Rather, they were bound in a web of social relations with their elite patrons and with their own lineage and household members and their trading partners. In exchange for their clients' skilled labor, the Tiahuanaco nobility provided both raw materials for the craft and artisanal pieces they wished to commission and, most likely, for the full-time craft specialists, their basic subsistence. The daily sustenance of these retainers and the junior lineages of the nobility were satisfied in exchange for their labor service, whether this was in the form of crafting precious objects or participating in the governance of the state. In the absence of money, a substantial quotient of the circulation of basic commodities in Tiahuanaco took place as informal barter among families and close associates—that is, at the level of the lineage (*ayllu*). The daily economic life of the ayllu was fueled by these kinds of direct, reciprocal relationships. But this form of intensely interpersonal exchange is radically different from that accomplished in an impersonal market. The point of direct, reciprocal exchange between patrons and clients, or between ayllu members, was not simply to effect a transfer of goods and services, although this was the overt purpose of the exchange. It was also, and perhaps more importantly, to build, express, and sustain a network of social relations. As with the modern Aymara communities of the high plateau, mutual labor exchange and interpersonal relationships were the life's blood of Tiahuanaco's economy.

But the lack of a market and Western-style commercial transactions, a tendency toward social homogeneity, political domination by eminent households, and a relatively small population does not mean that Tiahuanaco was an entirely closed, static community. The regal-ritual character of Tiahuanaco, and the mystique that inhered in the city because of its legendary role in native cosmology, ensured its preeminent status as a pilgrimage center. The awe-inspiring natural setting of the city and its remarkable human-created ensemble of temples drew people to Tiahuanaco. Countryfolk from the surrounding areas and from farther afield came to the city for public ceremonies, to participate directly in the state cults, and perhaps to bury their ancestors in the city's sacred ground. This periodic, temporary influx of pilgrims, who spoke a variety of dialects and practiced distinct customs, brought a dynamism to the texture of daily life in the city. The flow of foreigners and foreign ideas and beliefs to and from the city was intensified by Tiahuanaco's role as the central nexus of the llama caravan trade that extended across the south-central Andes and by its military adventures and conquests.

Tiahuanaco was a city redolent with the symbolism of power. As the principal seat of Tiahuanaco's ruling lineages, the city was the center of the royal court. Its temples, with their walls lavishly painted and encrusted with precious metals, became among the holiest shrines of the imperial religion. The city was simultaneously an icon of Tiahuanaco rule and a cosmogram, an image of Tiahuanaco's imagined universe. It was, for the people of Tiahuanaco, the ultimate place of wealth and power, social identity and prestige, cult and command. The architectural form of Tiahuanaco, together with its public ensemble of monumental stone sculptures, intensified the mythic aura of the city, imbuing it with a quality of the supernatural: a mystical space beyond the strictures of the profane world in which it was embedded.

But what did the city look like at its apogee? What meaning did the soaring ensemble of temples, palaces, and monumental art hold for the people of Tiahuanaco? These questions are simple, but the answers are not. They will lead us into a world of symbolism that is difficult to apprehend, one that links man, nature, and city in intimate and unexpected ways. In some sense, to truly grasp this world, one must first live in it, at least in the mind and in the imagination. We must come to feel the visceral impact of the high plateau's elements, its seasons, its changes, its peculiar rhythms. We must learn to appreciate what the ancients felt when they built their human environment to literally resonate with the natural world. They sought to construct their social world in harmony with the elements, with the forces and processes of nature. They pondered the glittering canopy of the stars and sought the movement and order within. They gazed across the mountain peaks and saw images of ancestral worlds. They made sense of themselves by careful reference to the environment around them, by mimicking and modeling themselves after the natural world in which they lived and from which they drew their sustenance. The ancients built their cities in the image and likeness of the heavens and the earth. Through this self-conscious mimicry of nature, they evoked the secure sense of eternal progression that they perceived in the daily arc of the sun, in the slow dance of the stars across the night sky, in the endless turning of the seasons. The urban order of the ancient world was transcribed from nature. If we understand this single principle, we can read many of the ancients' concepts and relationships to the world around them from the text of their built environments, their cities and towns, their temples and houses.

Yet the problem of understanding such embedded meaning is an extraordinarily intractable one. We are unaccustomed to perceive our own urban environments as imbued with this kind of symbolic coherence. Our image of the city is one of almost chaotic fragmentation, many disparate parts that make, at best, a mechanical, ill-fitting whole. Movement through the Western city from periphery to core does not offer the same sense of the inexorability of revealed truth that was designed into the archaic city. The social elites of London and New York never validated their status by emulating and symbolically appropriating the cyclical, reproductive powers of nature. There is an almost insuperable cognitive gap between the archaic, agrarian mind and the self-consciously "rational" mind of the industrial world: They inhabit and are engaged by separate realities.

Then, too, we must recall that cities and urban design played a distinct role in the agrarian world of archaic states. These were fundamentally nonurban, or even antiurban societies. Certainly that was the case of Tiahuanaco. The bulk of the population resided in the countryside, dispersed in small villages and hamlets. The dominant social reality was one which turned on the cyclical, seasonal rhythms of rural life, radically removed from the cosmopolitan world of the elites. The cities that did exist in societies like Tiahuanaco were few, and consequently exceptionally special. Most were centers of pilgrimage for the inhabitants of the countryside; a nexus of religious tourism and venal commercialism. At the same time, they were the focal points for, and the distilled essence of, publicly expressed notions of universal order. To exert any authority over the hinterlands, these cities required a coherent, immediately understandable design that expressed a sense of man's and, still more specifically, one's own ethnic group's place in the world.

Ironically, this sense of place, expressed with monumentality in the architecture of the cities, explicitly evoked a rural sensibility. The life of farms and fields in the countryside provided the model for the essential relationship between humankind and nature that profoundly influenced the internal design and social order of the city. The symbolic text written into the design of these cities was one that attempted to harmonize the productive, yet potentially destructive, forces of nature with the culturally created order of human society. The rural hinterlands of cities in the archaic world tangibly produced both food and symbolic meaning for urban populations. Such intense symbolic and historical relationships between urban and rural realities seem alien or quaint to us now, disintegrating under the heavy burden of industrialization and the globalization of economies. But we must vividly re-create these relationships in our minds if we are to grasp the social order that brought form and meaning to cities such as Tiahuanaco.

We see this singular principle, the mimetic reflection of nature and society, repeated over and again in Tiahuanaco and the cities it spawned throughout the high plateau. Tiahuanaco itself was a human icon of the natural order. The ceremonial core of the city was surrounded by an immense moat that restricted easy access to its centrally located public buildings. Inevitably, when we imagine a moat, we conjure images of medieval European castles with high, crenellated towers encircled by a deep ring of water. We think of heavy wooden drawbridges drawn up tight against a surrounding horde of armored knights. Intuitively, we understand the moat as a defensive device, a physical barrier designed to keep out enemies. But this was not its purpose at Tiahuanaco.

Tiahuanaco's moat had nothing to do with protecting its elite residents from marauding barbarians or the potentially hostile lower classes of the city. Rather, the moat was constructed to evoke the image of the city core as an island. But not just a common, generic island. The notion was to create, at the cost of a huge investment in human labor, an image of the sacred islands of Lake Titicaca which were, according to the great cosmogonic myths, the points of world creation and human emergence. Tiahuanaco's moat generated a dramatic visual cue that emphasized the ritually charged nature of social

Layout of the ceremonial core of Tiahua-naco. The moat encircling this sacred precinct transformed it into a symbolic island. (Copyright © by Alan Kolata.)

3840

3845

PUMA PUNKU

3850

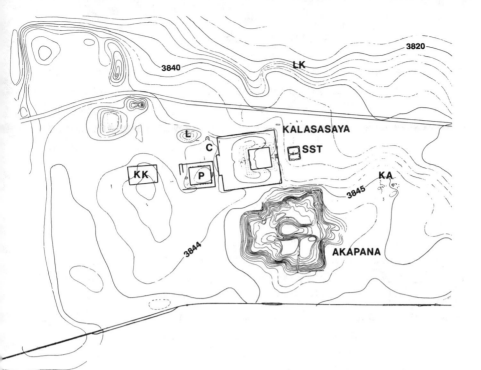

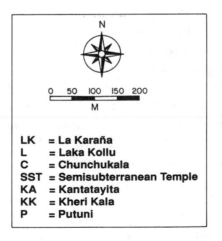

LK = La Karaña
L   = Laka Kollu
C   = Chunchukala
SST = Semisubterranean Temple
KA = Kantatayita
KK = Kheri Kala
P   = Putuni

actions that were played out in the center. In moving from the landlocked outer ring of Tiahuanaco's vernacular architecture across the moat into its interior island circle of temples and elite residences, the visitor to the city moved from the space and time of ordinary life to the space and time of the sacred. The interior sacred core was symbolically a human representation of the place and time of human origins.

In the Andean world, as in many other indigenous cosmologies, the time of origins was not a vague, temporally distant historical event to be remembered and commemorated in yearly ceremony. Rather, cosmological time was cyclical, regenerative, and re-created by human agency. Humans existed in the sacred time of cosmology, as well as in the profane time of daily life. The ceremonial inner core of Tiahuanaco was constructed as the theatrical backdrop for the recurrent social construction of cosmological order. And, of course, the parallel message embedded in this architectural text was the appropriation of the sacred by Tiahuanaco's elite. Within the ceremonial core of Tiahuanaco were constructed not only the principal temples of the city, but also the palatial residences of the ruling class. By living within this sacred inner precinct of the city, these elites were claiming for themselves the right—and assuming the obligation—to intercede on behalf of society with the divine, with the supernatural, to maintain harmony in the natural and social orders. The lineages of the elites conjoined historical time (the linear experience of time lived here and now) with cosmogonic time (the cyclical, regenerative time of myth).

Tiahuanaco's moat served to physically demarcate the concentrated, sacred essence of the city. The moat acted as a psychological and physical barrier, setting up by its very shape, dimensions, and symbolic representation a concentric hierarchy of space and time. Passage across the moat represented a change of both spatial and temporal frames of reference, a movement into the place and time of ethnic origins.

The contradiction inherent in its meaning to the people

128

of Tiahuanaco must have been clear to them; the central island of cosmogonic myth was believed to be the point of origin for all humans, but at Tiahuanaco, only *some* humans, the elites of Tiahuanaco society, appropriated the special right of residence in this sacred core. The barrier of water, then, also marked a point of transition that distinguished the residences of elites from those of commoners. Social inequality and hierarchy were encoded in Tiahuanaco's urban form.

There was, in other words, a principle of urban order at Tiahuanaco that we might describe as a concentric cline of the sacred that diminished in intensity from the city core to its far peripheries. Within this framework of urban order keyed to conceptions of the sacred, the inhabitants of Tiahuanaco occupied physical space in accordance with their relative social and ritual status. The upper echelons of the Tiahuanaco elite monopolized for their residences the innermost, and most sacred, core of their artificial island. Movement from the east of Tiahuanaco towards the civic-ceremonial core of the city entailed passage across a nested, hierarchical series of socially and ritually distinguished spaces.

The major structures within the civic-ceremonial core of Tiahuanaco are aligned to the cardinal directions. The perceived solar path establishes an east-west axis that bisects the city, and furnishes the principal avenue of circulation. This solar path emerges from and dissolves back into two salient geographic features to which indigenous peoples in the Valley of Tiahuanaco still orient themselves: the glacier-shrouded peaks of the Cordillera Real, particularly the three peaks of Mount Illimani, to the east (the emergent sun), and Lake Titicaca to the west (the waning, setting sun). The great snowcapped peaks and the lake are readily visible from the flanks of the mountains that enclose the valley, but both can be glimpsed simultaneously from the city of Tiahuanaco on the valley floor only from the summit of the Akapana, Tiahuanaco's tallest terraced platform mound. The summit structures of the Akapana (and the elites who resided there) were imbued with symbolic power derived, in part, from this unique visual frame of reference. From this summit alone could one track the entire celestial path of the sun from its twin anchors in the mountains and the lake.

That the elites of Tiahuanaco were conscious of, and purposely manipulated, this solar element of sacred geography to invest their capital with social meaning seems certain from key aspects of the architectural design of the Akapana and its companion terraced mound to the southwest, the Puma Punku. As the Spanish chronicler Cieza de León recounted in clear reference to the Akapana and Puma Punku, these two "sepulchral towers of the native Lords of Tiahuanaco" have their "doorways [facing] the rising sun."[2] Although not mentioned by Cieza, each of these structures possessed a second staircase, directly opposite those referred to in his account. That is, as we now know from recent excavations at these two structures, both Akapana and the Puma Punku possess twin axial staircases constructed centrally into their east and west facades. The concept of east-west axial entryways were also design features of other monumental architectural complexes in Tiahuanaco's civic-ceremonial core. What is interesting about these sets of axial staircases, apart from their simple presence and location, is that they differ dramatically in terms of architectural elaboration. In these structures, both sets of western staircases are significantly smaller in scale than their eastern counterparts. Furthermore, the western staircases lack the elaborately carved stone jambs and lintels that grace the eastern entries. This differential treatment implies that these buildings, and more specifically their points of entry and egress, architecturally encode a significant status hierarchy. That is, in Tiahuanaco's system of sacred geography, east was symbolically of higher status then west, and this symbolic hierarchy derives, ultimately, from the symbolism of the solar path; the ascending sun of the east is energetically more powerful than the waning sun of the west.

As with the concentric principle of urban organization, the

A view of the altiplano and the high, snowcapped peaks along the border between Bolivia and Chile. This vast, desolate plateau is the natural home of the llama and the alpaca, the most important animals of the Andes. (Copyright © by Flip Schulke; reprinted by permission.)

A view of Lake Titicaca, showing the ancient remains of raised agricultural terraces on the slopes. (Copyright © by Flip Schulke; reprinted by permission.)

Aerial view of the central monuments of the ancient city of Tiahuanaco.
(Copyright © by Flip Schulke; reprinted by permission.)

Closer view of the central monuments of Tiahuanaco. The Akapana pyramid rises behind the Kalasasaya, the Semisubterranean Temple, and the Putuni Temple and Palace complex in the foreground.
(Copyright © by Johan Reinhard; reprinted by permission.)

View of the Semisubterranean Temple and the sacred precinct of the Kalasasaya from the Akapana pyramid. (Photograph by Wolfgang Schüler; copyright © by Alan Kolata.)

Portions of the east facade of the Akapana pyramid. The "pyramid" itself is more accurately referred to as a terraced mound. The Akapana rises on seven superimposed terraces to the height of a five-story building. (Photograph by Wolfgang Schüler; copyright © by Alan Kolata.)

Monumental staircase to the Kalasasaya Temple. (Photograph by Wolfgang Schüler; copyright © by Alan Kolata.)

A view of the Ponce stela through the monumental gateway of the Kalasasaya. Weathered columns of sculptures more ancient than Tiahuanaco itself stand in the Semisubterranean Temple in the foreground. The rulers of Tiahuanaco actively sought out these sculptures to incorporate into the sacred structures of their capital. (Photograph by Wolfgang Schüler; copyright © by Alan Kolata.)

Detail of a ceramic incense burner in the form of a mountain lion discovered in excavations at the Tiahuanaco city of Lukurmata. (Photograph by Wolfgang Schüler; copyright © by Alan Kolata.)

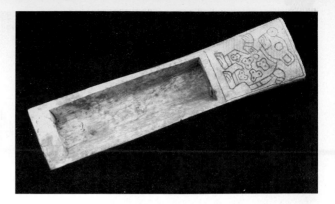

(Right) Snuff tray of bone with an engraved image of a Tiahuanaco priest-warrior costumed as a jaguar. The depression in this tablet once held powdered wilka, a hallucinogenic drug inhaled by the priests, rulers, warriors, and shamans of ancient Tiahuanaco. (Photograph by Wolfgang Schüler; copyright © by Alan Kolata.)

Polychrome ceramic portrait head of a turbaned Tiahuanaco ruler. (Collection of the Museum of Man, London, England; copyright © by Alan Kolata.)

Ceramic drinking cup with images of human trophy heads (upper band) and condors (lower band). (Collection of the National Museum of Archaeology, La Paz, Bolivia; copyright © by Alan Kolata.)

Copper mirror with a crushed lead flask and various pins of gold found with a sacrificial burial of a young woman in the Palace of the Multicolored rooms. (Photograph by Wolfgang Schüler; copyright © by Alan Kolata.)

The Gateway of the Sun at Tiahuanaco. The projecting central figure of the creator god Viracocha is one of the most famous images of ancient Andean art. The images carved on this gateway served as a complex—and still incompletely understood—agricultural calendar for the people of Tiahuanaco. (Photograph by Wolfgang Schüler; copyright © by Alan Kolata.)

Detail of the carvings on the Gateway of the Sun. (Photograph by Wolfgang Schüler; copyright © by Alan Kolata.)

Chrisostomos Choque, shaman, seated beside Lucas Choque, his nephew and apprentice, outside of Chrisostomos's hut. (Copyright © by Alan Kolata.)

The Choque family compound. Chrisostomos's great-grandchildren are fetching water from a well in the foreground. The Quimsachata Range rises in the background. Deep in the mountains is the shrine of Qorpa. Copyright © by Alan Kolata.)

Policarpio Flores and his family seated outside their house. Policarpio has just opened a textile bundle he carries with him during the planting season. Note the MasterCard sign in the window. (Copyright © by Alan Kolata.)

A textile bundle with seed potatoes and other traditional Andean crops. These are often used as ritual offerings at mountain shrines and in the agricultural fields of the Aymara. (Copyright © by Alan Kolata.)

View of ancient and rehabilitated raised fields in the Pampa Koani behind Roberto Cruz's house. (Photograph by Wolfgang Schüler; copyright © by Alan Kolata.)

Aymara women from the village of Lakaya harvesting potatoes on rehabilitated raised fields. (Photograph by Wolfgang Schüler; copyright © by Alan Kolata.)

principle of axiality generated by the solar path differentiated social space in Tiahuanaco. In effect, the solar path conceptually divided the city into two hierarchically ranked segments with distinct symbolic associations: the east conceptually linked to the celestial realm, the rising sun, and high prestige, and the west, evoking images of the setting sun, the underworld, and lesser prestige.

Concepts of sacred geography and the symbolic integration of natural landscapes strongly shaped the urban design of Tiahuanaco. The innermost core of the city, demarcated by the moat, was the heart of elite residence in the city, and the setting for one of the most important shrines: the Akapana. The inner core of the city represented the concentrated essence of the sacred, structured as an orchestrated architectural allusion to cosmogonic myths. If we have some insight into the overall structure, social partitioning, and symbolic structure of Tiahuanaco's urban design, what can we say about the meaning, function, and social characteristics of individual elements in its monumental and vernacular architecture?

The largest and most imposing single building in Tiahuanaco is the Akapana. Perhaps because of its massive and unprecedented scale for the Andean highlands, archaeologists early in this century assumed that the Akapana was a natural hill, a geological feature only superficially modified by the people of Tiahuanaco.[3] But the Spanish chronicler Cieza de León had it right nearly five hundred years ago when he described the structure as "a man-made hill, built on stone foundations."[4] The Akapana is, in fact, an entirely artificial construction of transported earth, clay, gravel, and cut stone, stepping up in seven superimposed terraces. The design, techniques, and materials of construction are fascinating in themselves, but even more so for the insight they provide concerning the function and meaning of this temple.

The Akapana itself is over two hundred meters on a side at its maximum extent, and rises to nearly seventeen meters in

131

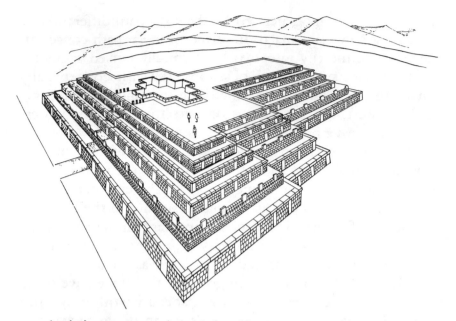

Artist's reconstruction of the Akapana pyramid as viewed from the northeast corner. (Drawing courtesy of Javier Escalante, National Institute of Archaeology, La Paz, Bolivia.)

height. The basal terrace is a monumental and strikingly beautiful revetment of cut stone with rounded, beveled edges at the joins between blocks. Vertical pillars were erected at the corners of the structure, as well as every few meters along the facade of the terrace. These pillars occur at intervals of approximately three and one-half meters. Between the pillars, the architects of Akapana set cut stone blocks in ashlarlike masonry, precision joined without mortar. This gigantic revetment wall was then capped with large rectangular blocks that projected slightly beyond its vertical face, much like modern coping tiles.

The upper six terraces of the Akapana riding on this foundation differ in architectural detail, mostly in that they lack the beveled edges of the foundation terrace. Excavations

132

along these upper terraces recovered tenoned sculptures shaped like the heads of pumas and humans that were at one time inserted into the facades, punctuating the flat, vertical surfaces of the terrace walls with gargoyle-like projections. Behind the retaining walls of the seven superimposed terraces, the builders of Akapana laid tons of earth and clay. The outward pressure exerted by this earth fill must have been tremendous, and, in some cases, Akapana's architects devised ingenious caissons of stone to contain the fill. The bulk of the clay and earth transported to construct the Akapana was excavated from the huge moat surrounding the civic-ceremonial core.

One material used in the construction of the Akapana offers an intriguing insight into the meaning of this structure for the people of Tiahuanaco. Within the construction fill of the upper terraces, interspersed between enormous layers of clay, are thin lenses of a bluish-green gravel. These small, waterworn pebbles completely cover the summit of the Akapana. Its presence on the Akapana can only result from human agency.

Why would the architects of Akapana go to such great lengths to incorporate this green gravel into the uppermost fill and surface of the structure's summit? It is apparent that this gravel had no structural role. Gravel in this quantity would have been exceedingly tedious to collect and transport to the construction site. The fact that the gravel occurs in distinct lenses within the structure and on the summit indicates that it was not simply a by-product, or accidental inclusion in the construction. What, then, is it doing there? Why would Tiahuanaco's architects invest so much labor in purposefully distributing this gravel inside and on top of the Akapana?

The answers stem from the origin and distinctive color of this gravel. This gravel is an erosional product of the Quimsachata and Chila mountain ranges to the south of Tiahuanaco, and it occurs naturally in a number of quebradas and intermittent streams that flow down from these mountains.

The source of the gravel is clear to anyone who lives along the base of the Quimsachata Range, and its exotic, visually arresting green color immediately attracts the eye. I believe now that the architects of the Akapana selected this gravel for inclusion in the structure precisely because of its potent symbolic associations with the sacred mountains of the Quimsachata Range, which were important spiritual points of reference, or wakas, for the people of Tiahuanaco.[5] The gravel was, quite literally, like pieces of the true cross, imbued with the spiritual essence of the mountain wakas. But, even more, the exotic green color of these stones conveyed an association with the life-giving springs, streams, and subterranean seeps that have their origin in the southern mountain ranges. Not only is the gravel the color of water, it is brought down to the broad plains of the Tiahuanaco Valley within these same surface streams and subterranean flows that furnish fresh water to most of the valley. This green gravel condensed in one material the symbolic essence of two Tiahuanaco sacred elements: mountains and water.

Such a conclusion is not without parallel in the ancient Andean world. One of the two principal plazas in Incan Cuzco, called Haukaypata, was covered with a layer of sand brought from the Pacific coast nearly five hundred kilometers away. The Spanish magistrate Polo de Ondegardo "had the sand removed in 1559 after finding that it was considered sacred by the local residents, who buried gold and silver figurines and vessels in it. Polo also relates that the original earthern surface of the plaza was venerated and carried to other parts of the empire."[6] The sand was apparently sacred because of its association with the waters of the Pacific Ocean. One of the places to which the original earth from the Haukaypata plaza may have been carried was the main plaza of the Inca sanctuary on the Island of the Sun in Lake Titicaca.

If we accept that the architects of Tiahuanaco shared similar concepts regarding the need to sanctify their capital's ceremonial structures through these audacious, labor-intensive schemes of symbolic transference, the question remains, Why cover Akapana, and not other structures, with this green gravel? Apart from the obvious fact that the Akapana is the most imposing structure at Tiahuanaco and the touchstone for the city's ceremonial complex, the great temple was conceived by the people of Tiahuanaco as an emblem of a sacred mountain. Akapana served as a human-created simulacrum of the highly visible, natural mountain wakas in the Quimsachata Range. Akapana mimics the form of a mountain, ascending in seven stepped terraces to visually dominate the urban landscape. Throughout the archaic world, there are countless instances of this kind of symbolic mimesis between pyramidal structures and mountain peaks.[7] Then, too, the layers of green gravel physically link Akapana with the Quimsachata Range; pieces of the mountains are quite literally built into the structure. But, more subtly, certain structural features of the Akapana intensify the mountain association and, even more specifically, the link between mountains and sources of water.

I had come to Tiahuanaco originally to conduct an intensive geophysical survey of the Akapana with the object of prospecting for subterranean passageways within the pyramid, concealing deeply buried tombs. And, in fact, over the course of my first months in Tiahuanaco, we detected many "anomalies" within the pyramid that indicated interior tunnels and voids. Although we were excited by these results and entertained visions of discovering a South American version of Tutankhamen's tomb, a lack of money to undertake the massive excavations required to reach them forced us to defer our plans and suppress our curiosity for an entire decade. By 1988, I was finally in a position to attack the mystery of Akapana's interior structures. Within days of beginning excavations on the summit of the Akapana temple, my research team found the completely unexpected solution to this mystery. The interior voids were not passageways and tomb chambers at all. Instead, we revealed a sophisticated and extensive system of subterranean channels and drains. Our visions of mummies wrapped in sumptuous textiles and bedecked in gold dissolved before our eyes. What we had found was another puzzle: Why was the entire pyramid riddled with drainage canals?

The system begins on the summit of the temple with sets of small, subterranean, stone-lined channels that originally drained Akapana's central sunken court. This court is now entirely destroyed by massive looting undertaken by the Spanish in the seventeenth century. (If there ever were royal tombs in the Akapana, they were probably discovered long ago and their precious grave goods melted down for the Spanish Crown.) The sunken court on Akapana's summit was not roofed, and huge amounts of water collected in the court during the altiplano's furious rainy season between December and March. These stone channels conducted water from the sunken court to a major trunk line that was buried deeper beneath the summit surface. This trunk line probably extended around the four sides of Akapana's summit, but we have direct evidence for it only on the north and west sides. On the west side, we excavated an extensive segment of this subterranean trunk line running in a north–south direction. The drain is rectangular in cross-section, and finely crafted of large, precision fitted sandstone blocks with an interior dimension that would have accommodated an enormous flow. This elaborate subterranean trunk line collected water flowing from the channels draining the sunken court on the summit and conducted it inside of the structure to the next lower terrace. Here the water emerged from inside the Akapana onto an exterior stone channel tenoned into the vertical terrace face. The water poured over the edge of the tenoned drain onto a stone channel on the terrace, flowed for a few meters on the surface, and then dropped back into the interior of the structure to the next lower terrace through a vertical drain. This process of alternating subterranean and surface flow on the stepped terraces repeated itself until the water finally flowed from the basal terrace of the Akapana through beautifully constructed tunnels. Eventually, the water descending from the Akapana's summit flowed into a monumental sewer system that was installed deep underground throughout the inner core of Tiahuanaco. This system drained into the Tiahuanaco River, and, ultimately, into Lake Titicaca itself. Although we were disappointed not to find tombs within the pyramid, what we did discover was a kind of intellectual gold. For now we had new, unanticipated clues to the function and meaning of the Akapana temple.

A much simpler and smaller set of canals would have accomplished the function of draining accumulated rainwater from the summit of the temple. As installed by the architects of Akapana, the system, although superbly functional, is completely overengineered, a piece of technical stonecutting and joinery that displays virtuosity. This elaborate drainage network possessed a dimension that goes beyond simple utility, a dimension that we can approach by posing a single question: Why is the water repeatedly and alternately threaded inside and on the surface of the structure?

The answer to this question lies in considering a more profound mimesis between Akapana and the natural mountains of the Quimsachata Range than the general visual similarity of stepped-terrace mounds and mountain peaks. This deeper symbolic association is grounded in certain ecological processes that characterize the Quimsachata Range. Rainwater pools in saddles and peaks welling up and then flowing down to the valley floor. The water quickly disappears into subterranean streams which periodically reemerge downslope, gushing and pooling in natural terraces, only to flow again down inside the mountain. The peculiarities of mountain geology and the erosive power of water combine to create this natural alternation between subterranean and surface streams. Runoff from the rains finally emerges at the foot of the mountains to recharge the aquifer of the Tiahuanaco Valley. And it is this aquifer that waters the valley's agricultural fields. The mountains were the sacred source of water that nourished people and their fields. Akapana was symbolically the human-created sacred mountain of Tiahuanaco. It partook of the spiritual essence of the Quimsachata mountain range, the image of which was evoked by Akapana's stepped-terrace shape, by its green gravel mantle, and by its cleverly constructed mimicry of the natural circulation of mountain waters in the rainy season. The course of water flow on the Akapana replicated the pattern of nature: pooling, dropping out of sight, gushing onto terraces, emerging at the foot of the mound. In a driving altiplano storm, the large subterranean drains inside of the Akapana may even have generated an acoustic effect, a vibrating roar of rushing interior water that shook the mountain-pyramid, much like the thunderstorms rumbling across the peaks of Quimsachata. In other words, the Akapana was Tiahuanaco's principal earth shrine, an intense icon of fertility and agricultural abundance. Although it may have had a particular association with the mountains of the imposing and immediately visible Quimsachata Range, Akapana's location in the civic-ceremonial core of the city suggests yet another kind of symbolic representation.

Akapana rests in the center of the conceptual island carved by Tiahuanaco's great ceremonial moat. Viewed in the larger context of its setting, Akapana becomes the mountain at the center of the island world, and may even have evoked the specific image of sacred mountains on Lake Titicaca's Island of the Sun. Here another aspect is layered into the meaning of Akapana. Akapana is the principal waka, the spatial centerpiece of cosmogonic myth. It is the mountain of human origins and emergence.

We know now that Akapana served as a key shrine in Tiahuanaco religion and elite ideology. But other elements of the structure revealed in recent excavations add fascinating textures to our understanding of its function and meaning. Although Akapana was a center of cult and ritual behavior, part of its summit was used for living quarters as well. Most of the Akapana summit was taken up by a centrally located sunken court, measuring approximately fifty meters on a side. Access to the court was gained by the twin axial staircases. Flanking the central court, at least on the northern side where we completed major excavations, were distinctly secular structures. Here we uncovered a well-constructed suite of rooms arrayed around a central patio that appear to have served as residences.

Beneath the central patio, a series of burials were uncovered. A file of seated adults, originally wrapped tightly in textile mummy bundles, faced a seated male holding a puma-shaped incense burner in his hands. Who might the inhabitants of such a sacred structure have been? The burials under the patio suggest that they were of an elite stratum in Tiahuanaco society. Although difficult to confirm, they may have been priests who served as the principal ritual practitioners for ceremonies that took place on Akapana's summit. This seems a plausible conclusion, particularly in light of the manner in which this residential complex was treated upon abandonment. We discovered a major offering that was associated with the sealing and abandonment of one of the rooms. This offering contained fourteen sacrificed llamas, a hoard of copper pins and plaques, hammered silver sheets, a miniature figurine of a sitting fox, a polished bone lip plug, mica, obsidian, quartz, and fragments of complex polychrome ceramics, including a miniature *kero* or ritual drinking cup, a puma-shaped incense burner, and a vase with an image of a resplendent crowned figure like that on the Gateway of the Sun. The offering itself was carefully arranged in a mannered, ritualistic fashion: The skulls and upper jaws of the llamas were found in the north and west sides of the room; the lower jaws of these animals were placed in the southeast corner; and the metal objects were concentrated in the northeast portions of the room. The polychrome ceramics, lip plug, mica, and fragments of obsidian and quartz stone tools were found immediately outside the entrance to the room.

The curious distribution of these objects, in many ways analogous to the Aymara shamans' misas, evokes a powerful

139

sense that we have excavated the final remnants of an important ritual. Radiocarbon dates from this offering cluster around A.D. 1150. Given that the offering itself rendered the room inaccessible, we may be witnessing here a ritual of closure, a ceremony during which the great Akapana earth shrine and the practitioners of its cults were symbolically interred at a time when the city was being abandoned.

The summit structures are not the only ones associated with Akapana. Terraces farther down the mound show evidence of surface buildings with foundations of andesite blocks and adobe superstructures. A series of small but finely wrought buildings were uncovered on the first terrace of the Akapana in excavations by Bolivian archaeologists in the mid 1970s. A number of these appear to be late constructions, perhaps even erected by the Inca after the abandonment of Tiahuanaco. The Inca incorporated Tiahuanaco as an important shrine in their imperial ideology, and were reputed to have built various structures in the city. But other such terrace structures are clearly associated with the florescence of Tiahuanaco.

Our own excavations on the northwest corner of Akapana revealed a fascinating, and, to date, not entirely understood set of ritual offerings associated with the foundations of the structure and with buildings on the first terrace. Here we encountered a series of twenty-one human burials commingled with llama bones and ceramics that date to the early Classic Tiahuanaco period between A.D. 400 and 600. What is curious about the burials is that most are incomplete. But the bones that are present from these skeletons were articulated in correct anatomical position. A good example of this unusual burial practice was an adult male, twenty-one to twenty-seven years old, who was found face down parallel to the foundation wall of the Akapana. His spinal column was complete, and his mandible (lower jaw) was in correct anatomical position, but his skull was missing. Another male, twenty-five to thirty years old, was discovered laying face down farther along the base of Akapana's foundation wall. Next to him in the same burial was a second young adult male buried face up. Eighteen of these burials lack skulls and several are missing lower limbs, arms, or portions of the spinal column. Among these remarkable burials, only one child was found completely intact and with a fully articulated skeleton. But this child, who was approximately two years old upon death, was also discovered laying face down and with legs flexed and crossed. Unlike the other burials of apparently robust young males, this child suffered from a severe degenerative bone disease that left it painfully crippled. This disease was, most likely, the cause of the child's death.

Who were these people, and why were only parts of their bodies buried at the Akapana? At first glance, we assumed that these individuals (many of whom were adult males from seventeen to thirty-nine years old) were dismembered prior to, or shortly after death, conjuring Aztec-style images of sacrifice at the hands of priest-warriors. But a fatal problem with this interpretation quickly emerged on closer examination: None of the bones showed evidence of cut marks, and there is little evidence of intentional physical violence. In lieu of a preternatural capacity to butcher a human body without leaving a mark on adjacent bones, the skulls and other body parts must have been removed postmortem, at some time after the corpse and its tough connective tissue had begun to decay. It is possible that these individuals died, or were sacrificed, and that their bones were later interred at the Akapana in the form of mummy bundles. Although some body parts, such as the skull and lower limbs, were removed in the process of assembling the mummy bundle, the remaining portions of the skeleton remained articulated in an anatomically correct position by the textile wrappings of the bundle.

But why did the people of Tiahuanaco remove individual bones, and particularly the skulls, from these burials? One clue to this intriguing puzzle comes from a tremendous offering of purposely broken clay vessels associated with five of these curious partial skeletons. This ceramic cache and its associated burials were uncovered within the destroyed room of a structure on the first terrace of the Akapana. The brightly painted ceramics are iconographically associated with the Classic Tiahuanaco period, and three radiocarbon dates fix the episode between A.D. 530 and 690. These dates, along with the identical burial pattern of partial skeletons, indicate that the offering was contemporaneous with those excavated along the foundation wall of the Akapana, perhaps even forming part of a single, ritual event. The ceramic offering consists of hundreds of fine polychrome vessels fashioned into bowls and keros that we found shattered into thousands of fragments. The polychrome bowl fragments from this ceramic offering have a consistent, standardized motif: painted bands of stylized human trophy heads. The keros display painted images of humans elaborately costumed as puma and condor figures. Trophy heads hang from the belts of these figures, or are worked into the elements of masks worn by the dancing celebrants portrayed on the vessels. Not infrequently, human trophy heads appear as the finials of staffs carried by the condor- or puma-masked dancers. The trophy heads, although eerily stylized skeletal images, are clearly representations of actual human trophy heads. Cut and polished skulls have been found in excavations at Tiahuanaco, leaving little doubt that the practice of taking heads in battle as trophies was a central symbolic element of Tiahuanaco warfare and ritual sacrifice. We know that the Inca took heads in battle and later transformed the skulls of particularly important enemy warriors into macabre drinking cups used to celebrate the victory over the vanquished foe.[8] It is not surprising that the people of Tiahuanaco adhered to similar practices.

If we can judge from the testimony of state art, the elites of Tiahuanaco were obsessed with decapitation and with the ritual display of severed heads. Grim images of decapitation abound in Tiahuanaco art. Many of these feature animal-masked humans carrying sacrificial knives and battle axes and wearing resplendent costumes studded with pendant trophy heads. A class of stone sculptures from Tiahuanaco, called *chachapumas,* portrays powerful, puma-masked humans holding a severed head in one hand and a battle ax in the other, as if to capture in stone the horrible and, one imagines, unforgettable moment of decapitation. We discovered one such chachapuma at the base of Akapana's ruined western staircase in the same context as the human offerings placed at the structure's foundations. This ferocious-looking sculpture, carved of dense, black basalt, seems poised in a crouch, ominously displaying in its lap a human trophy head with long tresses of braided hair.

Akapana's headless mummy bundles, associated with these lavish displays of trophy heads on ritual drinking cups and on monumental public sculpture, were interred at some time in the early seventh century. Given their state of selective dismemberment and their linkage to images of head taking, these human remains may represent the ancestral bundles of a conquered people. Few acts in the ancient Andean world could have been more intensely charged with the symbolism of domination than scattering the relics of ancestors and relatives at the foot of the conqueror's principal earth shrine. In the context of Andean ideology, this display of domination was simultaneously a symbolic act of incorporation of the conquered group into the social, cosmological, and political system of Tiahuanaco. The conquered group's ancestors were, in a real sense, infused into the sacred essence of the very shrine that was emblematic of Tiahuanaco's ethnic and cultural identity. The more profound act of domination here was not the simple taking of enemy heads, but rather the incorporation and assimilation of the conquered group's ethnic identity into the broader "body politic" of Tiahuanaco society. Domination here meant quite literally the loss of one's head, followed by the loss of the ethnic group's autonomous social identity. In addition to evoking the image of a gigantic earth shrine, the sculptures and esoteric offerings arrayed on and around the Akapana constituted a ritual text glorifying the political and ideological power of Tiahuanaco society, embodied in the actions of the warrior-priests who were at the apex of the ruling hierarchy.

The elaborate hydraulic features of the Akapana temple are replicated at the temple of Puma Punku, the second great stepped-platform mound at Tiahuanaco. As at the Akapana, the architects installed a system of tremendous internal canals that conducted rainwater from a sunken court on the summit into the interior of the structure. Ultimately, this water cascaded out from tunnels driven horizontally into the foundations. Precisely like Akapana, Puma Punku was designed to collect water and thread it through the structure from one terrace to the next. This terraced platform mound recapitulates, on a smaller scale, the intense symbolic associations inhering in the Akapana.

But why were two such hydraulic shrines constructed at Tiahuanaco? One solution to this question may derive from a fundamental structural feature of Andean societies: the division of social and ritual space into two parts. Anthropologists call this type of dual division or partitioning of society a moiety system. For instance, we know that the Inca capital of Cuzco was organized symbolically in just such a fashion, having been partitioned into two hierarchically ranked sectors, *hanan* (upper) Cuzco and *hurin* (lower) Cuzco, and further subdivided into quadrants defined by the four principal roads leading out of the city to the imperial provinces.[9] The Cuzco quadripartition rendered the capital an audacious microcosm of the empire, as well as an architectural metaphor for the Inca universe. In Cuzco, each of these two divisions were associated with specific lineages, or ayllus that were ranked in a hierarchy according to the degree of their kin relationship with the king and his royal lineage. These ayllus possessed territorial rights and access to sources of water within the district of Cuzco and were obligated to perform certain rites, such as sponsoring the celebration of agricultural rituals, or maintaining a particular shrine according to a complex cere-monial calendar. Tiahuanaco may have been organized in a similar fashion, spatially and symbolically partitioned into two segments, each with its own core of ceremonial architecture and sacred sculpture. Akapana and Puma Punku may have been the principal earth shrines and specific emblems of the sacred mountain for Tiahuanaco's moiety divisions.

Puma Punku itself appears to have been constructed in the Classic Tiahuanaco period, most probably between the seventh and eighth centuries A.D. Construction work on the Akapana, on the other hand, began prior to Puma Punku, although a more precise date for initial building activities is not yet clear. This chronological difference represents an intriguing, if somewhat speculative, possibility for interpret-ing potential changes in the function of these two great archi-tectural monuments of Tiahuanaco urban civilization.

At the time of the early-seventh-century event that led to the interment of ritual bundles and offerings at the foot of the Akapana, it is clear that the monumental drainage net-work of the temple that mimicked the alternating surface and subterranean flow of mountain waters was no longer func-tioning. The offerings of artifacts and human and animal remains in shallow pits at the base of the structure would never have been preserved intact, as they were discovered, if this internal drainage system still flowed with accumulated rainwater. In fact, one of the associated offerings from this event, a dog burial, was placed directly in front of a tunnel from which the water flowed out of the base of the pyramid. This indicates beyond much doubt that the great drainage system had ceased to function at some point before the ritual interments on the Akapana, or before circa A.D. 600.

If the Akapana's original symbolic association for the peo-ple of Tiahuanaco was as an earth shrine linked to sacred mountains as sources of fresh water, how can we interpret this potentially radical change in the function of the temple mound? One possibility, deriving from the pattern of offerings, is that at some point in the early seventh century, the intense ethnic and cosmological symbolism of the Akapana was appropriated by the Tiahuanaco elite (or perhaps even an individual king) to glorify their position and social standing within Tiahuanaco society. Given that the imagery of these ritual offerings are overwhelmingly focused on aggressive, martial themes (the display of trophy heads and the arrangement of mummy bundles lacking skulls and other body parts), we may be witnessing here the aftermath of a particular campaign of military conquest at which the principal temple in the capital city was rededicated to commemorate a transforming event in Tiahuanaco history. Such temple rededications, accompanied by a mannered, symbolically rich incorporation of ritual objects, were a common feature of fifteenth and early sixteenth century Aztec imperial society in the central basin of Mexico. Periodic rededications of the Aztec *Templo Mayor* were stimulated by the passing of a designated fifty-two-year cycle in the Aztec ritual calendar, and by extraordinary events in the lives of the reigning monarchs, such as accession to the throne or the successful conclusion of important military campaigns. If the Akapana offerings reflect a similar act of ritual temple rededication, then the closing of the monumental internal drainage system may reflect a premeditated reconfiguring of the structure's symbolic "text" by the Tiahuanaco elite to memorialize a historically momentous event. From a generalized earth shrine and sacred mountain, Akapana at this time may have become a more specific icon commemorating, and further legitimating, the right of the Tiahuanaco warrior-elites to rule in the city: a massive, brutal and public expression of self-interested propaganda. Although the old, deeply rooted association of Akapana as a sacred mountain would surely have persisted in the minds of the people of Tiahuanaco, the temple rededication imparted a new layer of meaning that more intensely related the qualities and actions of the ruling elites to the ancient earth shrine.

Around the same time that the symbolic associations inhering in the Akapana were being reworked, the Puma Punku complex was built according to a structural template that replicated the original Akapana design by incorporating a monumental internal drainage system. Although after the early seventh century water on the Akapana no longer seems to have flowed in highly visible, alternating cascades from surface terraces to subterranean chambers, this artful and symbolically rich mimicking of natural hydrological processes on artificial mountain-pyramids was not lost at Tiahuanaco—it simply was transferred to the Puma Punku. After A.D. 600, Puma Punku became the general ethnic shrine to earth, mountains, and water at Tiahuanaco, while the Akapana was transformed into a more personalized shrine of the Lords of Tiahuanaco: a monumental paean to, and sacred guarantor of, their right to rule.

The distinctive architectural arrangement of a central, stepped-terrace mound in the center of an artificial island city encoded in the Akapana and Puma Punku complexes reoccurs beyond the boundaries of Tiahuanaco itself. This concept of urban spatial order, which evoked the place and time of cosmological and ethnic origins and visually related built forms to sacred geography, was a central symbolic expression of Tiahuanaco elite culture. This symbolically dense architectural arrangement was extended to regional Tiahuanaco capitals in the altiplano such as Lukurmata, Pajchiri, and Khonko Wankané as a self-conscious emblem of Tiahuanaco dominion and legitimacy. In each of these regional cities, canals or moats carve the urban landscape into a ceremonial core of temples and elite residences within an island enceinte counterpoised against extensive sectors of vernacular architecture. At Lukurmata, the most intensively investigated of the Tiahuanaco regional cities, the central ceremonial complex, organized around a terraced mound, was furnished with a drainage network similar to that of the Akapana and Puma Punku. Here, too, rainwater collecting on the summit of the ceremonial complex was threaded through carved stone drains to the base of the artificially modified rock outcrop on which the complex was constructed. Water from the summit flowed into the principal canal demarcating the island-core of the site, and, ultimately, into Lake Titicaca. At Lukurmata, this canal also drained an adjacent sector of agricultural fields, unambiguously linking the summit ceremonial complex with agricultural productivity through the connecting thread of flowing water.

Two other structures at Tiahuanaco complete the tableau of ceremonial architecture in the city core visible on the surface today: the Semisubterranean Temple and the Kalasasaya. Both of these structures are adjacent to the north face of Akapana, and both contain remarkable examples of Tiahuanaco's monumental stone sculpture that add substantially to our understanding of the meaning and function of these buildings for the people of Tiahuanaco. The Semisubterranean Temple, as its name implies, is a structure excavated into the ground to form a rectangular sunken court, constructed of sandstone masonry. A monumental staircase on the south side of the structure descends into the temple, which was originally left unroofed, open to the elements, as was the central, sunken court on the summit of the Akapana. The Semisubterranean Temple at Tiahuanaco contains an eclectic assemblage of stone stelae and sculptures carved in various styles which were carefully arrayed in subsidiary positions around a centrally located, monumental *axis mundi:* the seven-meter-tall Bennett stela.

The Bennett stela, like other major anthropomorphic monoliths in the Classic Tiahuanaco style, portrays an elaborately costumed and crowned human figure pressing a banded kero, or drinking cup, against the chest with one hand and grasping a scepterlike object in the other. This monumental sculpture visually encodes the principal tenets of Tiahuanaco state ideology and cosmology. The essential agrarian focus of this ideology is recapitulated in specific images on the sculp-

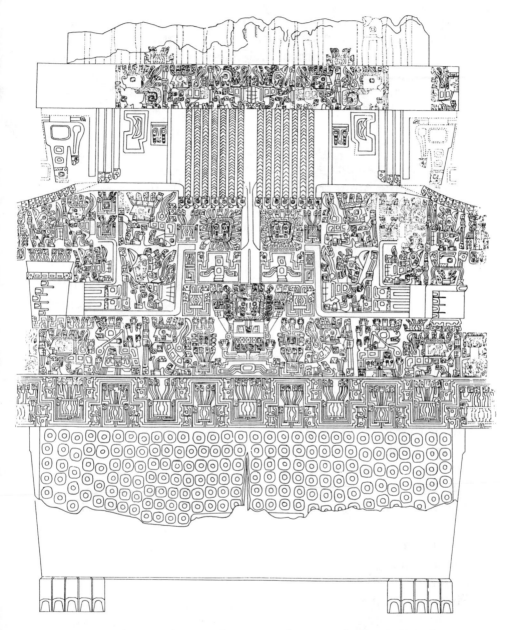

A drawing of the complex engravings on the Bennett stela.
(Copyright © by Alan Kolata.)

ture, which anthropologist Tom Zuidema, in a provocative interpretation, reconstructs as a representation of a twelve-month, sideral-lunar agricultural calendar.[10] He suggests that the doughnut-shaped circles portrayed on the short pants worn by the anthropomorphic sculpture represent day signs. Tie-dyed versions of these circles appear on textiles preserved in coastal Tiahuanaco tombs, indicating that the costume represented on the sculpture replicates actual clothing that was worn by humans, at least on ceremonial occasions. Zuidema interprets the number of circles on the sculpture, which total 177, as reflecting the number of days in six lunar months. Similarly, he suggests that the sequence of thirty figures shown in profile on the low-relief carving of the sculpture correspond to the thirty days of a month.

Several of the figures on the Bennett stela are associated with flowering plants, most notably the central human figure whose feet are transformed into plants. The image of a llama with a halter on either side of this central figure bears numerous representations of distinct flowering plants, both cultivated and wild, that conceptually associates llamas with agriculture and plant life. In particular, the llama figures appear to be draped with a textile that bears an emblem of a banded cup with a painted human face from behind which sprouts a maize plant. The association of the *kero* and maize plant immediately brings to mind the ritual drink, chicha, a maize beer which was central to indigenous Andean religion and politics. A plant sprouting from the back of the caped llama represents not a cultivated plant, but the columnar cactus *Trichocereus pachanoi*, a mescaline-bearing cactus that was sought for its hallucinogenic properties. Other images of this columnar cactus appear prominently on the Bennett stela, implying that the consumption of hallucinogenic plants was a key instrument for religious and ritual expression among the people of Tiahuanaco. We know that the consumption of plants with the capacity to alter consciousness are a common feature of shamanic ceremonies throughout the world. The occurrence of snuff trays, inhalation tubes, and other para-phernalia associated with the consumption of mind-altering substances in Tiahuanaco sites makes it clear that this was an important element of native Tiahuanaco religion also worthy of public commemoration on monumental state art.

The ritual content of the Bennett stela's rich iconography links agriculture, llama husbandry, and calendrics. Zuidema demonstrates that this conceptual linkage reflected social, symbolic, and ecological relationships between pastoralism and agriculture in the high plateau. As he notes: "While the crops are growing, the animals are kept away from the fields, but after harvest they are led into them [to permit llamas to graze on the remaining stubble and thereby through their dung regenerate the fertility of the fields]. Thus, crops and animals alternate in the same fields."[11]

The Bennett stela, along with other similar monuments at Tiahuanaco, is a highly compressed image of esoteric knowledge that emphasized the complementary relationships between agriculture and llama husbandry, the two economic pediments of Tiahuanaco's political power. The public monuments on which these intense images of ecological and productive complementary occur also represent idealized portraits of the ruling elite. The insistent message of a cosmically sanctioned, harmonious and rhythmic complementarity between farmer and herder reoccurs in standardized images on elements of elite costumes, such as tunics, crowns, and sashes, and on symbols of royal authority, such as scepters and staffs of office. Displayed on the greatest sculptural images of Tiahuanaco monumental art, this same message was integrated directly into the principal architectural ensembles at Tiahuanaco and its secondary administrative cities.

The intended meaning of this metaphoric association between images of agropastoral productivity and the representation of royal office, all framed in the context of a ritual calendar, could not be more clear. The elite of Tiahuanaco nourish and sustain the common people. Through direct intercession and identity with the divine forces of nature, they will guarantee the agricultural and reproductive success of the nation. The lords of Tiahuanaco were guarantors of reproductive success not only through ritual intervention with the supernatural forces that affected agropastoral production, but also through manipulation of a pragmatic body of knowledge: an effective agricultural calendar. The elite classes harmonized the potentially disruptive competition between farmer and herder by formally synchronizing productive strategies, adjudicating territorial disputes, and redistributing the crops and animal products.

Having decoded the essential meanings integrated in the form and iconography of the Bennett stela, what of the other sculptures arrayed around this central pivot in the Semisubterranean Temple? It is crucial to note that these sculptures were arranged in a subsidiary position with respect to the Bennett stela. These sculptures are also highly diverse stylistically, and some of them were clearly carved many centuries before the Bennett stela itself. At some point, the architects of the Semisubterranean Temple assembled an eclectic collection of sculptures that were temporally, stylistically, and most likely ethnically foreign to Tiahuanaco. These foreign sculptures were sacred emblems of the concentrated spiritual power—or, in Andean terms, wakas—of distinct ethnic groups. In the process of expanding their rule over the Lake Titicaca basin from the fourth century on, the warrior-elites of Tiahuanaco ritually captured these ancestral wakas and incorporated them in subsidiary positions in the ceremonial core of their sacred capital city. In so doing, they demonstrated both the ideological and secular superiority of the Tiahuanaco state. This process of co-opting local wakas is a familiar one in the native Andean world, replicated in the annals of Inca history. When the Inca subjugated a new territory, the principal wakas were brought to Cuzco and housed in a central shrine supported by the peoples of the conquered provinces. The provincial wakas, although honored and worshiped in a traditional manner in Cuzco, were, in effect, held hostage to the state cults of the Inca. Frequently, as in the case of the powerful lord of the Chimu state deposed by the Inca, the authorities of conquered provinces were held in captivity in Cuzco along with their nation's spiritual icons, and treated with elaborate royal hospitality.

Immediately to the west of the Semisubterranean Temple rises the imposing massif of the Kalasasaya. This structure is a large (approximately 130 × 120 meters), rectangular precinct elevated above the ground to form a low platform mound. Like the Akapana and Puma Punku temples, Kalasasaya was furnished with a central sunken court. Kalasasaya's walls were built of towering, rough-cut sandstone pillars that alternated with sections of smaller ashlar blocks of high-quality masonry. Entry to the Kalasasaya was through a monumental staircase that pierces the eastern facade of the structure. The massive facade of this building creates a powerful impression of "solidity, strength and overwhelming grandeur."[12] Kalasasaya forms a structural unit with the Semisubterranean Temple. They share elements of architectural design, including orientation to the cardinal directions, and an astronomical alignment that marks the vernal and autumnal equinoxes, which are critical markers in the agricultural cycle of the seasons. On the morning of the equinoxes, the sun bisects the Semisubterranean Temple and appears in the center of Kalasasaya's monumental staircase.

Kalasasaya was visually linked to the Temple through placement of a major stone stela in its central sunken courtyard. This sculpture, termed the Ponce stela after its discoverer, was engraved with designs similar to those of the Bennett stela. The Ponce stela faces eastward, gazing through Kalasasaya's monumental gateway toward the Temple. The Bennett stela was oriented with its face towards the west, as if returning the eternal gaze of its counterpart. If we have captured the essence of Andean religious thought, these two

The Ponce stela in the Kalasasya Temple. These commanding monolithic sculptures represented idealized portraits of ancestral rulers. (Photograph by Wolfgang Schüler; copyright © by Alan Kolata.)

monolithic sculptures, paired and placed in visual counter-point along the solar path, one facing east and the other west, may have been intended as representations of the ancestors of Tiahuanaco's ruling lineages: in Andean terms, wakas par excellence of ethnic identity and continuity.

This sculptural ensemble, evoking the ancient mystique of dynastic ancestors, sits squarely in the middle of Tiahuanaco's innermost island; in its day, it intensified the spiritual aura of the city's core. These sculptures brilliantly represented the essence of the Tiahuanaco elite's political legitimacy, their esoteric knowledge and their moral authority. These were powerful visual statements that linked Tiahuanaco's ruling dynasty with the mythic past, with the time of ethnic origins and with the principles of the natural world.

Flanking the entry courtyard in the Kalasasaya and facing the central pivot of the Ponce stela were a series of small stone rooms. These rooms were associated with elegant, sculptured-stone portrait heads of Tiahuanaco males, fre-quently portrayed chewing coca leaf. These portraits may have been representations of individual Tiahuanaco rulers. An intriguing interpretation of the use of these rooms is that they were designed as mausoleums to hold the mummified remains of deceased rulers, or elite ancestors. Ancestor wor-ship and the preservation and manipulation of mummy bun-dles were the bedrock of Andean religion, the basis of ritual in the social unit known as the ayllu. We know that similar, although much larger, above ground burial chambers for the social elites were an important element of the later Aymara kingdoms. These chambers took the form of impressive stone and adobe mortuary towers, known as *chullpas*. They are found throughout the old Tiahuanaco homeland on the high plateau. Among the Inca elite of Cuzco, ancestor worship took the form of an elaborate cult of the royal mummies which simultaneously fascinated and repelled Spanish chroni-clers like Bernabé Cobo, who vividly recorded this key ele-ment of indigenous spirituality in 1653:

[The Inca] had the law and custom that when one of their rulers died, they embalmed him and wrapped him in many fine garments. They allotted these lords all the service that they had in life, so that their mummy-bundles might be served in death as if they were still alive . . .

It was customary for the dead rulers to visit one another, and they had great dances and revelries. Sometimes the dead went to the houses of the living, and sometimes the living visited them.

[Royal relatives of the deceased] brought [the mummies], lavishly escorted, to all their most important ceremonies. They sat them all down in the plaza in a row, in order of seniority, and the servants who looked after them ate and drank there . . . In front of the mummies they also placed large vessels like pitchers, called vilques, made of gold and silver. They filled these vessels with maize beer and toasted the dead with it, after first showing it to them. The dead toasted one another, and they drank to the living . . . this was done by their ministers in their names.[13]

Although fascinating, this description of the lurid spectacle of the descendants of dead kings ministering to their ancestors' elaborately costumed, desiccated corpses with offerings of food and drinks fails to convey the subtle political and religious nuances embedded in the cult of the royal mummies. This practice symbolized something more than the simple veneration of ancestors. The elaborate feasting of the dead royals was organized around and intended as ceremonies of agricultural fertility: "When there was need for water for the cultivated fields, they usually brought out [the dead king's] body, richly dressed, with his face covered, carrying it in a procession through the fields and punas, and they were convinced that this was largely responsible for bringing rain."[14] Dead kings were addressed in toasts as Illapa, the weather deity who personified the atmospheric forces of wind, rain, hail, lightning, and thunder. The mum-

mies of the dead Inca kings were constantly paraded around
Cuzco and its countryside precisely because of their ability to
communicate with supernatural forces. The mummies were
regarded as members of the human community who had
been transformed into the avatars of a supernatural force. In
Andean thought, the body of the king had the capacity to
attract the rain and to ward off frosts and hail.

But there was a political as well as a religious dimension
to the itinerant mummies of the Inca kings. The public display of the royal mummies during state occasions, arranged in
order of seniority, served as an affirmation of the legitimacy
of Inca dynastic rule. On these occasions, the reigning king
would participate in ceremonial processionals throughout
Cuzco, literally joining the complete line of his royal ancestors, who were physically represented by their richly adorned,
mummy bundles. Who could contest the legitimacy of the
Inca when the entire dynasty, the distilled history of their ruling mandate, was visible to the nation? By these ritual actions,
the deceased monarchs and the living emperor symbolically
became one: embodiments of legitimate power, emblems of
agricultural fertility and abundance, and powerful icons of
national identity.

The mummy bundles of the Inca rulers were kept in a
number of places, including the principal temple of Qorican-
cha, the Golden Enclosure, where elaborate niches held these
and other relics. We lack ethnohistorical accounts of mortuary rituals and practice for Tiahuanaco to definitively associ-
ate the Kalasasaya structures with such behavior, and must
rely instead on archaeological evidence for our interpretations. In the case of the structures designed into Kalasasaya's
interior courtyard, that evidence is largely negative; the
rooms themselves were long ago emptied of their contents.
However, we can conjecture from their distinctive form and
placement that they at one time held objects of high cultural
value, which were precious and designed to be periodically
removed and displayed. Mummy bundles of ancestors,

among other objects of prestige and power, fit this description well.

The association of the Kalasasaya temple with the Tiahuanaco elite, the elite's lineage ancestors, and agricultural ritual finds confirmation in the iconographic record of another sculpture within this temple: the Gateway of the Sun. Perhaps the most famous stone sculpture in the ancient Andean world, the Gateway of the Sun was discovered in the northwest corner of the Kalasasaya, although its original location may have been the Puma Punku temple mound. The central figure of the Gateway of the Sun at Tiahuanaco represented a celestial high god that personified various elements of natural forces intimately associated with the productive potential of altiplano ecology: the sun, wind, rain, and hail. This celestial high god was most likely an ancient representation of Thunupa, the Aymara weather god (equivalent of the Quechua Illapa), manifested majestically in the lightning and thunder that rips violently across the high plateau during the rainy season. This weather deity is portrayed standing on a triple-terraced, stepped pyramid, perhaps even Puma Punku itself, holding a sling in one hand and an atlatl (a spear thrower) in the other. A frieze at the top of the sculpture depicts the forceful image of Thunupa displayed in full battle regalia, along with eleven faces, each encircled by a solar mask virtually identical with that of Thunupa, and thirty running masked figures shown in profile and looking toward the central figure. These thirty subsidiary figures are arranged in a symmetrical array, each side consisting of three rows of five figures each. Arthur Posnansky interpreted these images as a calendar in which each of the twelve solar-masked figures represented one month in a solar year.[15] Tom Zuidema interprets the iconography of the gateway in a similar fashion, although he assigns the names of the various months of the Christian calendar to different positions than Posnansky.[16] Zuidema suggests that the solar-masked faces stand either for the sun in each of the twelve months of the solar year, or for full moons in each of these months. In this interpretation, the thirty running profile figures refer to the days of each (synodic or solar) month.

However one reconstructs the precise structure of the calendrical information embedded in the complex iconography of the Gateway of the Sun, this monument, along with the Bennett and Ponce stelae, distills the essence of the Tiahuanaco elite's esoteric knowledge, a knowledge that was intimately linked to their key role in sustaining agricultural production. These sculptures clearly had multiple meanings and uses, and only a select group of elites understood them all. They were simultaneously sacred objects, studded with the images of gods, mythical beasts, and mystical symbols, monumental representations of the dynastic ancestors of the lords of Tiahuanaco, and clever repositories of esoteric, yet pragmatic, knowledge, like libraries of agricultural lore and practice etched in stone.

If the moat-encircled core of Tiahuanaco, with its splendid temple complexes, exotic ritual offerings, and monumental sculptural ensembles, was the religious focus of the city, a place for worship imbued with the essence of spirituality, it was also a place for living. Given the highly charged religious and political significance of Tiahuanaco's ceremonial core, it is not surprising that the right of residence within this sacred precinct was restricted to the elite lineages of highest status. Intensive archaeological investigations in one residential and ceremonial complex, the Putuni, offer fascinating, detailed insight into the daily life of the Tiahuanaco elite, who wielded both secular and sacred power.

In many respects, the Putuni is an architectural complex with uncommon, if not entirely unique, structural features at Tiahuanaco. Early in this century, Georges Courty, one of the principals of a French expedition to the site, commented that the architecture of Putuni was different from all the rest at Tiahuanaco.[17] He noted that all other structures in Tiahuanaco are distinctly above or below ground. Putuni, on the

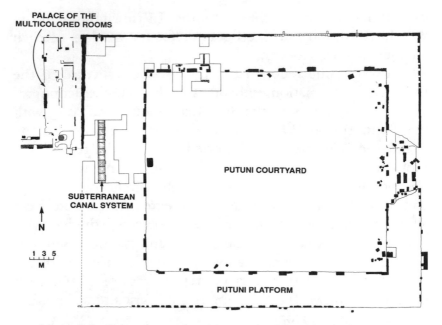

Map of the Putuni complex. (Copyright © by Alan Kolata.)

other hand, combines elements evocative of both elevated and subterranean architecture. The structure is an elevated platform approximately fifty meters on a side surrounding an open, partially sunken interior courtyard. On the east side of the complex, the French expedition uncovered a spectacular painted polychrome stone staircase that originally descended into the central sunken courtyard. (This staircase was promptly dismantled for shipment to Paris, where it remains today packed in excelsior-stuffed wooden crates, mislaid somewhere along the labyrinthine back corridors of the Musée de l'Homme.) The only extant access to the elevated platform surrounding the courtyard is an unprepossessing set of stone stairs tucked into the northwest corner of the structure. The top of the platform was most likely finished with carefully dressed paving stones, as were other structures in the Putuni complex. However, these paving stones have all been removed in looting and quarrying operations in Tiahuanaco over the past five centuries. The design of Putuni would permit large numbers of people to gather in the central courtyard, while a relatively few individuals were elevated above them, standing along the top of the platform.

Systematic excavations in the Putuni undertaken by my research team reveal some provocative new clues about the function and meaning of this special architectural complex. Perhaps the most telling discovery about the Putuni is that it was not an isolated, single-purpose structure, as previous investigators have assumed. Rather, the Putuni platform-and-courtyard complex represents the central focus of an ensemble of buildings that integrated intimate, private living quarters with open spaces designed for large, public convocations. In 1989 we discovered the elite residence of this ensemble, immediately adjacent to the Putuni platform. Our excavations revealed the partially preserved remains of an elegant, generously proportioned building. This structure, which we have called the Palace of the Multicolored Rooms, was constructed of stuccoed, painted adobe laid on foundations fashioned from beautifully cut stone blocks. The foundation stones were sunk into trenches in order to accommodate the overlying structure. Internal wall trenches and the alignments of the foundation stones indicate that the floor plan of the palace incorporated five large interior rooms. The original entrance to the palace, now utterly destroyed by centuries of unrelenting graverobbing, was a truly regal gateway, graced by a monumental stone architrave that displayed in low-relief carving two rampant pumas, ritually costumed and crowned. The floor of the palace was a distinctive surface of dense, hard-packed red clay. Clumps of charred grasses pressed into the clay floor indicate that, while occupied, the palace supported a thatched roof. At the time the palace was abandoned, or shortly thereafter, this thatch burned and collapsed inward, so that fragments from the roof were incorporated into the floor.

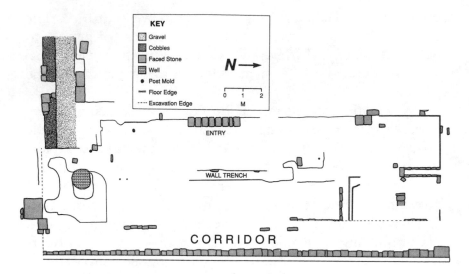

Map of the Palace of the Multicolored Rooms within the Putuni complex. (Copyright © by Alan Kolata.)

The Palace of the Multicolored Rooms and the adjacent Putuni platform-and-courtyard complex were constructed simultaneously during a flurry of urban renewal at Tiahuanaco. Both the Putuni palace and the temple platform were built over earlier residences that were purposely razed to accommodate the new building scheme. Radiocarbon dates on charcoal samples taken directly from the floor of the palace indicate that this urban renewal took place at some point between A.D. 780 and 900.

The Palace of the Multicolored Rooms derives its name from its brilliantly painted walls. Chips of spectacularly hued paints littered the palace floor. The colors of these mineral-based pigments include rich malachite green, deep cobalt blue, and an electric reddish-orange extracted from cinnabar. The distribution of paint chips recovered from the palace floor suggests that some rooms were painted primarily in monochrome, while others were embellished with multiple colors. Because the original adobe walls of the palace are not preserved above the foundation stones, any evidence of figural drawings or painted murals, similar to the icongraphically rich engravings on Tiahuanaco stone sculpture, is now long destroyed. Although any complete murals that might have animated the palace walls are lost, individual adobe bricks with adhering fragments of pigment preserve a record of the painting technique. The process began with a thin coat of white plaster that provided a clean, uniform substrate. Normally, one or two coats of intensely colored paint were then applied over this stucco-like base. But some brick fragments recovered from the ruins of the palace preserved from six to fifteen layers of paint. Frequently, these multiple paint layers were of a single hue applied again and again to the same surface, suggesting that particular colors carried important symbolic or decorative connotations. Although no paintbrushes or other instruments for applying the paint have been found in excavations to date, several different kinds of vessels with crushed, dry pigments were recovered. These paint receptacles included ceramic cups, translucent stone jars (one containing a brilliant cinnabar-based red pigment), silver tubes packed with cobalt blue pigment, and flat pieces of sandstone with multiple pigments adhering to the surface, suggesting that these objects served as palettes.

Although densely painted and clearly designed as an architectural backdrop for the display of wealth and power, the essential residential character of the Palace of the Multicolored Rooms is apparent. Our excavations uncovered facilities designed specifically for routine household maintenance, particularly within a major palace kitchen complex. This complex included pits with embedded ceramic vessels appropriate for storing food and drink, hearths for cooking meals, and wells, extending as much as four meters deep, that provided easy access to fresh water for drinking, cooking, and preparing fermented drinks, such as maize and quinoa chicha.

The palace, and particularly its kitchen complex, was served by an elaborate waste removal system of enclosed stone canals connected into the deeply buried drainage lines that undergird the core of the city. In the Putuni area, the main trunk line of this sewer system is truly a marvel of hydraulic engineering. The subterranean canal, measuring some ninety centimeters wide and one meter from base to cap, was built with precision-cut, closely fitted sandstone and andesite blocks. The entire sewer line was then packed in a thick cap of pure red clay, effectively sealing the structure. Excavations beneath the Putuni platform uncovered two deep tunnels capped with stone slabs giving access to the buried trunk line near critical junctions, which suggests that routine maintenance was performed. Wastewater in this remarkable system ran down a gently sloping two-percent grade leading into the Tiahuanaco River.

The palace was supplied with fresh running water through a system of enclosed canals that tapped into springs which still flow on the southern outskirts of the ancient city. Unlike most other preindustrial cities, Tiahuanaco, or at least its elite neighborhoods, boasted a secure and hygienic water system that segregated wastewater from the freshwater supply. The sophisticated design skills of Tiahuanaco's hydraulic engineers enabled at least some of the city's residents to live with a level of hygiene and luxury that is unmatched in the same rural areas of the altiplano today, and even in some of the barrios of La Paz.

The Palace of the Multicolored Rooms is an intriguing structure that offers glimpses into the opulent, and ritually charged lifestyle of the Tiahuanaco elite. Power, ritual, and spirituality interpenetrated every aspect of life among the elite. The rich, glowing colors painted on the palace walls and the elaborately carved stone entrance were displays of accumulated wealth and status, tangible reminders to the people of Tiahuanaco of the secular power vested in their rulers. At the same time, the display of wealth served a more esoteric, religious purpose. In many respects, the Palace of the Multicolored Rooms was constructed with an eye to ratifying the role of the elite as intermediaries with the supernatural forces of nature. The palace and adjacent Putuni temple complex are located within the city center, inside the concentrated, sacred confines of Tiahuanaco's moat. The palace was physically situated near the center of Tiahuanaco's metaphorical island, associated symbolically with the creation of humankind, and with the origins of time and of civilization. In essence, the palace occupants lived in the space and time of the sacred.

The intentional linkage of this elite dwelling with notions of the sacred was further intensified by a series of dedicatory offerings that were deposited in the foundations of the structure. Our excavations encountered a hierarchical series of ritual offerings of perhaps the most profoundly personal, emotionally powerful kind—human dedicatory burials. The most important of these dedicatory burials were shaft-and-chamber tombs sunk into the four corners of the structure at the time of construction of the palace.

The shaft-and-chamber tomb in the northeast corner was found completely intact, and its rich contents evoke well the wealth and ritual status of the palace occupants. To judge from the dress and tomb offerings, the burial was that of an elite female. The burial itself was located at the base of the shaft section of the tomb, with a slightly raised side chamber serving as a repository for a textile-wrapped bundle of grave goods. The skeleton was in a seated position facing north, with arms and legs tightly flexed against the body—a classic burial position in the Andes that results from placing the corpse in an egg-shaped mummy bundle. Although long decayed from the corrosive effects of high groundwater characteristic of the Tiahuanaco region, remnant fabric impressions and richly organic, blackened soil surrounding the skeletal remains indicates that this individual was once tightly wrapped in just such a textile bundle. The most spectacular grave goods were associated directly with the skeleton. At the time of burial, four copper bracelets were placed on the corpse's right arm. A stunning collar fashioned from hundreds of beads, delicately crafted in a rich variety of luxurious materials including purple lapis lazuli, cobalt blue sodalite, sky blue turquoise, coral-colored stone, and cream-colored bone, hung from the neck. A miniature gold mask with a repoussé image of a human face was discovered lying at the feet of the skeleton. This stylized gold mask has tiny perforations along its perimeter, suggesting that it was originally sewn to fabric as an element of costume. Along with this gold mask, an eclectic assemblage of grave offerings was found distributed around the original mummy bundle. These included clusters of exotic minerals; slender bone awls and bone tubes, one containing yellow pigment; a thin andesite scraper; and a red, globular ceramic vessel inside of which was placed a collection of beautiful grayish black obsidian chips. The small side chamber of the tomb to the north of the burial contained its own set of grave goods that were apparently wrapped in a textile bundle fastened with long copper pins. The centerpiece of this bundle was a perfectly preserved copper disc that served as a mirror, although, like the gold mask, it may have been incorporated as an element of costume since it too was perforated. Adhering to the surface of this disc was an elegant, long-necked flask fabricated from lead—a rare, if not unprecedented, use of this mineral at Tiahuanaco. Accompanying the lead bottle was a long-necked companion piece of polished red ceramic. Scattered around these central pieces in the side chamber were a series of smaller metal and bone objects, including gold and copper pins, bone tubes and needles, a copper spatula, a sandstone pigment palette, and lumps of white and yellow minerals. The precise significance of these grave offerings remains elusive, although it is not difficult to propose that the side chamber collection, in particular, represents items related to personal adornment, a kind of toiletry kit of the deceased.

The shaft-and-chamber tomb at the southeast corner of the palace contained fewer grave goods than the northeast corner tomb, although in some ways this interment is more interesting and evocative. This tomb contained two individuals, one of which was an adult in a seated, flexed position similar to that of the northeast corner mummy bundle. Underneath the skull of the adult was a second burial: a complete skeleton of an infant laid prone. Accompanying this double burial was a silver pin and a pair of deer antlers that were placed near the adult's skull. Antlers occur in Tiahuanaco ceramic iconography as elements of headdresses worn by costumed, masked figures in processions. Frequently, these masks portray snarling felines with imposing fangs, and are associated with scenes of decapitation and dismemberment. The individuals wearing these elaborate costumes may represent ritual warriors or perhaps shamans, cloaked in deer costumes. We know that this sort of shamanic connection between humans and deer was a common feature of Native American religions, and the clear ceremonial context of the cavorting costumed and antler-bedecked figures portrayed on these ceramics implies a similar association among the people of Tiahuanaco. If, in fact, the adult occupant of this shaft-and-chamber tomb was a shaman or priest, the sacred character of the Palace of the Multicolored Rooms was further underscored when this individual was interred at the time of construction.

The other two shaft-and-chamber tombs at the northwest and southwest corners of the palace are not preserved, although we do have clear evidence of massive looting in these areas, thus confirming their existence. A fifth shaft-and-chamber tomb, also heavily sacked, was placed under the monumental west gateway to the palace. All that remained of the contents from this tomb were some scattered pieces of human bone. The distribution of these tombs forms a distinct pattern in the palace: one at each corner of the palace and one beneath the principal entrance. This arrangement implies that these were dedicatory burials made at the time of construction to sanctify, or ritually charge, the palace.

Another kind of burial was associated with the construction of the Palace of the Multicolored Rooms. At the time the palace was built, its architects razed earlier structures to accommodate the new Putuni palace-temple complex. The rubble from previous constructions was leveled through an ambitious cut-and-fill operation. A layer of coarse gravel was then deposited over this construction fill. Finally, the continuous red clay floor characteristic of the late Putuni complex was laid down as the base for new walls. In the course of establishing the foundations for the palace, both complete and partial human burials were incorporated into the razed debris immediately below the subfloor gravel layer. During excavations in the southern part of the palace, these rather melancholy burials were frequently found pushed into the beds of old, abandoned drainage canals that once served earlier structures. The context of these burials makes it clear that they, along with their more formal shaft-and-chamber tomb counterparts, were made in a single episode at the time of construction of the palace. Unlike the elaborate shaft-and-chamber tombs, these subfloor burials contained no associated grave goods and were often found mixed indifferently with the bones of llama and alpaca. The numerous partial burials of humans and llamas found just underneath the red clay floor of the palace created a macabre foundation of bones.

We know that the burials were not accidental inclusions from the demolition process that created the palace's foundations because, although they lack grave goods, a number of these burials were carefully placed in the old canals. In one instance, nearly complete skeletons of a male-female couple were encountered locked in a poignant embrace. Most of the subfloor burials were not complete skeletons but rather collections of body parts. But these body parts were articulated—skull to spinal cord, pelvis to leg bones, wrist and hand to arm bones, and the like—indicating that flesh was still on the bones when the burials were interred.

The construction of the Palace of the Multicolored Rooms was clearly more than the development of luxury housing for the Tiahuanaco elite. The rituals incorporated into the construction transformed the buildings into a profoundly sacred space. In a sense, the Palace of the Multicolored Rooms was simultaneously an ordinary dwelling for satisfying the daily needs of its extraordinary occupants and a ritually charged space for expressing the intimate connection of the palace occupants to the sacred. If one of the primary roles of the Tiahuanaco elite was to act as intermediaries between the people of Tiahuanaco and the supernatural forces of nature, it is not surprising that their palaces were sanctified in this manner. Nor is it unusual that the private apartments of these elite were attached to larger public spaces. Tiahuanaco royalty did not simply intercede from time to time with the forces of nature; they constantly lived the role of divine intermediaries, and their special residences reflected this role.

From all this description of the ancient city, we can draw an important conclusion about the conduct and meaning of private life for the Tiahuanaco elite. Their role as interlocutors with the divine—with what the French anthropologist Maurice Godelier called the "invisible realities and forces controlling the reproduction of the universe and of life"[18]—demanded that they create symbols that linked them publicly with the realm of the supernatural. In the ancient Andean world, communication with the divine was achieved through the dead, through the long chain of deceased ancestors reaching back to the heroic, legendary time of human origins. Necrolatry—the worship and propitiation of the dead—was the sacred obligation of the living, as well as the most powerful tool for gaining access to the invisible realities and forces that controlled the continuity of the world. In this conceptual world, the living resided cheek-by-jowl with the dead.

From about A.D. 500 on, Tiahuanaco elite residences were organized into distinct barrios, or neighborhoods, that were insulated from public view by massive adobe walls set on stone foundations. Residential and service areas, such as communal kitchens, were clustered within the large compounds created by the barrio walls. These massive walls, with only a few narrow entrances, reduced access to the elite residences and afforded security and privacy to their residents.

During an extensive phase of urban renewal after A.D. 750, barrio walls were razed to accommodate construction of the Putuni temple and the Palace of the Multicolored Rooms. A similar process of leveling earlier barrio walls to accommodate new construction occurred in other areas of Tiahuanaco's core. This dramatic reconfiguration of the urban landscape resulted in a complete integration of ceremonial and elite residential areas. The leveling of the Classic Tiahuanaco barrio walls and the residences within permitted a significant redesign of the city. Large expanses of land within the moated sanctuary of the city center that were previously given over to elite residences were transformed into elegant temple complexes with fewer and more formal palatial residences adjacent to them.

While the center was being reshaped, outside of the core, the city witnessed a dramatic expansion in residential construction. The boom in construction in what was once the peripheral areas of the city resulted in a proliferation of dwellings that were much smaller and less elaborate than structures like the Palace of the Multicolored Rooms. Rather than fine ashlar masonry foundations, these more modest dwellings were built on river cobbles with adobe walls and thatched roofs. They exhibit none of the impressive architectural ornamentation of the central palaces. There is no evidence of monumental, carved stone gateways or polychromed walls. Although many of these structures were equipped with deep freshwater wells and small floor drains for wastewater, they were not tied into the impressive subterranean sewer lines of the city center. Moreover, unlike the palaces, the architecture outside the moat was not juxtaposed or integrated with ceremonial structures or large public plazas. Instead, we find repetitive ranks of simple structures that clearly served a residential function, like blocks of apartments.

All of these buildings featured cooking hearths, storage pits, wells, and small interior and exterior patios for craft activities such as weaving and the production of stone tools.

Who might have been the residents of this kind of architecture? It is tempting to conclude from the obvious differences in the quality of this architecture that the occupants were members of a lower class within the city. This may, in fact, be true. But other elements of these dwellings indicate that the residents were not entirely without privilege and access to wealth in Tiahuanaco society. Certainly, they did not form the lowest stratum of Tiahuanaco's hierarchical social world. For one thing, although not of the same quality and scale as the city's palaces, their houses were well constructed of stone, adobe, and thatch, and they were supplied with rudimentary but effective cooking and sanitary facilities. Perhaps more telling, our excavations of domestic structures outside of the moated core revealed that they took the identical cardinal orientation of the ceremonial and elite residential architecture in the city center. This alignment suggests that some kind of state planning was involved in the construction of these buildings. In effect, the elites enforced zoning regulations within the boundaries of the sacred city.

Objects once used by the occupants of these dwellings in daily life provide other clues to their relatively high position. Each of the excavated houses contained significant numbers of metal artifacts, principally copper lamina and plaques, pins, nails, and awls. Most of these items were intended as decorative and symbolic elements to be sewn into clothing. Costume was one of the principal public markers of ethnic and class status in the ancient Andean world, and the rich, metal-encrusted clothing worn by the people of Tiahuanaco was no exception. In general, metal objects were relatively scarce and were the product of intensive labor. As a consequence, they commanded high status. Their use in Tiahuanaco society, as was the case with the Inca state, may have been restricted to, or at least more prevalent among, the political and social elite.

171

In addition to metals, substantial quantities of cut and polished bone, malachite, turquoise, sodalite, and lapis lazuli
beads, along with beautiful pyroengraved llama bones with
elaborate iconography carried on them, were encountered in
these houses. These objects, of course, were not utilitarian, but
rather were associated with personal adornment and the display
of wealth. Some of the pyroengraved bones were fashioned
into snuff trays and tubes for the ritual consumption of hallucinogenic drugs, such as the powdered seeds of the leguminous plant called *wilka* by the Quechua-speaking natives of the
Andes. Other such engraved bone tubes were used as flutes. A
striking terra-cotta ring found in one of these houses carries an
embossed, stylized representation of a masked human wearing
an elaborate crown. The intaglio design makes it clear that the
ring functioned as a signet device for marking or sealing
objects as the property of the owner. Such signet rings are rare
in Tiahuanaco, suggesting that they were the property of a
restricted class of people. They may have belonged to elites of
a rank immediately below that of the royal lineages who were
charged with the day-to-day affairs of the state.

That the residents of these structures performed some
kind of public role in Tiahuanaco society is further substanti-
ated by another class of objects uncovered consistently in our
excavations. All of these houses possessed a high proportion
of fine polychrome ceramic vessels in their domestic repertoire. These highly polished, strikingly beautiful vessels (fine
basins, bowls, and drinking cups, or *keros*) were used exclusively as serving dishes for food or drinks. Fancy serving ware
and elegant drinking cups imply that the occupants engaged
in public feasting and ritual hospitality, both among themselves and perhaps with guests of equivalent status from outside the city. Public feasting imbued with an ethic of conspicuous, ritualized generosity was the essential social etiquette
that kept the wheels of politics and commerce moving in the
ancient Andean world. The relationship between city and

countryside was fostered and tightly interwoven through the mechanism of reciprocal hospitality between rural and urban elites. The politics of the native Andean world demanded face-to-face contact and an ethic of broad public participation. Elaborate public feasts and bouts of prodigious drinking were the standard forum for formalizing and expressing social ties among equals, as well as with one's social inferiors. Without these feasts, few public works would have been accomplished. What seems an inefficient, even outrageously wasteful, deployment of time and resources was, in fact, an essential political tool of the ruling elite. To be generous in food and drink was to give public evidence of a special capacity to provide for your constituency, and therefore affirmed your capacity to govern well.

The social life of Tiahuanaco as a city entailed not only the performance of religious and political duties by the elite (and near elite), but also many craft activities. Most of the households in Tiahuanaco were engaged in the production of textiles and basic kits of bone, obsidian, basalt, and chert tools, mainly for their own daily use. Still, even some of these household crafts served a ceremonial function. We found gold and silver laminae, exhausted obsidian cores, and fragments of turquoise and sodalite in the main sewer line beneath the Putuni palace-temple complex. These finds imply that certain crafts were practiced even within the highest-status households at Tiahuanaco. These remains are clearly the by-products of larger-scale craft production that were disposed of in a most modern fashion—by flushing them down the drain.

Who the actual artisans of these luxury crafts were remains unclear. We can propose two plausible scenarios. The elites may have retained gifted artisans to craft the luxury items that were so important to the performance of their regal and priestly duties. This was a common practice in the ancient Andean world. Specialized artisans were in great demand and given unusual privileges by other kingly courts of the native Andean world. That some artisans of particularly fine or specialized objects, such as textiles, gold, silver, and lapidary work, were retainers to Tiahuanaco ruling lineages is therefore a strong possibility. The other possibility is that the scions of Tiahuanaco's ruling lineages may have been obligated to learn an elite craft as a part of their training. The courtiers and kin of preindustrial kings were often esteemed artisans, crafting the symbols of their own spiritual and secular power.

If we concentrated only on the urban settings of Tiahuanaco civilization, we will draw a skewed portrait of life in the empire. The citizens of the capital were different from their rural counterparts. They were of different social statuses. They engaged in distinct occupations, and we might imagine at some level held divergent and contradictory beliefs. If the essential work of the capital was producing religion and politics, the work of the rural countryside was centered on activities that produced primary goods: farming, herding, fishing, and weaving. The rural commoners—the agriculturists, herders, and fishers—who lived and worked in the hinterlands surrounding Tiahuanaco's urban centers provided the surplus products that underwrote the complex system of public works that came to characterize Tiahuanaco civilization. These public works included audacious projects for reclaiming vast tracts of rural land as agricultural estates under the direct control of Tiahuanaco's ruling lineages. The surplus from these remarkably productive estates flowed into Tiahuanaco's urban society, providing the economic bedrock for the political power of the aristocratic lineages, and for unparalleled achievements in religious and political architecture and art.

The urban and rural milieux were intimately interconnected in the process of creating Tiahuanaco civilization. The challenges, structures, and subtle textures of rural life set the tone for religious expression and for political action in this civilization. Tiahuanaco's economy revolved around three intimately related systems of production: intensive agriculture, extensive llama and alpaca pastoralism, and exploitation of Lake Titicaca.

Perhaps the most important of these three forms of rural economic production was Tiahuanaco's remarkable system of intensive raised-field agriculture. This system of cultivation emerged as early as 1000 B.C. in the marshlands that surround the edge of Lake Titicaca. The history of wetlands reclamation for intensive agricultural production by the Tiahuanaco state is emblematic of the larger social history of the people of Tiahuanaco. The emergence, floresence, and ultimate collapse of intensive raised-field agriculture in the Lake Titicaca region recapitulates the trajectory of Tiahuanaco state expansion and decline. The fundamental basis of power for Tiahuanaco's elite was control over a secure, sustainable fund of agricultural products. Agricultural wealth financed other local and foreign ventures of the Tiahuanaco elite: construction of monumental temples and luxurious palaces, subsidies for artisan retainers, wars of conquest and territorial expansion, or reinvestment in the agricultural landscape. Tiahuanaco's raised fields were the keys to the extraordinary wealth that underwrote the brilliance and raw power of its civilization.

Tiahuanaco's raised fields were made of massive, elevated platforms of earth which served as planting surfaces. These raised planting beds alternated with adjacent irrigation canals. Tiahuanco's farmers built these fields with wooden digging sticks and foot plows equipped with hard stone bits to cut sod and break up soil. The foot plow was the principal agricultural tool of native Andean farmers. Little-altered variants remain in use today in rural agrarian communities throughout the Andean altiplano. The construction of the elevated planting bed was critical to the technological effectiveness of this extraordinary farming technique. By cutting and turning the surface sod and mounding it into an elevated bed, the ancient farmers of Tiahuanaco transformed and improved their fields, resulting in earth that could efficiently capture and retain water and absorb essential nutrients. The canals between the elevated planting beds contributed to the enormous productivity of raised fields by mitigating the effects of the two critical limiting factors of high-altitude farming in the Lake Titicaca basin: frost and nutrient-poor soils. One of the most important and abundant sources of locally available fertilizer was the rich, organic, nutrient-laden sediments that developed in the canals adjacent to the raised fields. The canals surrounding the raised fields were rapidly colonized by aquatic plants and, most importantly, by communities of nitrogen-fixing organisms such as free-living blue-green algae.

These plants were harvested directly from the surface of the water and incorporated into the planting bed immediately before sowing, or their decayed products were dredged from the muddy sediments of the canals and redistributed over the surface of the field. The high nutritive content of these decomposed aquatic plants and their capacity to fix atmospheric nitrogen counteracted the nutrient deficit that characterizes most altiplano soils. Apart from their capacity to sustain aquatic plants that could be exploited as forms of natural fertilizer, the canals between fields played a second vital role in maintaining the productivity of raised fields. Perhaps the greatest risk that altiplano farmers face on a daily basis during the growing season is the threat of crop loss from killing frosts. In the process of developing the raised-field system of cultivation, the people of Tiahuanaco discovered that the canals surrounding raised fields functioned as gigantic solar collectors, absorbing the energy of intense sunlight during the day and transferring this stored heat into and around the planting platforms of the fields at night. Through long experience of cultivating around the edges of Lake Titicaca, Tiahuanaco's farmers learned that the raised fields effectively protected crops from frost damage during subfreezing altiplano nights. For over five hundred years, the crops from these fields were the principal economic engine of Tiahuanaco society. In the world of Tiahuanaco, agriculture was power.

We return, then, to the land, to the elements of earth and water that permeated ancient Tiahuanaco society. The people of Tiahuanaco, like their modern Aymara descendants, worshiped and sacrificed to the land and the sky. Then, as now, priests and shamans interceded with the invisible forces of nature. Then, as now, they trembled in trances among the mountain peaks, seeking to transcend the limits of mundane perception, to peer into the numinous world of the spirits. Then, as now, they sought to gather the strands of spiritual power found in sacred plants, in the bodies of their ancestors, in the flow of blood and alcohol that permitted them to predict and influence the future. In their forbidding environment on the margin of habitability, their spiritual role is critical, for with each planting, with each harvest, society is created anew. Each cycle of the seasons invites risk and instills dread. If humans are to survive, every year the social and natural worlds must come into alignment. The specter of catastrophe hovers over all human efforts to dwell in the high plateau. And catastrophe did come to Tiahuanaco. Not with the suddenness of plagues or war propagated by the hand of man, but with a slow, inexorable turning of the natural world. Like all empires, Tiahuanaco, in its time, was forsaken by the gods and the ancestors. No amount of sacrificial blood flowing on the great earth shrines of the city would change its fate.

5

The World
Turned Around

The glacier knocks in the cupboard,
The desert sighs in the bed,
And the crack in the tea cup opens
A lane to the land of the dead.
"As I Walked Out One Evening,"
W. H. Auden (1907–1973)

OMETIME around A.D. 1150, the descendants of Tiahuanaco's creators performed a desperate ritual on the summit of the Akapana pyramid. On the day of the ritual, the sun illuminated a land clad in the doleful colors of parched grass and lifeless soil. The horizon was hazy with a powdery mist of dirt relentlessly scoured from the dry earth by the winds of the altiplano.

The celebrants ascended the seven eroding tiers of the sacred mountain-pyramid laden with riches, leading a small herd of young llamas. The great pyramid no longer sparkled and roared with the life-giving waters of the rainy season.

179

The secret tunnels within were long choked with debris, forgotten remnants of an earlier time.

Gaining the summit, the celebrants proceeded quickly with their sacrifice. One by one the native priests bent the long necks of the llamas backwards toward the west, toward the land of the dead. Then, with sure, practiced strokes, the priests struck deep with blades of translucent obsidian. Great bursts of blood spurted from arteries pumped taut with the terrible pressure of the animals' dying hearts. The priests caught the bloody torrent in elegant ceramic cups. Striding to the four corners of the temple, they cast the liquid in viscous, crimson streams to the ground below.

Having fertilized the dry earth, the priests returned with sacred, blood-smeared hands to butcher the dead animals. With great effort, they cut through sinew and tendon, muscle and bone, to decapitate the llamas. They placed the severed heads and upper jaws of the sacrificed beasts in the north and west corners of a room that had once been the priests' quarters. They carefully removed the animals lower jaws and piled them in the southeast corner of the room. Then, with the foundation of the sacrifice properly laid, the priests began to assemble the offering to the gods who had abandoned them.

First they placed copper pins, plaques, and figurines in the northeast corner of the room. A magnificent three-dimensional sculpture of a miniature fox, the tiwula, stood on the lime-plastered floor of packed earth, eternally frozen in the posture of a canine howl. Layered on top of the copper objects were countless sheets of pale, hammered silver. Then the headless bodies of the sacrificed llamas, still oozing blood, were packed inside the room. The last bodies were draped over the cut-stone threshold, blocking access to the dark interior where no one would ever live again.

In the rising heat of the day, the stench of spilled blood and the dull drone of torpid, black flies enveloped the room. Just outside the door, the priests burned pungent resins in an incense burner of painted clay shaped in the form of a powerfully muscled mountain lion. They lifted their eyes to the heavens and to the great, glistening mountain peaks over the horizon, intoning the long litany of the wakas, supplicating the ancestors. As white smoke rose up to a cloudless sky through the open fanged mouth and perforated anus of the clay puma, the priests poured libations of maize beer from lyre-shaped cups onto the ground. The keros they held were painted with a resplendent crowned figure whose impassive face, vacant of human expression, stares out eternally from the Gateway of the Sun. This was the manifold image of Viracocha and Thunupa: the creator-god in his guise as Lord of the Atmosphere. This Lord was a violent, unpredictable spirit holding thunderbolts in one hand and a spear-thrower in the other. He brought wind and rain, lightning and thunder, life and death, all with sublime indifference.

After drinking deep from their ruby-colored keros, consecrated to the Lord of the Atmosphere, the priests, in a sudden, whirling movement, shattered the ritual beakers on the ground. Then they slowly removed the jewelry with which they adorned themselves before the ritual, placing the sacred objects, imbued with the spiritual status of their owners, next to the smoking incense burner. A pile of gleaming polished stone and bone plugs drawn from their lips and septums lay next to earrings of gold, silver, and copper. From bundles of exquisite woven cloth, the priests drew amulets and razor-sharp flakes of quartz crystal and obsidian, scattering them before the gore-spattered threshold. The jewels and fragments of crystalline rock glittered brightly in the sun. But the great pools of llama blood spilled inside the sacrificial room had already begun to blacken and congeal. The dark contents within remained concealed for over eight hundred years.

The ritual was over. The priests dropped the remaining balls of resinous incense into the maw of the clay puma and watched the smoke swirl upward in the wind. On the distant western horizon, they glimpsed the soothing, azure blue waters of Lake Titicaca. But gazing down from the summit of the great temple, they could see before them only the colors of desolation: gray soil, yellow grass, brown leaves, withered and blackened stalks. They saw, too, a once invincible city abandoned.

As the priests descended the decaying terraces of the mountain-pyramid, they wondered if this time the Lord of the Atmosphere would take pity on them and help them to fertilize Lady Earth. On their long, dust-plagued walk home to their hamlets scattered in the fields and mountains, they passed through vacant streets strewn with garbage and the wastes of animals who were now Tiahuanaco's only permanent residents. The monumental walls of the old aristocracy lay in shambles. The decaying stone icons of kings and gods, once emblems of unimaginable spiritual power, now evoked only the stomach-churning awe of ruination. Devils of whirling grit scoured their faces, erasing the sharp, chiseled edges of their majesty. Few prayed before these broken, fading idols now. Their spiritual power had long since dissipated into the pitiless dry air. Now the idols' most constant companions were the animals of the field. Only the wind and the voices of ghosts echoed in Tiahuanaco's deserted halls and public squares.

The vibrant capital of Tiahuanaco had become a city of the dead. What events had transformed Tiahuanaco from an Andean Mecca into a necropolis? How had Tiahuanaco's rich, ancient world turned around?

The question of how and why a civilization disappears is one of perennial fascination, particularly when the disintegration happens so rapidly. Much as we may admire a civilization's glories, we are perhaps even more transfixed by the spectacle of decline and fall. For those of us schooled in the history of the Western world, this morbid curiosity is probably most strongly evoked by the collapse of the Roman Empire. Michael Ivanovich Rostovtzeff, the eminent Russian historian of Rome, eloquently posed the question about Ancient Rome that has engaged each generation:

> Why did such a powerful and brilliant civilization, the growth of ages and apparently destined to last for ages, gradually degenerate? . . . why did the creative power of its makers wax faint, with this result, that mankind slowly reverted to primitive and extremely simple conditions of life and then began to create civilization over again from the very rudiments, reviving the old institutions and studying the old problems?[1]

Perhaps in our collective fascination about the fall of empires, we seek cautionary tales; tales reminding us that our own cherished civilization may be fragile. Perhaps some of us look to ancient history as a guide, a means of identifying the universal causes of decline in the hope that we can learn to avoid the fatal mistakes of the past. Or perhaps more simply, death in its multiple guises is so mysterious that we feel psychologically compelled to explore its causes and its meaning.

Our gaze is drawn ineluctably toward tragedy. We all experience an ineffable fascination, tinged with horror, when contemplating the dissolution of a whole society. Who can fail to be moved by the heroic saga of Alexander the Great and his aggressive campaigns to impose Greek civilization in the deepest reaches of Persia and India? Yet the dramatic heart of Alexander's story is not his stunning military achievements, but rather his premature death, his empire's tragic denouement, and the bitter political intrigues that embroiled his successors.

But apart from sheer fascination, there is a rich intellectual harvest to be gathered by studying these cases of decline. Reflecting on the processes of a civilization's decay, we gain insights into its fundamental structure. When the complex, fully fleshed skin of a civilization's history begins to dissolve, its underlying anatomy is laid bare. We cannot hope to perceive and appreciate the inner structure and workings of civil societies without contemplating the forces that lead to their dissolution.

In all our efforts to understand the death throes of civilizations, one fact seems certain: Complex societies do not collapse for simple reasons. The end of empire, particularly global empires such as that of Rome, is rarely precipitate. Individual events, such as an invasion or the death of a leader at a critical juncture, or changing natural and social circumstances, such as the emergence of competitive powers, the interruption of strategic trade routes, and critical environmental crises, sometimes apply the coup de grâce. But such historically specific occurrences are rarely more than proximate causes of collapse. More often they are simply symptomatic of underlying ruptures in a society's political and social cohesiveness.

On this score, Rostovtzeff's own explanation for the collapse of the Roman Empire is instructive. Rostovtzeff located the cause of Rome's dissolution in the corruption of its once dynamic economic system. He argued that this corruption was exacerbated by a decay in the social consensus between the ruling aristocracy and the mass of the empire's citizenry. According to his analysis, deteriorating economic conditions in the third century A.D. generated empire-wide class and labor conflicts and sowed anarchy among the military which, in turn, shattered the elitist political structure of the state. The end product of this process was the fragmentation of the state. Political boundaries shifted and a multiplication of centers of local power arose. One symptom and cause of Rome's degeneration particularly intrigued Rostovtzeff:

> The old institutions are replaced by utterly primitive conditions; in social, economic and intellectual matters there is an unbroken reversion to barbarism. One feature of the economic condition is especially remarkable—the complete change in agricultural methods throughout the empire. Scientific cultivation backed up by capital and intelligence disappears utterly and is replaced everywhere by a system which merely scratches the surface of the soil and sinks lower and lower into primitive routine.[2]

Rostovtzeff's interpretation of the empire's decline as a product of the devolution of agricultural techniques illustrates a fundamental axiom of any theory of state collapse. Unless a civilization can assure a reasonable measure of economic well-being for its population, it will inexorably lose competitive advantage and either disintegrate through internal disaffection, or fall prey to competing powers that will dissolve or absorb its political structure.

A large part of any explanation of state collapse resides in the vicissitudes of the production and distribution of wealth. Rostovtzeff's explanation of Rome's decline emphasized the role of economic instability in causing social divisiveness. From his perspective, an emerging sense of economic and social insecurity generated a crisis of confidence in the aristocracy and eventually fomented bitter class conflicts to the point that political collapse became a virtual inevitability.

Rostovtzeff's notion that political and social instability in the core of the empire stifled innovation and investment in agricultural production in the countryside is particularly astute. In preindustrial states, economic well-being was largely synonymous with agricultural wealth. Commerce generated huge profits for state elites, but unless some of this wealth was invested in "landscape capital" for food production, the population who lived in the hinterlands was largely cut off from the flow of new wealth. This imbalance generated the social conditions for discontent and ultimately for rebellion.

Intensive farming was the fundamental engine of wealth in preindustrial states. Agriculture was an essential sector in the economy of these archaic states. There are certainly examples of preindustrial trading states, but these were subject to the vagaries of quickly changing political fortunes. Commerce-based states often coalesced, prospered, then disappeared quickly. By contrast, the great global empires of antiquity demanded strong agrarian infrastructures. Trade alone could never funnel into the cities the enormous

amounts of foodstuffs necessary to feed the urban populations that reached into the hundreds of thousands. Even with
well-developed agricultural estates, chronic food shortages
and periodic famines besieged cities throughout the ancient
world.[3]

The chain of food supply to these preindustrial capitals
was complex and often neither systematically organized nor
particularly well-managed. The ebb and flow of urban life in
the ancient world was intimately bound to the agricultural
cycle of the seasons, and the local hinterlands of archaic cities
became, in effect, remote urban gardens. Farming was as
basic to the economy of the cities as it was to the life of the
countryside. Agriculture was scaled to many different units of
production. Basic grains, fruits, and vegetables were produced on individual plots, on small family farms, on peasant
collectives, and on large plantations organized by local and
state aristocracies. City gardens were an important supple-
mental source of foodstuffs, condiments, and medicinal
plants. Livestock breeding was a common urban occupation.
The number of domestic animals within most archaic cities
far exceeded that of its human population.

Agricultural arts and the inherent mystique of the agrarian
lifestyle permeated archaic science, natural and political philosophy, literature, and religion. In most of the preindustrial
world, the king was the guarantor of agricultural success.
One of the primary cult obligations of royal households was
to perform agricultural rituals designed to ensure abundant
harvests. Rulers in these agrarian states were often symbolically associated with agricultural fertility. Not only was the
king perceived as the provider of political protection for his
subjects, in his role as a ritual practitioner of the agricultural
arts, he also provided daily sustenance for the common people. The relationship between political legitimacy and agricultural success could not be more intimate. Uneasy lay the
crown of a preindustrial king who presided over an agricultural disaster.

This link was even more direct in the pre-Columbian Andean world, where mercantile activities and markets were, on the whole, nonexistent or only weakly developed. In the ancient Andes, in lieu of unrestricted commerce and free-market exchange, there was no other source for generating wealth beyond the margin of subsistence than intensive agriculture. Here, agricultural success was the pediment of social power and agricultural failure the harbinger of collapse.

The fate of Tiahuanaco's millennium-long civilization was intimately bound to its agricultural fortunes. In time, the highly specialized wetlands agriculture so ingeniously deployed by Tiahuanaco's rulers became its undoing.

Over several centuries, intensively cultivated raised fields supported the explosive growth of Tiahuanaco urban culture. Abundant harvests of grains, potatoes, and other foodstuffs fueled the expansion of the empire's population, and financed Tiahuanaco's military adventures outside the heartland of the high plateau. The state's raised fields offered the promise of an inexhaustible food supply. Crop production calculations on restored raised fields suggest that, throughout Tiahuanaco's history, the exploitation of this rich wetlands system of cultivation was never pushed to its limit. Continuous cultivation, double-cropping, and strategic management of a hydraulic infrastructure that fed irrigation water to field systems all ensured an abundant supply of staple crops.

Stimulated by the astonishing productive capacity of the raised fields, Tiahuanaco's urban populations swelled to great size. Under the hegemony of the Tiahuanaco state, tens of thousands of people clustered together in cities and towns. But this very success, epitomized in the gold-clad cities of Tiahuanaco teeming with its aristocracy and vast body of retainers, generated the social conditions for collapse.

The urban culture of Tiahuanaco flourished in an improbably harsh, high altitude environment, an environment at the extreme edge of viable agriculture. Tiahuanaco's scientific genius was to redefine the physical limits of farming at this altitude by transforming the environment, by subtly changing environmental conditions to conform to the biological needs of major food crops. In deploying the power of the sun, Tiahuanaco's farmers literally changed the climate of their fields. In effect, they created an artificial microclimatic regime, one considerably more conducive to intensive agricultural production than the natural regime.

An intricate hydraulic network of dikes, reservoirs, check dams, aqueducts, river shunts, and canals provided a constant supply of fresh water to the raised fields and controlled groundwater levels on an unprecedented regional scale. This system ensured that Tiahuanaco agriculture could respond to normal fluctuations in climate and to the periodic droughts and flooding cycles characteristic of the Andean altiplano. And yet, sometime between A.D. 1000 and 1100, Tiahuanaco's vast landscape of agricultural fields was abandoned, its cities deserted, and its empire dissolved.

Why did such a successful, long-lived, and apparently resilient society fail? Archaeologists are rarely in a position to provide definitive answers to such questions. The partial quality of our evidence rarely permits us the luxury of saying: "You see, it happened just this way." On the contrary, the collapse of many ancient civilizations remains mysterious to us. But in the case of Tiahuanaco, over a decade of scientific detective work has finally yielded enough clues to solve the mystery. The collapse of Tiahuanaco's once-productive agroeconomy was the result of a natural catastrophe of unprecedented proportions: Tiahuanaco succumbed to a four-centuries-long drought that destroyed its capacity to supply its cities with food.

Based on a rich spectrum of new ecological and archaeological information, we now understand Tiahuanaco's political decline as the product of the deterioration and ultimate abandonment of its regional-scale agricultural systems. Under the burden of a declining economic base, the political structure of the empire fragmented and Tiahuanaco's royal dynasty eventually dissolved. In one of the most dramatic climatic changes ever experienced in the southern hemisphere, the carefully nurtured system of hydraulic agriculture disintegrated, and so dissolved the pediment of elite power and authority.

Tiahuanaco's farmers were incapable of responding to a drought of unprecedented duration and severity. In the prolonged decades of drought conditions, the fields produced insufficient crops to support the urban populations. Tiahuanaco's cities were abandoned and the state administration disintegrated. The royal dynasty, tied so intimately to the success of its agricultural estates, lost both its fundamental source of power and its social relevance.

The psychological impact of this drought must have been devastating. The people of Tiahuanaco were accustomed to dominating the essential elements of their environment. These were a people capable of diverting great rivers and reshaping intractable mountain landscapes—virtuosos in the art and science of farming. Their consummate skill in controlling stone and water, land and people converted their society into one of the truly brilliant achievements of native Andean civilization. And yet, the elaborate urban world they created proved vulnerable precisely in the manner they least expected.

Over the centuries, Tiahuanaco's urban food supply had come to rely upon an intensely productive, yet highly specialized form of cultivation. After all, raised-field agriculture could stand many different kinds of environmental stress through clever use of aqueducts, canals, and dikes. But, in the face of such a profound drought, no agricultural system could be expected to survive for long especially under the rigorous environmental conditions of the altiplano. The people of Tiahuanaco themselves did not perish en masse, but their special form of social organization, their economic power impelled by imperial conquests and intensive production on rich agricultural lands, their cities studded with the monumental displays of glory, all of these disappeared.

This is a classic evolutionary tale. Successful adaptations are frequently responses to prevailing environmental conditions. Normal fluctuations in these conditions cause gradual modifications in the original adaptation. But abrupt, profound shifts in environmental conditions can generate intolerable stresses that force radical change. Highly specialized adaptations are resilient within a given range of variation. But unanticipated catastrophic events that fall outside this range suddenly convert a resilient system into a brittle one. Like a rubber band stretched beyond its inherent elasticity, at the point of maximal tolerable stress, the structure snaps.

After the decline of Tiahuanaco, urban civilization disappeared in the Lake Titicaca basin for nearly four hundred years. Central organization and the management of intensive agriculture, craft production, long-distance trade, and other sources of wealth broke down. Throughout the south-central Andes, human populations dispersed across the landscape, settling into smaller, easily defended settlements. The demise of the Tiahuanaco empire brought with it widespread political instability. The "Pax Tiahuanaco" imposed by the empire could no longer repress interethnic hostilities, and the former provinces of the empire dissolved into polities bitterly contesting land, water, and other natural resources. The political disturbances and economic chaos that followed in the wake of Tiahuanaco's collapse are reflected in the characteristic style of settlement of this period: a fortified village clinging to steep mountain slopes. Vast stretches of formerly productive land in the highlands and along the coast were abandoned as populations retreated into protected redoubts, subsisting principally on the production of small-scale agricultural terraces in arable pockets. The cosmopolitan luxuries of cities and towns were exchanged for an aggressive fight for survival in an increasingly intractable countryside.

Although the immediate cause of the empire's decline was associated with uncontrollable environmental forces, the decline may also be viewed from a longer term perspective as

190

the product of evolutionary fate. In the process of shaping their society, Tiahuanaco's aristocracy unconsciously violated a cardinal rule of successful adaptation: They encouraged their economy to become increasingly specialized. Rather than diversify the technology of food crop production, they invested heavily and increasingly in more refined elaborations of raised-field cultivation on wetlands and in the hydraulic infrastructure that supported this specialized technology. The strategy of Tiahuanaco's aristocracy was eminently sensible and successful for many decades. But their chosen agricultural technology was also heavily water-dependent in what is, in the end, an arid environment. Under conditions of uncertainty, the foremost evolutionary imperative, as any good investor in the stock market knows, is to maintain a diversified portfolio of potential adaptive responses. During the long centuries of successful agricultural adaptation to their rigorous environment, the people of Tiahuanaco invested so heavily in a single strategy that they ultimately paid a fatal price for overspecialization. Raised fields demand a constant, voluminous supply of water. Under normal climatic circumstances, the great waterworks commissioned by Tiahuanaco's aristocracy functioned with admirable efficiency to supply the demand. But even Tiahuanaco's sophisticated agricultural engineers could not anticipate what began to happen at the end of the tenth century.

For a decade or more after it began, they may not even have been aware of the subtle shift in climate that would bring their world to its knees. At first, Tiahuanaco's farmers would have noticed only that the rains came later and more sporadically than before. They had experienced annual fluctuations in rainfall many times over the course of their lives, every farmer has. This would not have seemed unusual or especially threatening. After all, most of the fields were tied into the great network of canals and reservoirs constructed by their kings. If rain didn't feed their fields, the king's canals would.

191

But, as drought conditions persisted from one year into the next, the volume of water in the rivers began to drop. The old intakes of the irrigation canals began to draw less and less water and, each year, the area of land under cultivation began to decline. Tiahuanaco's rulers struggled to make up food shortages in the cities by importing grains and tubers, and by distributing food from public granaries. But urban demand was too great to rely on imports alone. Doling out stored foodstuffs was, at best, a temporary solution. In the face of increasing demand, season after season of declining harvests rapidly depleted palace warehouses.

In time, river water declined to the point at which the canal intakes were converted into sterile, useless spigots. The complex irrigation networks that had served the cities so well became emblems of the king's failure. Harvests declined. Food shortages and, in particularly bad years, famine began to haunt Tiahuanaco's cities. People in the countryside faired no better than the city dwellers as the tempo of tributary demands from Tiahuanaco's aristocracy increased in a desperate attempt to stave off the impending food crisis.

Although we have no contemporary narrative of the famine's impact on Tiahuanaco society, we can conjure a vision of the sheer human devastation through a harrowing account of famine in another part of the ancient world drawn from *The Chronicle of Joshua the Stylite,* which recounts this story of famine provoked by a plague of locusts:

> The famine was sore in the villages and in the city; for those who were left in the villages were eating bitter-vetches; and others were frying the withered fallen grapes and eating them, though even of them there was not enough to satisfy them. And those who were in the city were wandering about the streets, picking up the stalks and vegetables, all filthy with mud, and eating them. They were sleeping in the porticoes and streets, and wailing by night and day from the pangs of the hunger; and their bodies wasted away, and they were in a

sad plight, and became like jackals because of the lean-
ness of their bodies. The whole city was full of them and
they began to die in the porticoes and in the streets.

Children and babes were crying in every street. Of
some the mothers were dead; others their mothers had
left, and had run away from them when they asked for
something to eat, because they had nothing to give
them. Dead bodies were lying exposed in every street,
and the citizens were not able to bury them, because,
while they were carrying out the first that had died, the
moment they returned they found others.[4]

Although not as dramatic as a plague of locusts, the slow
effects of chronic drought on Tiahuanaco's cities provoked
intense human misery. The drought inflicted on Tiahuanaco
was an insidious, lingering killer that played cruelly on the
emotions. Some rain always fell in the spring, reviving hope
that this year would be different; that the seeds would swell
with water, take root, and flourish in the sun. But the world
had turned around; the rains of spring disappeared, evaporat-
ing in the bone-dry air before they fell to the parched earth.

After a decade of drought conditions, the levee systems
along the rivers served now only as hulking, bitter reminders
of the ensuing disaster. The great artificial reservoirs, excavated at huge cost, turned first to gnat-infested mudholes and
then to barren patches of cracked earth. In the initial years of
the great drought, raised fields farthest from the shores of
Lake Titicaca were abandoned first. Farmers began to pursue
the declining groundwater toward the lake. Each year they
had to excavate deeper into the earth to tap into the water
table. Eventually, even their drinking wells became perilously
deep and virtually impossible to use.

After a century of drought conditions, only patchy remnants of raised fields were still successfully cultivated. A few
deep, protected gorges near the lake still ran with sufficient
water during the summer to coax out a single harvest. But
the great agricultural estates on the plains around Lake Tit-

icaca—the once inexhaustible breadbasket of Tiahuanaco civilization—withered.

Predictably, some years were better than others; abundant rainfall swept across the parched plateaus, and dry rivers ran again in wild torrents. At times, several good years followed one another, renewing hope that the cycle of drought was finally broken. But then the drought returned with a vengeance.

The battle to restore the altiplano to its formerly productive conditions must have been a desperate one. New canals were cut, new hydraulic schemes were hatched—only to fail again. Gradually, in the face of repeated failure, people began to drift away from the cities. The ruling elite lost their social credibility, along with their powers of moral persuasion. They no longer commanded the economic, political, and spiritual authority to keep the populations attached to their households. Tiahuanaco society demanded that the elite display great generosity in return for the subordination and loyalty of the masses. Without the means of distributing tangible goods and services, the lords of Tiahuanaco were stripped of their social superiority and of their capacity to mobilize their subjects. Even more, the persistent lack of vitalizing rain made it clear to everyone that the king and his court had failed in their most essential ritual task: to harmonize the world of man with the forces of nature. Now, because of their failure, a Pachakuti had befallen Tiahuanaco. The Spirits of the Earth and the Sky had abandoned them. A new social and moral order was imminent.

Economic insecurity bred political instability and social unrest. Tiahuanaco civil society shuddered under the impact. Prominent lineages, families, court retainers, and state administrators saw their social roles begin to dissolve in their lifetimes. Court life disappeared, and with it the city itself. The cosmopolitan culture that was Tiahuanaco left no heirs. After the decline and fall of Tiahuanaco, the Andean high plateau was ruralized for nearly four centuries. Populations scattered into the countryside in search of survival. Many migrated out of the altiplano altogether into the forested slopes that cling to the eastern ramparts of the Andes. The glittering cities of the high plateau lapsed into lichen-encrusted ruins within a few generations. For Tiahuanaco, it was the end.

How do we know for sure that there was such a cataclysmic climate change at a time so far in the past? What physical evidence do we have for a drought of unprecedented duration? We have never experienced a drought of such proportions ourselves. Is such a climatic phenomenon even possible?

The answer to these questions is a fascinating tale in itself. Until recent developments in the scientific investigation of climate history, we would never have been able to construct such a compelling portrait of the decline of Tiahuanaco civilization. The causes would have remained simply another unresolved mystery of the ancient world. But interdisciplinary environmental research has opened new vistas into the Andean past. The study of paleoclimates is an esoteric field, pursued by an eclectic group of scientists who search for clues to climate fluctuations in annual rings of ancient trees, in laminations of lake sediment and glacial ice, in ratios of oxygen isotopes in lake and ocean water, in changing profiles of pollen which preserve the ancient history of forests and crops.

Research using these methods has shown that the history of a catastrophic shift in environmental conditions is sedimented into the Andean landscape: in the crests of remote, ice-clad mountains and in the muddy depths of Lake Titicaca. Like the Aymara, paleoenvironmental scientists believe that the history of the world is infused in the landscapes around them. To the Aymara, each mountain pass, ravine, stream, and boulder inscribes a unique history, a kind of text of the memory that can be recalled only if one possesses the keys of knowledge. The yatiri know each of the landscape's features intimately, and they recount their histories in great detail. The worldview of the Aymara and the paleoenvironmental scientist converge on this point: They both appreciate that

the land around us is a product of the past, a physical repository of history, a record of events congealed in rock and
mud, ice, and water. Both attribute enormous significance to
the most subtle details of that record.

In searching for the causes of Tiahuanaco's decline, we
are fortunate to have one of the most highly resolved records
of climate history on earth to study. This record is preserved
in the massive ice sheets of the Quelccaya Glacier situated in
the rugged Cordillera Blanca mountain range of southern
Peru, less than two hundred kilometers northwest of Lake
Titicaca. The climate history established through scientific
exploration of this ice cap applies directly to the historical
development of the empire.

Lonnie Thompson of Ohio State University's Institute of
Polar Studies is one of the main protagonists in the effort to
document the long-term climate history of the Andes.
Thompson leads an intrepid interdisciplinary research team
laboring under extreme conditions on the remote Quelccaya
outcrop to develop a detailed history of climatic fluctuations.
Over nine consecutive summers between 1976 and 1984,
Thompson's team battled wind, cold, and the effects of
extreme altitude to drill cores in the glacial ice, gathering a
rich sampling of meteorological information. The team struck
paleoenvironmental pay dirt in 1983 when it managed to
extract two long ice cores (one 155 meters and the other 164
meters long) extending from the summit of the ice cap to
bedrock. These cores yield a continuous record of snow accumulation extending back 1500 years. Subsequent laboratory
examination of samples from the Quelccaya cores offers us an
exceptionally detailed record of climate variation in the south-
central Andes over the period from A.D. 400 to 1980.[5] The
ongoing research of Thompson's team will eventually extend
this unique, long-term climate record backward to the periods
of the early political formation of the Tiahuanaco empire.

The basic data extracted from the ice cores are measurements of annual snow accumulations, together with concen-

trations of dust microparticles and other contaminants embedded in the snow. During the dry season (May–October), prevailing winds from the altiplano transport particles of dust and organic debris toward the Quelccaya glacier where they are deposited in annual dust layers. These particles serve as datable boundaries within the snow layers and also as indicators of unusual events, such as volcanic eruptions or regional-scale earth movements like those resulting from intensive agricultural activities.

The highest peaks of the Andean range receive significant precipitation in the form of snow throughout the year, but most especially during the wet season, when air masses originating in the Amazon basin pump huge quantities of moisture into the high Andes. About eighty percent of the annual precipitation in the Quelccaya area falls during the wet season. Extreme elevation—in the case of the Quelccaya ice cap 5,670 meters (nearly 18,500 feet)—and permanent low temperatures prevent significant melting and evaporation of surface snow. These atmospheric conditions result in annual deposition of snow in stratigraphically distinguishable layers on the glacier.

The amount of snow that accumulates varies seasonally and from year to year. Interannual variation can be measured. In simplest terms, snow accumulation on the glacier is an excellent proxy for regional precipitation patterns: a large layer on the ice cap signals heavy annual rainfall at lower altitudes; smaller layers imply lower rainfall. But the practice of measuring the thickness of accumulated snow layers in the Quelccaya cores is more complicated than this simple equation implies. The deeper Thompson and his team drilled into the ice cap, the thinner the annual snow layers became. This is because the weight of the overlying mass of ice compresses the layers below. Over time, older layers of snow, converted to ice by this process, thin and flow outward from the center under the enormous pressure of the glacial burden. The compressive forces on underlying snow accumulations vary over time as the glacial mass grows. This means that the actual layers in the core do not directly represent the original thickness of fresh snow deposited each year at the surface of the ice cap. Thompson successfully developed a mathematical model to compensate for the variation in the thinning of the annual snow layers.[6]

The record so constructed reveals numerous wet periods, along with a prolonged dry period between A.D. 1000 and 1400. My colleague Charles Ortloff, an engineer and extraordinary avocational archaeologist, reanalyzed Thompson's data for the period from A.D. 800 to 1400 to clarify the extent of drought conditions in this period so critical to our understanding of the decline and fall of the Tiahuanaco state. His subtle reanalysis demonstrates that over successive two-hundred-year intervals from A.D. 800 to 1400, the mean annual snow layer thickness progressively declines. Although vigorous fluctuations in precipitation exist over individual years, there is a significant decline in mean annual precipitation beginning after A.D. 1000. The cumulative extent of this decline is astonishing: Net annual snow accumulation in the period from A.D. 1000 to 1400 declines fifteen percent from previous periods. This dramatic decline in annual precipitation is graphically conveyed in the accompanying illustration. This graph expresses in the abstract fashion of science an enormous social tragedy

If the Quelccaya glacial record were our sole evidence attesting to one of the most severe climate changes of the past millennium, we might remain justifiably skeptical. But work by my colleague Michael Binford of Harvard University on sediments extracted from Lake Titicaca strongly corroborates the ice core evidence. Michael is trained as an ecologist and specializes in the esoteric field of paleolimnology—the study of ancient lake sediments. These sediments are like a library of environmental history. For the past decade, he and I have worked closely together to correlate long-term changes in the landscape with intensive human activities. His

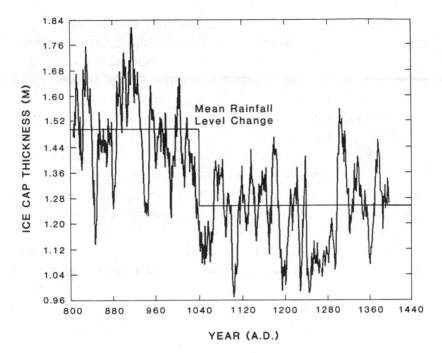

Average ice cap thickness values from the Quelccaya glacier, illustrating the dramatic decline in mean rainfall levels in the south central Andes after A.D. 1000. (Figure based on privileged, unpublished data courtesy of Lonnie Thompson.)

team of ecologists includes experts in the analysis of pollen; plant and animal fossils; geochemistry; and geochronology.

According to sediment cores extracted by Michael's team the lake level was significantly higher than usual between A.D. 350 and 500, implying increased precipitation. This period of elevated lake level is indicated in ancient pollen collected from one of our cores and is marked by a dramatic rise in certain aquatic plants and planktonic algae. The sediments in this section of the core have been radiocarbon dated from about A.D. 300 to 700, with the highest lake level peaking at around A.D. 500. The increase in aquatic plants and algae is coincident with a decrease in sedges, such as the Lake Tit-

199

icaca totora reed. This particular distribution of ancient pollen indicates that during this time lake levels rose over the core site, drowning the sedges and promoting the expansion of aquatic plants and algae. Subsequently, the sediments in the upper sections of the core show a dramatic decline in deeper water plants and algae, and a resurgence of totora, which is a shallow-water plant. According to our research team's palynologist, Barbara Leyden, this pollen distribution in the upper third of the core reflects a lowering of lake levels. Age estimates on these sediments place the decline in lake level precisely in the period of desiccation after A.D. 1000 recorded in the Quelccaya ice cap.

Analysis of a second core extracted in 1992 confirmed our inferences regarding changing lake levels based on the ancient pollen. In this core, paleoecology team members Mark Brenner and Jason Curtis of the University of Florida examined long-term lake level fluctuations as they are reflected in the fossilized shells of tiny mollusks embedded in the lake sediments. Changing ratios of different oxygen isotopes in these shells offer another means of creating a record of the climate. Two key isotopes of oxygen are found in these shells, and they behave differently from one another in response to climate. The ^{16}O isotope evaporates more rapidly than ^{18}O. Therefore, in environmental conditions characterized by higher evaporation, the concentration of the ^{18}O isotope increases in shell samples. Determining the ratio of ^{16}O to ^{18}O isotopes provides a reliable measure of the evaporative conditions prevailing at the time a shell became part of the sediment core. The ^{18}O oxygen samples in the interval in question indicate highly evaporative conditions, a drying trend, and, by inference, falling lake levels, all coinciding with the pollen record.

A third core extracted by our team from another part of Lake Titicaca offers even more intriguing insights into the extent and duration of the climate change. This core exhibits a marked hiatus in sedimentation which occurs in an interval dated to between A.D. 900 and 1400. This hiatus tells a particularly shocking tale of just how abrupt and catastrophic climate change can be.

The core contains a segment taken in water over twelve meters deep, in which the accumulation of sediments to the lake virtually ceased. The only compelling explanation for this phenomenon is that the core site was completely desiccated at the time of this sedimentation hiatus. There was simply no standing water under which wind and waterborne sediments could accumulate. In other words, at some point between A.D. 900 and 1400, the level of Lake Titicaca declined as much as twelve meters from its previous high stand. This means that the entire small basin of Lake Titicaca (the Lago Menor or "small lake" in Spanish), which today has an average depth of ten meters, dried up completely. This part of Lake Titicaca simply ceased to exist. We cannot determine yet if this catastrophic decline occurred relatively rapidly in a matter of years or decades, or if the process of desiccation proceeded more gradually over the course of these five centuries. Historic records from the basin indicate that the lake level can fluctuate as much as five meters in a single decade. From the archaeological patterns of the abandonment of the raised-field systems, I suspect that the lake level began to fall rapidly after A.D. 1000, and that the twelve-meter decline was completed in a matter of a decade or two.

Whatever the precise timing of this extreme climatic event, the social, economic, and environmental impacts on human society were devastating. This enormous drop in water levels in a lake as large as Titicaca, over 8,500 square kilometers in area, indicates that the drought that began after A.D. 1000 was of far greater severity and duration than the infamous "Dust Bowl" conditions that afflicted the United States between 1928 and 1934. Yet, in the United States, these conditions caused extreme economic hardship and social dislocation. Thousands of people were forced to abandon their family farms, which converted to virtual deserts before their eyes.

Given the remarkable severity of this great Andean drought,

it is not surprising that paleoenvironmental scientists have identified contemporaneous periods of climatic anomalies in other
parts of the world. A drought of such scope and persistence
cannot fail to be related to, and have significant impact on, the
global ocean-atmosphere circulation system that is the source of
earth's weather. Scott Stine of California State University at
Hayward recently identified severe droughts in the Sierra
Nevada mountains of California and in southernmost Patagonia
through the analysis of relict tree stumps stranded in modern
lakes and along present day stream courses.[7] These relict stumps
are rooted firmly in deep water indicating that substantially
lower water levels prevailing in the past were succeeded by
flooding. By taking radiocarbon assays on the outermost,
"death-year" tree ring of these stumps, Stine dated the time of
inundation. Then, by working backward, counting successively
older rings in the interiors of the stranded stumps, he was able
to determine the duration of the preceding intervals of desiccation. His results signal sustained droughts between A.D. 892
and 1112 and A.D. 1209 to 1350—precisely the time of the
great Andean drought.

On the opposite side of the world, in Europe, even
though there were substantial secular variations in precipitation, the tenth to fourteenth centuries were characterized
overall by consistently mild winters and abundant rainfall. H.
H. Lamb referred to this interval as the "Medieval Warm
Epoch," during which vineyards appeared in England, and
extensive stands of wheat and barley flourished in southern
Iceland.[8] The interconnectedness of the ocean-atmosphere
system and the fact that the earth's total water budget is
always in equilibrium makes these contemporaneous,
medieval climatic anomalies in distant parts of the globe eminently understandable. In essence, for every (climatic) action,
there is a reaction. If a severe, chronic drought develops in
the Western Hemisphere, there must be a response in the
Eastern Hemisphere in the form of a regionwide, aggregate
increase in precipitation. The important point is that this

medieval climatic anomaly was a global phenomenon, and that the individual expressions of climate fluctuations in various parts of the earth were severe and extraordinarily persistent. Although the period of dessication that descended on the Andean altiplano was not unique (there was a similar episode of great aridity in the region prior to 1500 B.C.), it was certainly unprecedented from the standpoint of the people of Tiahuanaco.

We have solved much of the mystery of Tiahuanaco's collapse. We know now that the people of Tiahuanaco were confronted with a drought unprecedented in both severity and duration. From our archaeological research in the old sustaining hinterland of Tiahuanaco, we know too how they responded to this environmental crisis. After A.D. 1000, intensive agricultural production on a grand scale disappeared. Although there are still substantial numbers of human habitations in Tiahuanaco's hinterland that date after this time, they are widely dispersed and most are very small. Most dramatic of all, the cities of Tiahuanaco became virtual ghost towns after this time; no radiocarbon dates on ordinary households are associated with these urban centers past A.D. 1000. Put simply, under the impact of widespread environmental crisis, Tiahuanaco's cities were depopulated. The Lake Titicaca basin, one of the greatest demographic centers of native Andean civilization, became a land without cities for over four hundred years. When cities and urban culture fail, so do the larger political systems in which they are embedded.

But what happened to the population over the course of the empire's decline? Did they die off from malnutrition and starvation? Did they migrate to other more productive regions unaffected by the drought? Did they change the way they made a living? The short answer to these questions is most likely yes on all counts. If we consider recent, devastating droughts in Africa and other areas of the developing world, we see that people respond to grave climatic deterioration in all these ways. Who can forget recent images of delirious African children languishing in the dust, deformed by distended bellies, their growth grotesquely stunted by bones depleted of marrow and minerals? Even in the United States today, under much less extreme social and environmental circumstances, lands in the arid West are being abandoned at a rapid rate for lack of sufficient water. A whole culture of once productive farmers and ranchers has virtually disappeared. The battle over the dwindling waters of the once great Colorado River is a germane reminder that even the richest industrialized countries are still profoundly dependent upon this most precious of natural resources.

The people of Tiahuanaco did not have the luxury of industrial technology to help them overcome their own water crisis. But they did have some means of response as shown by the archaeological record. Our archaeological investigations show that entirely new environmental zones were colonized for the first time in millennia. Virtually vacant in Tiahuanaco times, high mountain valleys blessed with meadows, springs, and local aquifers suddenly became crowded with small sites. Remote valleys that were peripheral to Tiahuanaco's agricultural economy for centuries served as fragile lifelines for the dispossessed.

Many migrants ventured even farther afield to colonize lands in an entirely different ecological setting: the warm, subtropical yungas on the eastern slopes of the Andean chain. If the history of human occupation is an accurate indicator, the yungas were not as seriously affected by the great Andean drought because this region enjoys an entirely different climate than that of the altiplano. The yungas is more Amazonian than Andean in terms of temperature and rainfall. Here wild rivers originating in the ancient glaciers of the Cordillera cut and gouge the hard rock of the mountains in spectacular displays of headward erosion. Waterfalls cascade violently for hundreds of meters down vertiginous slopes, which become increasingly humid and forested as they descend through roiling banks of damp fog from the high mountain passes. Gnarled evergreen shrubs, dripping with parasitic wild orchids, cling tenaciously to the fractured black shale and basalt clad mountainsides. Enclaves of flat land with deep, rich soils are encrusted in the chaotic jumble of rock formations that form the eastern edge of the Andean chain. Here labor-intensive terracing is a way of life, and it significantly expands the amount of land that can be reclaimed for agricultural production. The upper margins of the yungas abut the treeless, windswept steppe of the mountains. The lower margins merge gradually with the true tropical rain forest of the Amazon basin. The yungas are a zone of radical landscape transition, of movement from the dry, frozen edge of glaciated tundra, where biological activity seems virtually paralyzed, to the suffocating humid heat of the tropical forest, swarming with insects and redolent with the organic smells of decaying plant and animal tissue. Nowhere in the world is this transition between radically divergent biozones completed more abruptly and dramatically as in the yungas. Here the natural vegetation is an exuberant mix of trees, shrubs, vines, and wild fruits. Walnut, mahogany, cedar, and ironwood palm tower overhead. Aromatic woods and shrubs like sasparilla and saffron grow in profusion. Strawberries, oranges, lemons, and coffee grow beside maize, hot peppers, manioc, and potato. Avocados, bananas, pineapples, mangoes, guavas, melons of all kinds, and papayas flourish in the rich soils and mild climate.

The constraints to agriculture in the yungas are not set by climate or soil, but rather by topography. Arable land in the yungas is at a premium: The broken, tectonically folded landscape concedes little in the way of flat land to the hopeful farmer. After A.D. 1000, we see evidence of heavy colonization of the yungas. A whole new culture with a heritage clearly traceable to Tiahuanaco emerges in this region. The town of Iskanwaya was one of the principal products of this migration. Apparently defying the laws of nature, the site is hewn from the unyielding rock of the Cordillera. But, even more impressive than the town itself, are the countless contour terraces that undulate gracefully along the mountainside. Now long-abandoned, these terraces were once fed by networks of canals that drew sweet water from seams in the mountain's face. The Tiahuanaco empire had regularly exploited these warm, humid lands for crops unavailable in its high plateau heartland, crops such as corn and coca. Now the land of exotic, high-prestige crops became their new breadbasket.

Great movements of human populations became the norm in the time of the great drought. The entire south-central Andes was roiled in bitter contests of competitive exclusion as humans fought for access to dwindling resources. Apart from migration to more favored climatic zones, refugees of the shattered empire invested increasingly in llama and alpaca herds. These tough animals, cousins of the camels, are extremely well-adapted to arid conditions, and can convert even the most unpromising, silica-infused plants into forage. But the shift to nomadic pastoralism also entailed dramatic changes in the structure of the prevailing social order. Civil society became more dispersed, mobile, and inchoate. The ideology of Tiahuanaco could no longer hold the empire's disparate populations together. There were no longer any fixed capitals and centers of prestige from which the elite could rule. In the high plateau, once-prosperous farmers were transformed into subsistence cultivators clinging to the bare edge of survival, surrounded by mobile, aggressive, and potentially hostile pastoralists.

This state of political instability in the Lake Titicaca basin persisted until the late fourteenth century. Only in the decades immediately prior to the emergence of the Inca on the high plateau around A.D. 1440 did well-organized kingdoms associated with Aymara speakers begin to reassert their authority over large expanses of productive territory. In the fifteenth and sixteenth centuries, coincident with the return of normal precipitation levels, the Lake Titicaca basin was again under the sway of powerful political coalitions. The French ethnohistorian Thérèse Bouysse-Cassagne identified at least twelve Aymara *señorios* or kingdoms in the highland territories of the old Tiahuanaco empire, including the King-dom of Pacajes in the region of Tiahuanaco itself.⁹ Two of these kingdoms, the Lupaqa and the Qolla, centered on the western shores of Lake Titicaca, appear to have been orga-nized nearly at the state level, restoring some of the political power once wielded by Tiahuanaco alone. The Lupaqa and Qolla sustained a series of heavily populated towns and domi-nated relatively large territories, including distant colonies on the coast of Peru and in the yungas on the eastern slopes of the Andes. By the mid-fifteenth century, these two native kingdoms were in a bitter battle for political supremacy of the lake district. If their further development had not been trun-cated by the Inca conquest of their territory, the outcome of the contest between the Qolla and the Lupaqa might have been the emergence of a new Tiahuanaco-style empire.

Instead, the imperial armies of the Inca moved swiftly to gain the submission and rich tribute potential of the native Titicaca basin kingdoms. Appealing to a mythical association with the ancient Tiahuanaco dynasty, the Inca constructed a powerful identity with the past, appropriating the mystique of Tiahuanaco's distinct civilization as their own. The Inca con-quered farther and faster than Tiahuanaco ever had. But unlike Tiahuanaco, their impact on the local population was short lived. The coercive techniques liberally applied by the Inca—calculated military violence, garrisoning of provinces, uprooting and resettling of populations in alien social set-tings—were effective, but these measures were costly and short-term solutions to the problem of political integration. Coercion, when applied indiscriminately, inevitably generates hostility in subject populations.

In 1532, another wave of conquerors stormed the Andean world and transformed it forever. After the Spanish van-quished the ill-fated empire of the Incas, they began at once to implant European modes of economic and political behav-ior. Their attempts to restructure the native Andean world in terms they could understand, and better manipulate, were immeasurably aided by the scourge of virulent diseases to which the natives had little resistance. In province after province of Alto Peru (the Spanish term for the great Andean altiplano), colonial tribute lists record the terrible toll on natives exacted by foreign diseases and by other introduced evils, such as forced labor in the deadly mines of Potosí in southern Bolivia. In some provinces, as much as ninety percent of the indigenous population disappeared within fifty years of the Spanish conquest. Some fled the foreign invaders, disappearing into the trackless deserts of the high plateau, or into the lush forests east of the Andes. Many were murdered in the aftermath of the conquest or died rapidly from smallpox or measles. Others suffered an even more agonizing fate: They were consigned to the mines to labor for their Spanish overlords until death. For the miners, death came slower, but it came surely and in bitter ways: starvation, exhaustion, poisoning from the mercury used to extract the precious silver, despair. The waves of killing pandemics kept coming. A contemporary account from Peru in 1585 vividly captures the terror and the terrible social cost of these epidemics:

> They died by scores and hundreds. Villages were depopulated. Corpses were scattered over the fields or piled up in houses or huts . . . The fields were uncultivated; the herds were untended; and the workshops and mines were without laborers . . . The price of food rose to such an extent that many persons found it beyond their reach. They escaped the foul disease, but only to be wasted by famine.[10]

It was not long before the sophisticated agricultural techniques worked out by the natives of the high plateau over the millennia were lost to the world. The population that survived the conquest was not large enough to justify investment in terraces and dams, dikes, and aqueducts. The Spanish overlords were more interested in precious metals, cattle, and a few crops that fueled their mining industry—vineyards for wine, olives for oil, and a few cereal grains to sustain their workers. The once-innumerable banks of fertile agricultural terraces fell gradually into disuse, the once-vast herds of llamas and alpaca dwindled, and the once-vital network of caravans and colonies atrophied, bringing isolation to the native populations where there had once been alliance. The native Andean peoples have lingered in this state of marginality to this day.

But the great agricultural heritage of the Andean past remains, inscribed deeply in the landscape. Ancient terraces still shape the contours of mountain valleys. Although abandoned and, in places, eroding away into the valley bottoms, they retain the capacity to affect the complex cycles of sediment and nutrient flows on the land. Some contemporary communities still farm these terraces, but on a scale much reduced from the past.

If Tiahuanaco's world was turned around by an unmanageable ecological disaster, the vestiges of its monumental agricultural legacy still persist in form, although, over the past eight hundred years, not in function. The elevated planting beds and the ghostly tracery of canals still cover the valley floors around Lake Titicaca. Ironically, Tiahuanaco's cultural descendants farm the heavily eroded hillsides well above the old raised fields, struggling to extract a viable crop from the stony earth, unaware that their own ancestral culture had solved the most intractable problem of cultivating the high plateau. Today, in three out of every five years, the Aymara Indians' crops succumb to serious frost damage. Aymara farmers are barely able to meet their minimal subsistence needs, and so increasingly they are abandoning their traditional homelands to escape the bitter realities of rural poverty. In the past decade, the trickle of Indian migrants from the country to cities such as La Paz has swelled into a torrent. These migrants are trading a marginal existence in the countryside for what has become for many an even more marginal lifestyle in the city, where thousands now languish idle, unemployed, and without a permanent home. But they still come, because they perceive the city as a place of opportunity for themselves, and even more for their children.

Once we understood that raised-field agriculture was the key to ancient Tiahuanaco's economic success, I was struck by the irony and the paradox of the contemporary Aymara condition. By any economic measure, farmers in the distant past were significantly better off than those in the present. Rural populations in the Tiahuanaco empire were an order of magnitude larger than they are today, and, by all the physical evidence we have gathered, they enjoyed a much healthier and prosperous life than today. These discoveries rapidly erode our cherished notions that the human condition is one of inexorable progress, and that modernity inevitably increases well-being.

As I realized the full implications of our research, a simple question occurred to me: Could raised fields become the key to prosperity on the altiplano once again? A seemingly simple experiment—restoring the ancient raised fields to production—promised a solution to this provocative question. Could a technology from the past help resolve the problem of modern rural food shortages and chronic poverty? Our efforts to resolve these questions is the final part of this tale. It is a quest in progress with an outcome as yet undetermined, but one that has become part of the Aymara future still unfolding.

6

Restoration

JUST after dawn on June 21, 1986, I met Cosme Uruchi in the plaza of Lakaya. Cosme was a jilakata, an elder of his community, and the patriarch of an old, many-branched family. Virtually everyone in Lakaya is related by blood to Cosme, or can claim a spiritual kinship with him. By local standards, the extended Uruchi clan is land and cattle rich. More importantly from the perspective of the Aymara, they are people rich. Most of the Uruchi had remained in Lakaya over generations and the family grew exceptionally large. The Uruchi could count on the hands and resources of many relatives when the time came to raise a house, harvest a crop, or sponsor a festival.

But Cosme enjoyed special deference in Lakaya and beyond. Although he was nearly eighty years old at the time of our encounter, the respect he commanded was not simply that of an elder. Cosme had been a guerilla fighter with a fearsome reputation. During the social revolution that rocked the Bolivian altiplano in 1952, he was in the vanguard of native warriors. Carrying only his vintage Mauser into battle, Cosme led his community against the landholders who had held them in bondage and ill-disguised contempt for generations.

211

Although ill-equipped, Cosme's peasant militia was tough, disciplined, and when necessary, ferocious. They seized the huge, whitewashed hacienda houses surrounded by soaring stands of pungent eucalyptus. For centuries, the estates of the elite jealously gathered the best resources of a harsh land to themselves—the sweetest, ever-flowing springs, the blackest soil, the richest minerals of the mountains. The great houses perched dreamlike, shimmering in artificial mantles of manicured lawns and well-tended gardens. In a surround of sere land, they alone burst with color: the crisp white of lime-plastered adobe walls cutting sharp geometric lines across the earth; the rich, mellow evening glow of roofs clad in thick red clay tiles; the extravagant crimson and magenta shades of bougainvillea. In 1952, the human magma of resentment and dreams long denied finally erupted through the crust of repression that had contained it. Cosme and his forces occupied the land, expelling the hacienda owners and their families forever. During the revolution, other landowners were not so lucky to escape with their lives.

After the initial exhilaration of victory, the bitter legacy of prerevolutionary days lingered in the native communities of the high plateau. The newly dispossessed landlords, long haunted by visions of an armed, unified mass of Indians on their doorsteps, retreated to the safety of the cities. For years afterward, land disputes roiled the altiplano, splitting communities apart seam from seam and instilling profound distrust of all outsiders' intentions in the minds of the Aymara. Back in Lakaya, Cosme had known bitter days on the front line of the revolution, and learned not to expect too much from the *q'ara*, the white-skinned foreigners who had repressed the Aymara for centuries. He had lived long enough to see it all, to recall the endless, hollow promises of government officials. He knew that he cultivated his own land now only because he and his compatriots had taken their destinies into their own hands.

And so, in the cold, predawn hours of a winter solstice

thirty-four years after the revolution, I was on my way to meet an Indian warrior. As I drove through the early morning darkness over the treacherous mountains from Tiahuanaco, I was accompanied by Cesar Callisaya, my longtime guide to the Aymara world, and by Oswaldo Rivera. I had met Oswaldo literally the first time I stepped off a plane at La Paz's airport in the summer of 1978. He was then one of Bolivia's up-and-coming archaeologists, and he immediately took me under his wing. Within a year, we began working together to explore the ancient history of the Aymara. Pursuing our research, we grew close in friendship, and he, like Cesar, is now my *compadre,* my spiritual kin. For years we have shared the same hardships, pleasures, and dreams in the land of the Aymara.

Bonfires inexplicably burned on distant slopes, lending a surreal cast to our expedition. Clouds of smoke from brushfires massed and swirled through the quebradas. As we crested the pass that led down through folds of eroded rock toward Lakaya, a sliver of sun broke the jagged skyline of the distant Cordillera Real. We were suddenly bathed in pale light. I had the Toyota's heater on full-force, but still felt chilled. Plunging down into the shadow-dark gorge on the other side of the mountain, we passed small farmhouses mortised into the stony hillsides on either side of us. Black figures scuttled in front of adobe doorways illuminated by flickering candles and kerosene lamps. Wisps of wood smoke rose from mud chimneys. Roosters crowed in hidden courtyards. We saw no one on the road. It was still early, even for the farmers of the high plateau. Most people were taking their morning meal of quinoa porridge, bread, and heavily sugared coffee before the day's work. Our road finally leveled out as we shuddered across a boulder-strewn quebrada that ran down to the lakeshore. Within minutes we saw light glimmering on the wind-whipped surface of the lake. From our vantage point, the lake seemed sinister, displaying an impenetrable, obsidian-colored surface, wave-flecked with morning light. It looked as unspeakably cold as I felt.

The full disk of the sun cleared the Cordillera as we reached the turnoff to Lakaya. Although heading inland now, we skirted the lakeshore for a few kilometers more. I had come to know each of the villages and hamlets we passed with a kind of paradoxical intimacy. Rosa Pata, Tilata, Huacullani, Lukurmata, Chojasivi, Lillimani, Lakaya Alta, Lakaya Baja, Quiripujo, Korila, Wila Jawira. The litany of names was magical, exotic, although their everyday reality was not. I knew their rutted, muddy streets, their rotting facades, their tiny bodegas filled with soda crackers and Coca-Cola. Most especially I knew their eroding adobe churches, decrepit on the outside, yet glowing inside with racks of candles melting before luminous icons of Catholic saints. Whenever I entered one of these chapels on the high plateau, I was surprised to discover that the saints still exerted their unfathomable pull on my imagination. Perhaps the desolate feel of these places, the inhuman scale of the land subsuming them, broke through the protective layers of cynicism that had come to seem so natural to me.

Once I realized suddenly that in some strange way I felt deeply connected in spirit to the Aymara: We shared a long tradition rooted in the beliefs, the doctrines, the stories, and the rituals of our common faith. The roots of my Catholicism reached back a thousand years to Poland, to the land of my ancestors, while theirs was transplanted unbidden into their world by the militant forces of Spain over five hundred years ago. Different paths to the same City of God. But then my Catholicism was all I knew. The Aymara also faithfully kept Lady Earth and Lord Sky and the animate spirits of the land. Their faith was enriched by strands of deep belief I touched only tangentially. Their Mother Earth was a lived reality, one they fed every day with the fruits of their labor.

Every year I crossed paths with these villages and came to know that, although looking much the same on the surface, each possessed a peculiar character of its own. Each had its own history. Some were progressive, others deeply conservative; some were implacably hostile to outsiders, others anxiously looked for opportunities in the faces of strangers. In one dimension, these villages were painfully familiar to me. As physical places, I knew them well, much better than the hometown I had left behind. They even held for me those dense layers of accreted memories, friendships, joyous reunions, and bittersweet leave-takings that create and impart an unforgettable sense of place. But still they were not my personal frames of reference. Time and again I would visit a village after a few months absence to find a strange, changed place. The streets and houses, schools and chapels were all the same, looking as familiar and static as ever. But the feel of the place had changed. Like some great tectonic plates abruptly slipping under intense geologic pressure, the familiar landscape of friendship and acquaintance had suddenly shifted. Where once I was welcomed, I now met impassive stares. Where once I was stoned by a furious farmer, I was now greeted by welcoming smiles and easy laughter. The unchanging shell of these small villages barely contained the mercurial flow of belief and rumor, gossip and memory that constantly reshaped the intimate architecture of social life. I felt, at the same time, both insider and alien. I was more than a tourist, but much less than a native. I shared food and laughter and countless moments with these villagers, yet the social skin that encased their lives would never be my own.

The road to Lakaya took us first through the cooperative of Huacullani with its tiny trout hatchery and its large herd of dairy cattle. The day's work had just begun. Small clusters of women and children were leading the cows to pastures scattered throughout the marshes on the lake's edge. Broods of rooting pigs zigzagged behind in darting, single-minded lines, pausing only to thrust their snouts into patches of disturbed black soil and steaming piles of dung. Just ahead, Wila Kollu, Blood Hill, backlit in deep-shaded silhouette, carved its distinctive profile against the near horizon. The crescent-shaped outcrop seemed like the prow of some magnificent ocean liner soaring above the undulating reeds of the marshes. Astride Wila Kollu, an elegant acropolis of intricately worked granite and andesite temples once commanded the landscape for many kilometers around. On this morning of a late-twentieth century solstice, the first radiant spindles of dawn still converged on points of spiritual power within the ancient temples. Light played in a clever, predetermined sequence across one vandalized facade after another. The ancient gateways, although cracked and lichened over, continued to focus the sun's first solstitial rays across sunken courtyards. But the true targets of their luminous energy, the sacred stone images of Lady Earth and Lord Sky, were long gone, shattered into the earth or exiled to the fluorescent-lit corners of museums. Now the sun streamed under the lintels, across the recessed spaces of the vacant temples, and, unfocused by the hand of man, dispersed across the lake.

Crowding around the base of this mystical hill were the close-packed ruins of ordinary houses, workshops, and urban gardens entombed beneath one thousand years of sediment. This was Lukurmata, one of Tiahuanaco's dead cities. Today only a handful of people live on the old town's terraces, coaxing their subsistence from the moldering detritus of the past. Now, at harvest time, the once luridly painted temples take on natural color again: a vibrant pastiche of purple potato blossoms, crimson stalks of quinoa, and verdant green leaves of barley.

Our road resected the heart of the ancient town whose temples had been in ruin since the close of the tenth century. We drove across a slight knoll on the west side of Lukurmata, knowing from our excavations that this was yet another shrine riddled with the rich tombs of the Tiahuanaco faithful. Beneath the earth of Lukurmata the ancients rest. But their great stone calendars, still animated by the sun and the stars, stubbornly persist in marking the passing of the seasons. Indifferent to the modern world, they will keep their own track of time, until the temples and gateways erode to dust.

Only then, when their last monuments no longer tap into the rhythms of the natural world, will the people of Tiahuanaco recede completely, irrevocably, into the past.

As we climbed the small rise to the village of Chojasivi a couple of kilometers from Lukurmata, we saw our destination.

The ancient town of Lakaya perches on a prominence giving the impression that layer upon layer, age upon age of human actions had slowly accreted to form the whole. And this is not far from the truth. When the plaza in the middle of the town was leveled in an ill-planned paroxysm of civic improvement, the bulldozer struck and cleaved in two an old stone idol of Lady Earth. The profaned sculpture was quickly spirited away in the night and, so rumor has it, buried again in a secret mountain cave as an offering to Pachamama (or perhaps from fear that the broken idol would walk again and seek its revenge?). In the earthen spoil of the great steel blade, Bolivian archaeologists desperately tried to salvage Lakaya's ancient history. Bones of humans and animals, old building stones, and shards of pottery spilled out in vast, wanton quantities. The earth below was a conglomerate of spongy bone, broken crockery, and cracked rock. Man, more than nature, created the foundations of this ancient town. Lakaya was one of the major towns of the Tiahuanaco empire, and in some sections it is even more ancient than that: its foundation stones were laid over three thousand years ago when humans first began to live in permanent settlements in the altiplano. After the fall of Tiahuanaco, the town was recolonized by the Inca.

Today Lakaya is a strange place. In some ways it is no longer a town at all. Almost every day it is vacant, its houses, bodegas, and chapels tightly shuttered against intruders and the dust; its people mostly scattered across the land, tending to sheep, to fields, and to business in La Paz. But on Thursdays, the town revives, like Lazarus rising. The plaza becomes the epicenter of a raucous market. Battered blue buses (flagships of a notoriously dangerous fleet) block the road and

217

clog the broad expanse of the plaza. Lashed precariously to their roof racks are giant cloth bundles filled with everything imaginable. Anything one really needs in the countryside can be bought here: potatoes, oca, chuño, loaves of pressed salt, coca leaf, sacks of flour, bags of noodles, eggs, white peasant's cheese, fresh fish from Lake Titicaca, the occasional can of Nescafé imported from Brazil, llama fetuses, cane alcohol, rubber sandals cut from old tires, nylon cord, and Adidas sneakers. The merchants ring all sides of the plaza hawking their wares. In the middle, children play, dogs fight, drunks drink, teenagers flirt, friends meet, and the ancient ones sit on benches absorbing the heat of the sun. The market opens in the biting chill just after dawn and ends before noon. Only a few locals linger in the plaza into the early afternoon, and then they too disperse. For six hours, one day a week, Lakaya becomes a merchant's Brigadoon and then lapses back into its normal state of lassitude.

The purpose of our expedition was to talk with the townspeople about the ancient corrugated landscape below the town, that vast sweep of wetlands running to the lake and the river where the people of Lakaya have long pastured their animals. We had a special interest in those lands, which we believed held the secret to the wealth of the Tiahuanaco people one thousand years ago. We hoped to unlock those secrets again, but we needed the people of Lakaya and other communities along the lake's edge to do it.

The harvests had been bad for several years running. The aftermath of catastrophic flooding on Lake Titicaca between September of 1985 and April of 1986 was still painfully evident. In that seven-month period, the level of Lake Titicaca rose nearly three meters, inundating nearly thirty thousand acres of farmland and driving thousands of people from their homes. Salinated water covered the once productive fields to depths of one meter, and many homes were destroyed by the onrush. This was the latest catastrophe in the eternal cycle of drought and flood that plagues the altiplano.

We had come to Lakaya with a mission that was central to our work in Tiahuanaco. We planned to propose an experiment to the townspeople to reintroduce them to an ancient way of increasing crop production in their ravaged fields. After years of research, we had realized that raised fields were the secret to Tiahuanaco's remarkable longevity and economic success. For over eight hundred years, the ancients sustained opulent cities in a landscape that today barely supports a few thousand hardscrabble farmers living on the razor-thin edge of survival. Our archaeological research showed that Native American populations in the Lake Titicaca basin were better off prior to the sixteenth-century European conquest of the region than they are today.

To fully understand the Tiahuanaco empire's prolonged economic success, we had to experimentally re-create the techniques and conditions of ancient Tiahuanaco agriculture. The ancients had hit upon a remarkable form of highly productive, yet sustainable, agriculture. Most likely, they had invented raised-field agriculture through years of trial-and-error experimentation, constantly trying to reclaim the swamplands along the shores of Lake Titicaca. After hundreds of years of cumulative, hands-on experience, they developed one of the most sophisticated forms of hydraulic agriculture known to the preindustrial world. Putting the ancient fields back to work was the only way to determine just how productive the system was, and how many people raised-field agriculture could support in the unpromising conditions of the altiplano.

Years before, in early September of 1982, Oswaldo and I had ventured out to the small village of Chokara, in our first attempt to promote raised-field agriculture as a "new" solution to the age-old problem of making a living on the altiplano. But this earlier attempt could not have been more poorly timed. Our arrival in Chokara coincided with the onset of one of the worst droughts in the altiplano in the past forty years. The farmers of the altiplano fear a lingering drought more than any other single natural disaster. Local history tells a tragic story of the catastrophic effects of chronic drought; more than once the altiplano has been transformed into a virtual desert, incapable of supporting large, concentrated human populations.

Normally, rain falls sporadically in the altiplano during the month of September, when many communities begin to plant. This early rainfall, a precursor to the torrential downpours that begin in earnest in December, is critical for the healthy germination of seeds. But in the fall of 1982, the sky was cloudless. The omens and auguries of August had signaled a bad agricultural year, and now the yatiri's predictions were coming disastrously true.

Not realizing the ominous predictions for the planting season, Oswaldo and I stood on the high, wind-raked ridge above Chokara with the leaders of several families, looking out across a spectacular land tatooed to the horizon with ancient raised fields. We enthusiastically proposed that they excavate the dense sod clogging the ancient canals of the raised fields, reconstruct the elevated planting beds, and then fill the canals with water from the springs that gushed out below the village. In return for their labor, we would provide them with seed potatoes and some inexpensive hand tools—mattocks, shovels, and wheelbarrows. Oswaldo and I naively conjured images of a verdant landscape of corrugated fields crowned by ripening grain come January.

As the wind whipped dry soil into the air from the pampas below, the people of Chokara expressed their skepticism. They liked our idea of donating seeds and tools to the community, and were happily prepared to accept this. But they were decidedly cool to the prospect of the hard labor that would be needed to work the heavy clays of the pampas in an area they had never used for farming. Even worse was the necessity of diverting scarce water to fill the canals permanently.

An elder of the community who seemed slightly drunk angrily declared: "That is virgin land. Land that has never seen the sun before. If we open it up, we will have many problems with Lady Earth. No, that land should not be touched. It is for our cattle and that's all. Tell these outsiders to get out, leave us alone! What do they really want here anyway? Maybe the *wiracochas* [white-skinned outsiders] are bringing us this drought."

As if on cue, others began to chime in with hostile comments and more than vaguely threatening questions. We suddenly found ourselves defending our motives, denying accusations that we were really government officials or maybe fronts for private investors who wanted the peasants' lands for their own purposes.

As Oswaldo and I fielded the angry questions of the people of Chokara, I recalled that once in the altiplano I had been stoned by a farmer who didn't appreciate an outsider walking unannounced across his land. Then the odds were one to one, and I managed to retreat. But here the odds of survival if things truly got out of hand seemed hopeless. We were outnumbered, and our only means of escape was a rag-top Russian jeep with no door locks, a cracked windshield, bald tires, and a disturbing habit of stalling out at critical moments. To make matters worse, we were standing near an old cemetery studded with rock cairn grave markers. Any single stone would be enough to crush a gringo's skull.

I was cursing myself for not having had the foresight to bring Cesar along for this first attempt to restore Tiahuanaco's raised fields. He had saved us before from problems just as explosive as these. Now we were on our own. With outward calm, Oswaldo turned back to the the crowd, which was becoming more agitated, and began to speak.

"Brothers, you misunderstand what we are saying. We do not want your land. Remember that we worked together here just last year. Over there, out by the Katari River? Do you remember that we came to study the ancestors? You worked with us side-by-side. You know that I have a *compadre* here. Sixto Quipse. You all know Sixto. Go ask him about me. He will tell you I've come here for many years to work with you.

He will remind you that I sponsored the school in Korila. Your children go to school there. You must remember that Doctor Alan and I were sponsors; we donated desks and books, don't you remember any of this? Come. Let's go look for Sixto together. He will speak for me."

Oswaldo's speech was brilliant; everyone began to calm down as they thought about Sixto and the school. Oswaldo threw me the keys to the jeep and I opened up the back, motioning to the leaders of the group to get in. They began to demur. Some said they needed to tend to their cattle. Others said they had work to do in their fields.

Oswaldo calmly remarked:

"Well, it looks as if you have more important things to do right now. The Doctor and I will have to return to the city soon. But we promise to come back next week to talk about this again. We'll meet with the people of Korila, too. I think when you have time to think about this you will agree with us. But discuss this among yourselves. We'll come back for your decision."

We beat a hasty retreat. Later that night, in La Paz, I asked Oswaldo how close he thought we had come to serious trouble on the ridge above Chokara. As eternally optimistic and trusting of people as Oswaldo was, I didn't expect him to reply with such gravity. "I thought they were going to stone us," he said. "We were very lucky today."

Four years later, in Lakaya, we finally made a second attempt to get an Aymara community to restore the old Tiahuanaco fields to production. The Lake Titicaca drought had dragged on through 1983 and into 1984, and then the floods hit unexpectedly in 1985. The effects were as though the locusts of Pharaoh's Egypt had been loosed on the land. Finally, by mid 1986, when the flood had begun to subside, we had our first real chance after Chokara to try again. We were nothing if not persistent.

I had learned much about diplomacy among the Aymara in the intervening years, and felt much better prepared to make our case. But even so, with the memory of drought and floods so recent in the minds of the Aymara (natural disasters that they believed could be caused by the presence of outsiders), the debate was not going to be an easy one. Foot-dragging, disinformation campaigns, prevarication, and brinksmanship are common negotiating techniques among the Aymara. All too often these machinations, worthy of Machiavelli's Prince, devolve into a paralysis of will and action. More than anything else, bitter internecine squabbles, most with convoluted local histories, debilitate these Aymara communities; at times, they seem incapable of making any collective decision at all, much less of taking action for the common good. During the course of my years with the Aymara, I have witnessed many times the perverse effects of personal jealousies and the fear on the part of some that the benefits of a community undertaking would not be equally distributed. These internecine quarrels and fears destroyed many projects that had the potential to help lift rural Aymara communities from their abject poverty. Centuries of social and cultural repression, race and class prejudice, lack of economic and educational opportunity, all these and more took a savage toll on the Aymara psyche. They had been forced to live in a Hobbesian world, in constant tension between the desire for individual security and gain and the promotion of the common good.

With a better appreciation of the sensitivity of the proposal we wanted to make in Lakaya, I was determined to elicit the support of one of the community's most respected members: Cosme Uruchi. Oswaldo and I asked Cosme and the other leaders of Lakaya to arrange a meeting for us with the community, where we would make our best pitch about the merits of the raised field experiment. Our meeting took place in one of the lasting if incomplete glories of the revolution—the community schoolhouse. After the revolution, schoolrooms sprouted throughout the countryside and rural teachers, mostly of mestizo background, took up residence in the Aymara communities. The education offered by this system was poor at best, and many ill-paid teachers, stranded in remote rural hamlets, continued perpetuating racial myths of Indian inferiority. Still, it was education. Something, no matter how rudimentary, was better than nothing at all. Lakaya's schoolroom was typical. Its roof was corrugated tin. Its walls were decaying adobe, and its windows were cracked. In the afternoon, the bitter wind rising off the lake would whistle and moan past the cellophane tape seaming the glass together. Storms rattled the panes in their ill-fitting frames, loosening bits of dirty, rock-hard glazing compound with each violent thunderclap. Inside, several rows of plain, warped wooden benches and small clusters of tables and chairs faced a long blackboard occupying the length of one wall. Colored chalk dust filled the cracks in the gunmetal-gray cement floor. A huge, hopelessly out-of-date political map of Bolivia was strung from nails next to the national flag. There were no books, or bookshelves to hold them; lessons were taught by rote. But vivid posters—some standard government issue, others homemade—were plastered everywhere: *Cuidate! Lava las manos antes de comer* (Be Careful! Wash your hands before eating); *No al analfabetismo!* (No to illiteracy!); *Oprimido pero nunca vencido!* (Oppressed but never conquered!)

In contrast to the scant materials of the schoolhouse, we made use of an impressive array of visual displays for our presentation to the community: detailed topographic maps; low-altitude aerial photographs which revealed the massive sweep of ancient raised fields around Lakaya; and even a dramatic view of Lake Titicaca taken from a satellite, which captured in a single, vivid image the great mountain chains and vast, undulating grasslands encircling the deep, azure-colored waters of the lake.

Cesar rose and began a long eloquent monologue in

Aymara. I turned on my tape recorder to capture the debate that was about to ensue. I carried the tape recorder along to each of our formal encounters with Aymara communities. I wanted a permanent record of our exchanges to protect us from later fabrications or distortions of our words. Often, the communities would ask me for a copy of the tape for similar reasons and, most especially, to indelibly record any promises made. These tapes have become a precious personal record—an irreplaceable chronicle of my years on the altiplano. Although fragmentary, they still evoke a true sense of our evolving relationships with the Aymara.

Cesar, ever the consumate diplomat among his people, explained our proposition this way: "You know the wiracochas. Do you remember? We first came here eight years ago to dig the mounds. We have worked together often. We excavated the houses of our ancestors together. Now the wiracochas have a new project. They want you to open up *chakras* [agricultural fields] where you take your cattle to pasture. You all know the land how it rises and falls, like waves on the lake. The wiracochas have studied your land. In the nayra-pacha, our ancestors grew crops there. There were no cattle then, but our grandfathers grew potatoes and quinoa. All around here was a garden."

One of the Lakayans quickly broke into Cesar's monologue, saying: "Excuse me, brother. This land you speak of, we never plant there. Our grandfathers never planted there. It's much too wet, our potatoes would rot in those marshes." And so the debate began.

Cesar persisted in making our case: "But you see, hermanos, that is why we are here. To show you how you can grow potatoes on the lakeshore. Look at these photographs. Do you see all these swirling lines? These are the mounds on your pastureland that look like a washboard. Do you know what these are? They're *suka kollus* [the Aymara term for raised fields]. *Chakras* made by our ancestors. The mounds bring the plants up out of the water, do you see? The mounds keep the potatoes from rotting. The *suka umas*, the canals between the mounds, keep the soil moist, but not too moist. The mounds will give you good drainage. You will get very good harvests from these fields, just like our ancestors."

At that point, I jumped in: "Look here on this map. Do you see how many of these suka kollus were built in the past? Look. From the shore of the lake, from Huacullani, all the way out to the Rio Catari, and back over here to Cerro Catavi. We have these over in Tiahuanaco, and all the way to Jesus de Machaca. You know that we find suka kollus in Peru, too?"

As I talked, I pointed to these sites with a crooked stick on the topographic map that we had pinned up over the blackboard. "Your ancestors made these. They harvested potato and quinoa and tarwi from these suka kollus. They were rich in the past, you see. They ate well because of these suka kollus. But today, look, your harvests are really poor, aren't they? Every year your soil erodes away, right down the hillside. You have to move these fields every few years, isn't that true? You have to let your chakras rest. Why is that? Because your soil doesn't hold nutrients. But even if you plant your potatoes you might lose them because of the frosts. But the suka kollus will protect your crops from frost."

Despite my promises of plentiful produce, the crowd remained gravely skeptical. Then one of the younger members of Cosme's family voiced their worries eloquently. Anacleto Uruchi was only in his thirties, but he was already a well-respected leader of the community. He argued that what Lakaya really needed was state-of-the-art farming equipment and fertilizers, and insisted that the community must demand these things from the government. Agricultural extension agents rarely came through Lakaya, and the villagers had no access to credit that would permit them to upgrade their equipment and production techniques. At the same time, they saw that the larger agricultural cooperatives with sufficient cash to buy fertilizer could extract considerably higher yields from the same area of land than they could. The natural conclusion was that what Lakaya lacked was modern techniques and agrochemicals, and that the solution to their poverty was to agitate for these services from the government.

Anacleto saw us as an impediment to his people's progress, rather than as promoters of their economic welfare. Here we were, proposing that the people of Lakaya experiment with an ancient form of agriculture, rather than trying to help them gain access to what they perceived as modern techniques of cultivation. We were making claims that they could get much larger yields using raised-field agriculture, without the application of chemical fertilizers. We were asking the people of Lakaya to return to the past rather than aggressively move into the future.

For Anacleto, raised fields were pure fantasy. His people would have to invest an enormous amount of labor to get the raised fields working again, and without fertilizers, he argued, the yields would probably be just as low as on their fields on the stony hillsides. If truth be told, we weren't ourselves absolutely certain that the raised fields would perform as well as we were promising. We were just speculating, making conjectures. Reasonable conjectures, perhaps, but conjectures nonetheless.

We were once again losing the interest of the community, and we were forced to resort to a bargain I did not want to make. We agreed to give the community food as compensation for their work if they would attempt the experiment. For every month they worked with us we would give them flour, cooking oil, and sugar. The community leaders would keep lists of everyone who worked, and, after every twenty days, we would give each worker an allotment. This way, we explained, they took no risks by participating. If they worked with us, even if the suka kollus didn't produce a single plant, they would be given food, so their work would not be in vain. And, if the suka kollus really did work as we hoped they would, they would also get the benefits of the harvest.

I had tried to avoid making this agreement because I

feared that on these terms our project would appear to be yet another concept imposed and paid for from outside the community, rather than a true grassroots initiative managed by the Aymara Indians themselves. The only way for raised fields to function again in a way that would contribute to the long-term economic well-being of the communities would be if the people themselves understood the advantages of the system, if they perceived the benefits that would flow from its own merits, and not simply from the money and food that were temporarily attached to it from outsiders. But we had run out of other options, and I desperately wanted to get the project underway.

Our offers threw the meeting into a raucous free-for-all of opposing views and passionate arguments. Then, suddenly, Cosme Uruchi stood up and solemnly declared: "Doctor, you can do this on my land. My family will help you. We will make your suka kollus. Give us your seed and your tools and we will begin."

I had not expected that Cosme would speak to me directly in such a meeting. I assumed he would want to keep me at arm's length and discuss the entire matter in Aymara with Cesar and Oswaldo. In a state of surprise, I managed to blurt out only the single-word response, "When?" Cosme simply replied, "Tomorrow."

Then Cosme asked the community assembly for the floor. Rising slowly from his chair, he began a rapid monologue in Aymara. He spoke with such speed that Oswaldo and I could barely understand a few words, and these few were rare and isolated, like the tips of icebergs in an otherwise impenetrable sea. I saw that even Cesar was straining to absorb all the nuances. Later I asked him to translate the gist of Cosme's words so that I had a better idea of what had transpired.

Cosme first addressed the principal families of Lakaya, reminding them that they were all "brothers and sisters." He said directly to them: "We share the same blood, this same blood we have shed together." He recounted some of their experiences from the time of the agrarian reform, when the communities first secured title to their lands, to their present struggles to make a living from their tiny plots. He recited the litany of problems familiar to them all: frost, hail, drought, and floods; lack of tractors, and lack of fertilizers, lack of credit. But then Cosme veered off in another direction: "Hermanos, we all know these problems. But our biggest problem is lack of faith. Without faith, we cannot have hope. Our children are leaving us. Only the old people till the land now. Only the old people sacrifice to Lady Earth. Even they are forgetting our debts, our obligations. This is why our crops are failing. We must bring our childen back to the land; they must learn to honor Lady Earth. This is something we can do with our own hands right now. But we must ask for Lady Earth's blessings, so that we may open the land and expose it to the sun. If the coca sorteo is auspicious, let us try this year. If these suka kollus do not produce potatoes for us, we will have lost nothing; at least we will have been paid in food. So, brothers and sisters, let us cast the coca and decide."

With that, Cosme sat back down. While Cosme spoke, the entire room had fallen silent and attentive, except for a few whispered conversations in the back. Now everyone began talking at once.

Cesar finally managed to focus the crowd's attention on him. "Brothers, sisters, you have listened to Tata [father] Cosme. You have heard his opinion about this matter. He offers to work on his own lands. Do you agree with him? Do you want to participate too? Let us cast the coca now. Here, we will bring the coca and beer. Tito, go get us the coca. Who among you will cast the coca? Do you have a specialist here who will do this?"

Cesar, deftly exploiting Cosme's own words, was quickly bringing the issue to a head. He produced a fresh bag of coca leaf that we had brought from Tiahuanaco, and held it up before the crowd.

"Look," he said, "here is the coca, and here we have the beer. Who will cast the coca?"

The crowd was leaderless for a moment. No one knew exactly how to respond, and, for awhile, we all milled around. Finally Tomas Uruchi, one of Cosme's nephews, stood up and said, "My uncle is right. Let us cast the coca and see if we should do this."

With that Tomas asked his wife to spread her awayo on the floor of the school room. He began to cast the leaves repeatedly onto the worn, brown blanket. Tomas gave a running commentary on the way the leaves fell in clusters or singly onto the awayo. Each configuration of fallen leaves was distinct. Yet cumulatively, after repeated throws, the coca revealed, not quite the future outcome of a projected course of action, but rather the sense of luck or foreboding that attached to that action. It was a way of divining what was auspicious and what was not, as if the coca registered the Aymara equivalent of the petitioners' karma, the spiritual condition of their souls that would influence future actions. Divination with coca leaves revealed the balance between the strengths and weaknesses, the harmony and discord of the soul.

Divination and the taking of oracles is a practice as old as humankind. In the ancient Andean world, divinatory actions took many forms, of which the casting of coca leaf was one; the reading of llama and guinea pig entrails and induced hallucinatory trances were others. The reading of coca leaves is an ambiguous, open-ended proposition. No one can compel the leaves to fall in a particular way. Human manipulation of divine chance seems limited. Still, I got the distinct feeling that Tomas would reveal that the coca gave its imprimatur to our proposal—which was, in fact, precisely the result.

I believe that Cosme's speech in favor of restoring the raised fields was what compelled Tomas to give a positive reading to the coca he had cast. What was important to the Aymara was the social relationships among the witnesses to the divination. Once the consensus of the community was

intuited by the diviners, the prognostication became a valida-
tion rather than a prediction. The coca leaves imparted ancestral and divine approval to this consensus.

Because of Cosme's special status and history in Lakaya,
particularly his epochal role in the revolution, his words carried extraordinary weight within the community. With so
many intimate, interlocking relationships in Lakaya, Cosme
enjoyed the privileges of hard-earned authority. But this was
no imperious, absolute authority; royalty, divine right, and
the last Aymara kings disappeared one thousand years ago
with the empire of Tiahuanaco. Cosme's authority was more
indirect, personal, familial—the kind of authority that comes
from living a long life in a small, rural world where shared
responsibilities, daily communication, and mutual aid are
virtues of necessity.

So it was decided that the Lakayans would supply the
labor necessary to reconstruct, plant, maintain, and harvest
the raised fields. In return for their labor, they would receive
tools, seed, a monthly allotment of food, and, of course, the
fruits of the harvest. Cesar later told me with a shrug and a
laugh that the people of Lakaya envisioned fields of blackened, frost-stricken stalks, rotted to mush.

We had assembled a parcel of about ten acres for our
experiment. Our agreement with Cosme and the extended
Uruchi clan was to begin work immediately. We did our part
as quickly as we could: acquiring seed, buying new picks, mattocks, and shovels, and negotiating for the donation of flour,
oil, and sugar from Caritas, the Catholic relief agency, for our
food-for-work program. Within a short time we had rented
storerooms in Lakaya and filled them to capacity with our
provisions. For several days running, we returned to Lakaya to
iron out the details of the project. Cosme, Tomas, and Anacleto gave us a list of laborers who would begin the restoration of the ancient fields. I noticed that over sixty of the nearly
ninety people on the list carried the name Uruchi. Like classic
machine politicians in Chicago, Cosme was doling out patron-

age, rewarding his immediate family with jobs. I was taken aback for a moment and felt rather uneasy about the list. Although nepotism was considered normal, and even a moral obligation among the Aymara, it did not lessen the festering resentment among those left outside the chosen circle.

The potential for undisguised hostility and even covert actions against the project was high. Again I rationalized the problem as one that was, in truth, unavoidable. With our modest cash flow, we simply could not employ everyone in Lakaya. Even if we had the impulse to try, we could not force Western concepts of fairness, equal opportunity, and participatory democracy on the community. In the family-dominated, face-to-face world of the rural Aymara villages, such abstruse notions are virtually meaningless. The Aymara have their own sense of democracy, one centered around the universe of kin and neighbors, not on the abstraction of "universal citizenship."

By mid-July we seemed poised to take off. Everything was ready: supplies, people, land. We set several dates to inaugurate the work, but each time the community called it off. First Anacleto and Tomas had to attend a meeting of provincial leaders of the peasant's union. Then, badgered by their schoolteacher (an embittered ex-Communist party activist who loathed us and feared our intrusion into "his" village), the community decided repairs to the school were their first priority. By early August, work on restoring the fields was deferred again for a series of local and national holidays: Dia del Indio (August 3), National Independence Day (August 6), Feast of the Assumption of the Virgin (August 8). Religion and politics seemed to be conspiring against us.

In fact, unknown to us at the time, from the moment we had struck the agreement with the village on the day of the solstice, the people of Lakaya were embroiled in a furious, private debate about us and our project. Although written into the village records, our accord seemed to have little legal weight, and was, by no means, a done deal. It was a hard fact suspended in a social limbo of conflicting opinions. In fact, the contract itself became the catalyst for renewing long-simmering conflicts within the community. The deep memories of old insults, assaults, thefts, and adulteries welled up and irrupted. We became the crux, the convenient emotional touchstone, of old family feuds.

I should have known better. I cannot remember all of the times that we had come to apparent rock-solid agreements with villages, only to have our fondest notions of the sanctity of contracts unceremoniously overturned. In the high plateau, such agreements have a short half-life. They are like unstable isotopes, undergoing constant, spontaneous mutations.

We had both strong advocates and bitter opponents within Lakaya. The intensity of the feeling was what I failed to appreciate; one clash between the sides devolved into a drunken free-for-all. While this debate raged beneath the placid surface of Lakaya, Oswaldo, Cesar, and I constantly returned throughout August, trying to negotiate new starting dates for the work. We appealed to Cosme to use his influence. Each time he agreed, but nothing seemed to come of it.

Finally, as August grew to a close and the time for preparing the fields on the hill slopes was fast approaching, we called on Cosme with an ultimatum. We knew that if we allowed the work on restoring the raised fields to slip into September, we could forget our experiment for the rest of the year. There would be simply too little time for the villagers to add this extra burden to their daily routine. Their survival depended on caring for livestock and their traditional fields of subsistence crops, even if these fields failed often and barely provided a living. We could not ask them to risk substituting the unknown quantity of raised fields for the dry-farmed plots of land they had cultivated for generations. High risk–high return was not an acceptable strategy to the rural Aymara with whom we worked, especially when the "high return" end of the equation was based on the assurances of a couple of q'ara archaeologists, who hadn't grown a single potato in their lives.

As we stood with Cosme Uruchi that day, high in the fields above Lakaya, the same raking light that illuminated the deep creases of Cosme's face brought the corrugated landscape of ancient raised fields into sharp relief. They looked incredible, like massive, rolling waves of earth trailing off to the horizon. Even I found it difficult to believe that we were looking at a completely man-made landscape. Every landform around us bore the distinctive spoor of humans. The wrinkled pampas of raised fields, the artificial, straight-rule course of diverted rivers, the eroding steps of ancient terraces—from the bottom of rivers to the tops of the mountains, everything was transformed by man. Over the ages, the environmental impact of humans here was, in a word, total.

We challenged Cosme to explain the delays, and finally he began to reveal the community's misgivings. "Doctor, *Ingeniero*, it's true we've had some problems. The people in Lakaya Baja don't trust you. [Lakaya was divided into two sectors: upper—*alta*—and lower—*baja*.] They think its impossible to grow anything on the pampas. But you know what they've been saying, what they really believe? They think you are looking for gold. They reminded everyone that last year you were here digging in the *kontus* [archaeological mounds] and taking away pots. They said that in the night you secretly took away gold and silver. I tried to tell people that wasn't true, but some believe what they say."

This was a familiar story for Oswaldo and me. Our archaeological excavations never failed to attract the suspicions of some communities. They feared opening up the ancient tombs, but they were also intensely jealous of the imagined wealth inside. We had found substantial amounts of gold and other precious objects in our excavations in Tiahuanaco. This had only fueled rumors throughout Aymara country. In fact, we rarely found truly valuable artifacts outside the confines of Tiahuanaco's ancient cities, but perceptions and rumor were more powerful than reality.

Faced once again with community resistance, and at the

limit of our patience, we decided to use a hard-line negotiating ploy. We responded to Cosme by saying that we were sorely disappointed, but that we would have to move on to another community at this point in order to be sure that we could get the experiment underway before the planting season ended. We told him that we had explored the possibility of conducting the experiment in another village. I could see that our hardened stance had an impact on Cosme. He looked surprised and a bit concerned. The thought that we could switch communities probably hadn't occurred to Cosme. I wondered if he was worried that he would lose face in Lakaya, or if he was thinking about the jobs, seeds, tools, and food for the community. We turned to pick our way back down the road. Cosme remained, looking pensive. I gave him a final wave from the road and called back over my shoulder: "We'll be back tomorrow, Don Cosme, around noon." With that we left him standing in the growing shadows settling onto the hill slopes.

The next day, we traveled to Lakaya one last time to see what the impact of our threat to pull our project out of the town had been. When we arrived, we were greeted by a large assembly of the community. Cosme made no mention of our decision to move the project, but simply announced that the community leaders had met the night before and that work would begin that Monday.

It was a miracle that any decision was ever made. Still, the Aymara knew that they had to work together. Under their unforgiving social and environmental circumstances, they needed each other to survive. But they were wary of being taken advantage of by their neighbors—as much as by outsiders. Just as for their distant ancestors, reciprocity and mutual aid were social goods: You help me bring in the harvest on my fields, I'll help you on yours. But reciprocity here was not born of an ethic of social harmony alone; it was a pragmatic transaction, carefully tracked, measured, recorded, and balanced. No person wished to give more than he or she got in return—either directly, in equivalent amount of work, or indirectly, in prestige, status, and standing in the community. All negotiations became a tortuous exercise of balancing power, competing desires, and potential outcomes. But now, after all the indecision and squabbling, and without fully appreciating the portent of the work they were about to undertake, the people of Lakaya were ready to embark on a process of recapturing the ancient wisdom that had been lost to their people for a thousand years.

Although we were personally convinced of the productivity of the raised fields, we didn't yet have empirical evidence of how productive they would be when restored. I was reluctant to make too many promises to the Lakayans about the outcome of the experiment. But Oswaldo was never one to permit his passionate commitment to causes to be constrained by the cautious temperament of science. That day he sensed the need to strengthen the commitment of the community. In order to bolster their enthusiasm for the project, he addressed the gathering by describing the raised fields as a new green revolution for the altiplano, but one that would be sustained without damaging the environment with pesticides and petrochemicals. With a sweep of his hand against the horizon, he gestured towards the great landscape of long-abandoned raised fields. He revealed his dream of revivifying the entire ancient ecology of raised fields and restoring the marshlands to production again. I had always intensely admired Oswaldo's commitment to helping the rural Aymara communities of his homeland. His passion and commitment to Bolivia and, most especially to the Aymara, were incredible. Yet I worried that his vision might become mere hype, a beautiful but hollow promise. Until the people of Lakaya actually began to put picks into the earth to clean the old canals and to restore the ancient fields, I would remain skeptical.

When we returned the next Monday we found a full complement of workers waiting impatiently for us. They were anxious to begin, and a few had even begun to scratch tentatively at the earth before we arrived. Fortunately for us, there was considerable confusion among them. They really didn't know where to begin, since they didn't yet have a clue how a raised field was supposed to look.

Depending on local conditions, the ancient fields varied considerably in size and complexity. Field platforms ranged from three to ten meters in width, and some were hundreds of meters long. The canals, too, took on different forms and dimensions depending on the source of their water and their position in the complex hierarchy of primary, secondary, and tertiary channels that fed distinct sectors of the pampa. In Tiahuanaco times, the entire artificial landscape of fields and canals was knitted ingeniously together into a complicated, regionwide system of hydraulic agriculture. For the moment, though, our ambitions were more modest. The ten-acre area that we had selected with Cosme contained abandoned raised fields that were among the best preserved in the entire Lake Titicaca basin. Field platforms still stood a meter or more tall, and the outlines of the ancient canals were clearly graven on the surface of the land. Our only difficult decision was to estimate how deep to cut the canals and how high to mound the excavated soil on the adjoining platforms. From our archaeological excavations, we had a reasonably clear idea of the dimensions and contours of the original raised fields. I quickly sketched an idealized "blueprint" of the fields, complete with approximate dimensions, on a piece of paper. This sketch became the model from which the leaders of the crews worked.

Cosme had divided the workers into twelve crews. He assigned each crew a specific segment of the ancient field system for restoration. With proper coordination, this segmentary division of labor was a remarkably efficient technique. It was also an ancient device for organizing labor in the Andes. Archaeological sites on the central coast of Peru dating back to the second millennium B.C. exhibit telltale evidence of segmentary labor. Soaring walls of rubble fill and masonry were

divided into distinct vertical segments. Each segment represents the product of an individual work gang working side by
side with other gangs. By the fourth and fifth centuries A.D.,
segmentary wall construction had become the norm in the
great adobe brick temples of the legendary Moche kingdoms
on the north coast of Peru. The social implication of this
construction pattern is clear. Each vertical stack of adobe
bricks was the product of a specific work gang, most likely an
ayllu, village, or some other distinct social group. These social
groups paid their mit'a obligation, the labor tax, to their
overlords by fabricating the adobe bricks and constructing
designated segments of the Moche temples. Subsequently,
the Inca used similar methods for organizing and tracking the
progress of their construction crews.

Cosme's segmentary division of labor was a contemporary
adaptation of an ancient pattern familiar to any native of the
high plateau. One advantage of this form of labor became
clear that first day as we began the experiment to restore
Tiahuanaco's raised fields. After we shared an obligatory toast
to Lady Earth, and a simple meal of *q'ispiña* (quinoa bread),
fried eggs, rice, and ch'uño, the restoration work began under
our direction. As the crews worked, they talked constantly and
called out back and forth to each other. Occasionally, peals of
laughter rang out, especially from the young women wielding
heavy mattocks who were working hard, shoulder to shoulder
with the men. It wasn't long before I realized that shameless
flirtation and bawdy stories were the source of most of the
laughter. The crews were competing with each other to tell
the funniest and slyest stories with the most clever double
entendres. Cesar translated the rich nuances of Aymara for
me. Within minutes I, too, was laughing, even if my grasp of
the stories was imperfect. The gist of the jokes was enough,
and some of the crew members were great comedic actors;
their exaggerated gestures and pantomime were hilarious and
made certain intentions perfectly clear, even to a gringo. As
the day wore on, the stories became more explicit and the

flirtation became more obvious. Although good cheer prevailed, I could sense a subtle shift in mood. The competition among the work crews had become serious. The good-natured banter took on a slightly acerbic edge, a sharpness I hadn't noticed before. The crews began to measure the amount of work that each group had accomplished. Verbal sparring was now accompanied by out-and-out competition to see which crew would complete their designated segment first. Cosme became a kind of coxswain of the whole operation: exhorting all the crews to work hard, comparing their progress, keeping the verbal challenges from escalating out of control. It was astonishing to watch. Just when I thought they ought to be exhausted from hacking and shoveling through the heavy sod of the pampas, the tempo of the work gangs picked up.

Cosme's brand of managed competition was working wonders. Huge amounts of work were completed in a relatively short time with this informal system of friendly competition. I noticed that the competition expanded from gauging the amount of work each crew was doing to the quality of the work as well. Crew chiefs became extremely conscious of how closely their restored raised fields corresponded to the sketch I had provided them. They were particularly interested in creating aesthetically pleasing raised-field patterns. Beauty, especially the transcendent beauty of a manicured field, and the impeccable performance of creative work was important to them.

The planting surfaces of the raised fields were restored by stacking a few courses of cut sod blocks (called *tepes*) along the two long sides of the projected platforms. Then rich organic soil from the ancient, silted-in canals was piled between these side walls of sod onto the old eroded platform surfaces. The sod blocks stabilized the edges of the planting surface, and permitted the creation of crisp, beautifully contoured planting surfaces. As the restored raised fields took form, the crews would often step back and critique their own

239

work, frequently consulting with me, Oswaldo, or Cesar. They began to take a real intellectual interest in the project to restore their ancestors' forgotten agricultural system. Often, they expressed their own opinions and offered their own solutions to construction problems. Even if they were still skeptical about the final outcome of the project, they had become fascinated with the raised fields.

By the end of September, the people of Lakaya had managed to reconstruct nearly five acres of ancient fields. We had an equivalent area to restore before planting, which we now planned for late October. We were slightly behind the original schedule which Oswaldo and I had formulated back in La Paz. Still, I was content; given the difficulties of introducing radically different methods to native farmers, our experiment was on a remarkably fast track.

Throughout early October, we planned the logistics of planting our restored fields. But the week before planting, an unforeseen complication threatened to undermine the entire project. We had contracted to buy seed stock of several potato varieties that was certified to be disease- and fungus-free. But when we took delivery of the seed, we discovered that nearly thirty percent of the stock was infected with a bacterium that carries the daunting scientific name of *Erwinia carotovora*. The common name for this bacterium ought to be simply "rot," since this is its devastating effect on potato tubers. Instead of healthy seed, we had, in effect, purchased tons of useless potato mush.

Of course, we complained to the vendor, who expressed "shock" and "total surprise" at the condition of the seed stock which, he assured us, had been in perfect condition. Eventually, over howls of protest, we wrested our money back by threatening legal action (and a retaliatory publicity campaign in the newspapers). But we were now faced with the problem of acquiring high-quality seed from someplace else before our promised distribution in Lakaya. Our credibility was again squarely on the line. We had to move fast.

Through a series of contacts with government officials in the Ministry of Agriculture, Oswaldo identified a new source of certified potato seed in Puno, just across the border in Peru. Through some miracle, he managed to extract the necessary customs documents and agricultural clearances in record time. We sent our agronomists in our tired old truck with sagging springs over the border. After two days, they returned to Tiahuanaco with our precious cargo—which, to our relief, was disease-free.

The following day we were on our way to Lakaya, laden with seed. We made a triumphal entry into the plaza, and then threw back the heavy olive green tarpaulin covering the seed. I grabbed some off the back and held it up for Cosme to admire. Cosme and the other crew chiefs inspected the seed, then smiled and nodded in approval.

We distributed the seed to the participating crews right there in the middle of the plaza. I insisted that everything in our experiment to restore the raised fields be done publicly. Predictably, the distribution of the seed potatoes attracted an unusually large crowd, many of whom had seen us arrive from distant fields on the mountain slopes and had walked down to the village to see what was happening. I sought notoriety to insure that everything we did was transparent to the community. I wanted to reduce the probability of accusations from hostile villagers that we had made secret agreements against the will of the community or that we were involved in dark conspiracies.

I had another motive as well. I wanted to attract the hardcore skeptics in the community. I wanted them to observe all our activities, to lure them into interacting with us. This way, if the restored raised fields actually did produce rich harvests as we were projecting based on our archaeological research, our toughest critics would have witnessed it firsthand. We would win over all but the most implacable enemies.

Our success with Lakaya was critical to the entire future of a larger plan for restoring the raised fields system. We wanted to bring the system back to a large territory, not just to one tiny village on the edge of Lake Titicaca. News travels like wildfire in the altiplano, jumping rapidly from one community to the next, so that even the most isolated hamlet is privy to distant goings-on in a matter of days, if not hours. By the early 1980s, Aymara-language radio stations had sprung up throughout the altiplano, accelerating this process of transmission so that it is now virtually instantaneous. The rural Aymara villages are linked in an amazingly efficient altiplano-wide web of gossip, stories, and hard news. Openness was our best and, pragmatically speaking, our only sensible option.

Cesar organized an efficient accounting system to keep track of the seed distribution. Each crew chief signed a receipt for his or her portion of the seed. Then Oswaldo, Cosme, and the other principal leaders of Lakaya countersigned. We made two copies of each document: one for us, and the other to be appended to the community's permanent records. In the end, we toasted each other, and with great solemnity, made our libations to Lady Earth, and, most especially to Lakaya's own wakas and achachilas. We implored them to look with favor on our fields, to bless them, to make them productive. The stage was set for the next important event: the planting ceremony. Before leaving Lakaya with our now empty truck, we set October 28 as the date for the communal ceremony.

Oswaldo had invited the press and half the diplomatic corps to the ceremony. I disagreed with him about this, thinking it was premature for us to expose our experiment to such publicity. I was worried that we would inflate expectations well beyond our capacity to deliver, and the fragile experimental edifice we had so painstakingly contructed would come crashing down around us. But Oswaldo was determined. I conceded on this issue even though my misgivings lingered for days.

In the end, Oswaldo's intuition to publicize our restored

raised fields right from the start proved both shrewd and lucky. We arrived in Lakaya early in the morning to find Cosme and the community already mobilized. They had set up a series of three *arcos*, arched frameworks of wooden poles swathed in colorful, aniline-dyed textiles, leading down from the main plaza to the raised fields. Each archway had its own color scheme and sported whipalas, multicolored pennants, and Bolivian flags snapping in the chill wind.

The arcos always reminded me of the centrality of ritual portals, of points of spatial and temporal transition in Aymara thought and perception. The arcos were never erected at random; their precise location was divined to ensure good luck and prosperity. They are an Aymara form of geomancy. With them the yatiri take the pulse of the life forces that course through the physical world. The ritual portals are sited to capture, or perhaps better said, channel the flow of natural, procreative energy in the earth. With them the Aymara strengthen their human-created agricultural landscapes, to ensure their fertility. Of course, sacred portals associated with agricultural abundance are not a recent phenomenon in the religious thought of the Aymara. We need think back only to the monumental gateways and ritual portals of Tiahuanaco, oriented to the solar path, to realize that this concept is an exceptionally ancient and embedded one in the inhabitants of the high plateau. We changed status and states of mind as we passed under the arcos towards the raised fields. They were visual touchstones that reminded us that a special event would soon take place. They marked the field of the spirit, the bounded space to which we would soon call the ispallas, the avatars of the plants, imploring them to descend and infuse the seeds with their genesic energy.

Virtually the entire village of Lakaya, as well as many Aymara from neighboring villages, turned out for the ceremony. Within the hour we began the most important elements of the ceremony. Cosme was the principal officiant. He invited three fellow yatiri to help him perform the prayers and libations to the achachillas and wakas of the community. They quickly assembled four misas with the help of the crew chiefs. Oswaldo and I contributed layers of misterios, coca leaves, and cigarettes.

I always took a rich, sensual delight participating in the fabrication of the misas. Sight, sound, and smell were all piqued in the process of assembling the disparate elements of the misa. The yatiri carried the ritual offerings to the four quarters of the newly restored raised fields, doused them with alcohol, and, invoking the spirits of the plants, set them aflame. Placed on beds of dried dung, they burned furiously with a hot, blue flame for a few moments, then gradually subsided into charred masses. Four pillars of white smoke rising straight to the sky boded well: The spirits of the earth and sky would not fail to notice.

The band assembled for the ceremony immediately struck up a discordant, high-pitched tune—the song specific to the time of planting. (In seven months' time, they would return for the harvest song.) Spurred on by the music, lines of men began to hack furrows across the raised fields perpendicular to the canals. Groups of women followed closely behind with sacks of seed. They dropped the seed potatoes at regular intervals along the new furrows and quickly covered them over with soft earth. Then they moved to the next furrow.

Oswaldo and I waded into the middle, and with the video-tape camera of a La Paz television station rolling, planted our first potatoes in the restored fields. To see the glistening channels of blue water and the freshly mounded raised fields churning up a haze of dust from the impact of the mattocks was the culmination of a dream. The planting of the platforms proceeded rapidly. The first step in realizing our vision of restoring an ancient technology to production was complete.

With the planting complete, we sat on the ground to share the communal meal. The textiles laid on the earth were heaped with potatoes, ch'uño, and beans. Several men and women of the community, who turned out to be the crew chiefs of the raised-field restoration, were mounding enameled tin plates with huge chunks of roast pig and lamb, and passing them down the two lines of guests on either side of the table. I asked Cesar to distribute the beer and soda, but to hold back on the cane alcohol; I didn't want the occasion to devolve into a drunken melee. Everyone ate with great relish, although I managed to consume only half of a plate.

In late October, the altiplano seems at its most benign. Temperatures are mild and the extreme aridity of winter is forgotten. On the day of the planting, the sun was extraordinarily bright, but not unpleasant. By late afternoon, the glare of midday diffused into a more gentle, enveloping light. The plains all around us were suffused in tones of gold: yellow light reflecting off thatched roofs and dry stalks of barley in last year's fields. The sky was deep blue and the air was preternaturally clear. As I ate, I stared at the distant Cordillera. Every wrinkle and dark texture on the surface of the mountains seemed to stand out in high relief that day. Only the highest peaks were obscured behind a mist of airborne ice crystals pulverized by the winds. I felt the deep sense of awe and mystery every human feels when confronted with such unalloyed majesty. I wondered at the incomprehensible magnitude of the geological forces that thrust these immense fields of rock up from the earth's mantle.

After the aptapi, the band reassembled and began to play flute- and drum-driven music that inspired the Aymara to dance. For the Aymara, dancing is pleasure, but, then too, dancing is magical. At first, the men and women formed two opposing lines and danced with hands linked. All of the men wore wine-red wool ponchos with blue and black stripes. Yellow marigolds and fresh green leaves were tucked into the bands encircling their felt fedoras. Their hats were chocolate brown, and sweat-stained, forming the perfect dark ground against which the marigolds glowed like hot, orange coals. The marigolds were emblems of sympathetic magic, evoking the collective desire that the newly planted fields take on the flowers' beauty and vigor. The women wore multiple skirts, shimmering satin blouses, and pastel-colored shawls. A few of the younger, unmarried women wore elaborate chains of beads that fell from headbands provocatively obscuring their eyes, noses, and mouths. The colored curtains of beads swayed and vibrated to the dance, first revealing, then hiding the lustrous brown eyes behind the masks.

We clasped hands and danced in a sinuous, counterclockwise path around the newly planted fields. Their hands were strong, callused and as tough as rawhide. Shuttling back and forth, as if they were weaving a phantom textile on the ground, the women sang a high-pitched song of prayer. Their song invoked Lady Earth to take pity on them and charged the spirits of the plants to descend upon the fields. While they danced, they called down the ispallas, the spirits of the plants, begging them, cajoling them to infuse the plants with life. Roughly translated, the song they sang, repeated continuously with subtle variations, went like this:

> Come, come, come down here from wherever you are.
> These are your dominions, and here you must sit.
> You will come here from wherever you would rather be.
> Here you will sit, and here you will produce. You
> will not rest, you will not sleep. Be seated here.

The song reveals much. The invocation to Pachamama and the ispallas is both request and demand, a perfect inflection of the dynamics of Andean reciprocity. With our offering of the four misas, we had fed the earth. In the Aymara moral universe, the procreative forces of the earth now had an obligation to feed us, by ensuring that the newly planted crops would flourish. The cycle of reciprocity was demanding: a cycle of call and response that could not be broken. If, despite these invocations, a crop did fail, the Aymara look to themselves to see if some member of the community committed a secret sin, or if the offerings made to Lady Earth were insufficient in some way, not completely impeccable.

Our serpentine dance took us spiraling around the fields, again and again. From time to time, we paused to drink and to toast the wakas with small clusters of men who seemed intent on spilling devotional rivers of beer and cane alcohol on the ground. Then we were drawn back by the women again. We danced until dark, oblivious to the creeping chill of night. Finally, under hails of joking abuse from the women, we managed to pull ourselves away, exhausted. Just before midnight, we left Lakaya for the return trip to Tiahuanaco. The first, and most crucial phase of our experiment was over. As we climbed the mountain road behind Lakaya, an enormous, nearly full moon illuminated the pampas. We could see small bonfires still burning down below. The people of Lakaya continued to make magic, to dance and sing and drink to Lady Earth far into the night.

The next few months were a waiting game; time seemed to pass interminably as we anxiously watched for the plants to germinate and develop. We returned often to the fields to monitor growth, and to assure ourselves that the people of Lakaya were managing the fields well. My biggest fear was that, once planted, they would ignore maintaining the raised fields in favor of other activities. Once, we arrived to find the water in the raised-field canals dangerously low. We discovered that Cosme and Tomas had diverted the feeder canal, which was drawn from a local spring, in order to water some livestock. They didn't fully grasp that the water levels within the raised-field canals needed to be maintained in order to mitigate the impact of frost. After a long, difficult argument, we managed to convince them of this, and we never had that problem again in Lakaya. Everything was a process of learning, of rediscovering the secrets of the ancients. We were reinventing a wheel that was lost in antiquity: We had the basic blueprint in the form of the ancient abandoned fields, but the living, dynamic process of producing plants on those fields had been lost for many generations.

The rains fell generously that year; not too much, not too

little. Growing conditions were perfect. By early February, the raised fields were in full bloom. The visual impact of the growing crops in the pampas below the village was stunning. The plains surrounding the raised fields were covered with patches of unpromising, yellow-green grass and irregular pools of standing water. But the raised fields, rectilinear rows clad in intense emerald green, fairly burst with vitality.

During the festival of Candelaria (February 2) that year, I walked with Cosme through Lakaya's raised fields. In restoring the raised fields to production, we had, without fully realizing the environmental implications of our efforts, re-created a rich microecology of wetlands in plains that, over the past five hundred years, had been single-mindedly reduced to grazing grounds. The raised-field canals—once clear, running streams of water—had become murky incubators of aquatic life: water ferns, watercress, water milfoil, common weeds, blue-green and golden-brown algae, and exuberant stands of totora reeds. Thick mats of plants now colonized the canals, creating convenient islands for thousands of water walkers: black ibis with long, recurved beaks; tiny frogs and the occasional toad; long-legged insects skating insouciantly across the surface. Small fish, migrating in from Lake Titicaca, darted among the submerged plants which swayed gracefully to the rhythm of the slow currents below. Oxygen bubbles in long, continuous streams welled up from the bottom. The pungent, sulfuric smell of rotten eggs wafted about. Pollen and seeds, spores and microscopic eggs floated in the millions in ragged, hazy clumps on the open water of the canals, or swirled through the air on the slightest hint of a breeze. Pulsating warmth and light seemed to emanate from the raised fields themselves, as if the sun, not just its reflection, shone inverted from the canals.

The growing crops on the field platforms were shaggy and unkempt. We had intercropped quinoa and potato, cañawa, and tarwi. Only barley stood in nearly monospecific stands. Emerging lettuce and turnips, onions and beans hugged the ground. Along the edges of the fields, grass grew from the sod blocks that formed the field borders. Ducks and other shorebirds floated and bobbed on the canals. The whole impression was one of biological chaos, a riotous mosaic of irrepressible plants and animals, thriving in the richly organic microenvironment of the fields. This looked nothing like the precise, orderly rows of tall corn stretching to the horizon that I remembered from my childhood days on Wisconsin farms. Just across the last raised-field canal, the adjacent pastures appeared barren and still in comparison.

Candelaria was an important day. Around that time, the Aymara collect a few developing potatoes from their fields to examine them for their quality. They carefully place the immature tubers in the *tari*, a small woven bag used to hold ceremonial items, and bring them back to their houses. There they inspect them minutely, commenting on the number and placement of eyes, the texture of the skin, and the quality of their flesh. Then they perform libations and call to the ispallas of the potatoes so that, as a yatiri, Roberto Choque, once told me, the "potatoes will continue to solidify." According to Roberto, the "spirits of the ispallas are the spirits of the fields, the spirits of the harvest, the forces within the seeds of the edible plants." Roberto confided to me that these forces are so powerful that they could pull him into a trance when he reads the coca leaves. The forces of the ispallas flow through the shaman. The word "*ispa*" can mean twins; it also describes a large potato thought to be struck by lightning, which is then called a "potato with two faces."[1] The ispallas, shamans, twins, lightning bolts, and the proper growth of food crops are all cognitively entangled in the mind of the Aymara. These conceptual associations are never completely transparent to the outsider; they fold back one on the other, intermingle, and make curious leaps in apparent logic. They are part of the complex, ancient vision of the world that the Aymara still hold.

The procreative forces of the earth reside in these signs

and symbols and interpreters of the ispallas. Through them, these forces of life can be influenced. And so, during Candelaria, the Aymara take magical, ritual steps to ensure the health of the growing crops. Cosme and Tomas collected the immature tubers from our raised fields, and brought back several tari filled with them to Cosme's compound. There, with dozens of people milling about, we inspected them.

Everyone was astonished. The tubers we held in our hands were huge for their stage of development, much larger than those taken the same day from the dry-farmed fields on the hill slopes above Lakaya. All the potatoes from the raised fields seemed healthy, without signs of the pests and pathogens that plague the farmers of the high plateau. We saw no damage from fungus, aphids, or worms. Cosme cast coca leaves. All the auguries were positive. If conditions held, we could anticipate a tremendous harvest. We passed Candelaria and later Carnival in euphoria.

We tried to monitor the restored raised fields at least once a week. Each week the crops seemed to double in size. Barley, winter wheat, and oats were ripening, and the potato tubers beneath the ground were nearly mature. Splashes of crimson and gold painted the field borders where we had planted quinoa, as if a child had outlined the green fields with a bright, waxy crayon.

Toward the end of February, Oswaldo and I were in Tiahuanaco drawing up plans for the first harvest in early April. The logistics of gathering the harvest, weighing it, and distributing the produce among the various work crews was daunting. But on the morning of the twenty-seventh, we woke up to a winter wonderland that should not have been.

A hard, hard freeze had gripped the altiplano. I arose around 5:30, chilled to the marrow. As soon as I opened the door, I knew we had grave problems. On the mountains south of Tiahuanaco, I saw the fires burning. Smoke rose from a hundred columns. Up on the mountains, farmers desperately stoked their bonfires, trying fruitlessly to ward off the frost. Cesar came out into the courtyard. The look on his face confirmed what I already knew: Sajjra wiphina, the spirit of the frost, had descended, dragging his long, white hair over the earth. The old man must have been furious to strike so deeply with his sack of frozen lightning bolts. Snow covered the high peaks, and the ground was overlain with a filmy, crystalline lace of ice. Through my leather boots, I could feel the stiffness of the mud. Puddles had turned to ice, and Cesar's drums of drinking water were crusted over as if this were August, the dead of winter, and not the middle of summer. We later discovered that the temperature had dropped to 23°F. during the night.

We all shared hot coffee heavily laced with sugar, and then headed off to inspect the damage. My jeep refused to start. The battery was frozen and the intense cold had snapped a fuel line. We weren't going to make it over the mountains to Lakaya that day. Instead, Oswaldo and I took a walk through the ruins. As we passed by the decayed foundations of Tiahuanaco, we tried to convince ourselves that the frost was localized, and probably didn't extend much beyond the Tiahuanaco Valley. After all, Lakaya was nearer the shores of Lake Titicaca, where the deep reservoir of water moderated temperatures. We had just about concluded that our painstakingly restored raised fields would be fine when we took a turn through the potato and quinoa fields just outside the ruins.

The devastation was complete. Stalks of quinoa that had stood erect and taut now drooped as if sapped of life. The once-green leaves and dense seed heads were blackened. If it was possible, the potato plants were in a state of even greater ruination. The beans, tarwi, and oca were all damaged. Even the most resistant crops were affected, showing frost-burned leaves. As we walked the fields, my body felt leaden. For the first time, I had experienced something approaching the eternal anxiety—and now, the true despair—of the farmer. It looked as if all our efforts to restore the raised fields were in vain. It was clear from the blackened plants around us that this had been an unusually acute frost for midsummer. Like Oswaldo, I believed that the raised fields would protect crops from frost, but not one this bad. This one was a killer. Now, I thought all we could do was assess the damage in Lakaya, and try to put as positive a spin on the situation as we could with the community. We had made promises. In the teeth of this crisis, with their crops ravaged by the frost, the people of Lakaya would be waiting for us.

The frost had affected all of the altiplano, not just the Tiahuanaco Valley. There were already reports of major crop damage on the radio. Worse yet, the cold was going to linger for several days. The temperature was expected to plunge below freezing again during the night. There was nothing much to do.

Oswaldo and I talked into the night, replotting strategy, assuring each other that we would continue with the raised field restoration experiment no matter what the situation was in Lakaya. The cold seeping through the windows and under the door finally drove us to our sleeping bags. Even though I wore silk underwear, a woolen sweater, and a knit hat inside my mummy bag, it was not enough to ward off the cold immediately. I spent the first half hour shivering in my bed. Around two or three in the morning, the Old Man, Sajjra wiphina, visited us again.

The trip over the mountains to Lakaya the next morning was shocking. The two nights of hard freeze shriveled and blackened the green mantle of crops that normally blanketed the hillsides. Yet again, the farmers of the altiplano were being pushed to the edge. From what we saw driving through the back country, catastrophe was not too dramatic a word. I wondered if this would drive more farmers to the city, temporarily if not permanently. Frosts are a common, accepted element of the Aymara farmer's risky life, but this one had come at the worst time in the growing season and it clearly had hit the entire altiplano. By the time we crested the mountains between Tiahuanaco and Lakaya, the sun had melted the frozen dew. On the slopes, tiny rivulets of water were gathering momentum and particles of clay on their journeys to the flatlands below.

We found Cosme in his family's fields above the village. Most of his crops were destroyed. Only a few of his hardiest quinoa and "bitter" potato plants had survived the hard frost. Like most Aymara farmers, Cosme spread the risk of crop failure by cultivating a variety of plants in different plots scattered across the face of the mountain. This was his only defense against total disaster. Now he was in his fields, salvaging as much of the harvest as he could. He and his family were collecting the immature tubers from the affected plants. Some of the quinoa still looked promising. A few scattered plots seemed relatively untouched by the frost. These turned out to be planted with *rucki,* probably one of the most frost-resistant potatoes in the world. Despite these small successes, after gazing about I guessed that Cosme had lost well over three-quarters of the food crops on his fields. His neighbors had done no better.

We commiserated with him, informing him that the disaster was shared by his compatriots in the Tiahuanaco Valley; in fact, the situation was worse away from the moderating, microclimatic effects of Lake Titicaca. Still, this was cold comfort to Cosme.

We stared off towards the raised fields. To my surprise, they looked no different than on the day of Candelaria: rich, blue-green patches, starkly visible against the surrounding dry pastures. Of course, at this distance, it would be impossible to assess frost damage at a glance. We set off to find Anacleto and Tomas.

As we walked across the pampas towards the raised fields, Anacleto came running up. He had been drinking, and although not drunk yet, he was well on his way. He was voluble, almost shouting:

"Doctor, Ingeniero Oswaldo, you must see this. Early this morning, after the frost, I came down here with my cattle. I saw a mist covering the suka kollus. I could barely see the plants. And when I walked into the fields, everything was green! The frost didn't damage the potatoes."

We had no idea what this "mist" that Anacleto was talking about was. He wasn't making much sense. We must have looked skeptical or confused to Anacleto. He continued rapidly:

"Look, look see for yourselves. The potatoes are fine."

We had come up to the edge of the restored raised fields. Just as Anacleto had said, the plants didn't seem to be damaged at all, at least along the canal borders. We spent the next couple of hours walking among the fields, astonished. The temperature had risen so much during the day that I removed my down jacket, and still I was sweating. I contemplated taking off my sweater. To see us walking through the barley in shirtsleeves, no one could have imagined that we had just experienced one of the coldest nights on the altiplano in the past few years. Birds and insects flew about, and the crops retained a healthy, emerald green cast. Everything looked normal.

There was damage of course. No cultivated plant could ever escape unscathed from those freezing conditions. Some of the foliage was burned by the frost; a number of quinoa seed heads were blackened; and all of the corn plants that we had planted in a burst of experimental enthusiasm had keeled over dead. But the overall crop loss looked amazingly low.

Oswaldo and I were ecstatic. The raised fields had performed exactly as advertised. Even Oswaldo's enthusiastic claims seemed modest now. We had our first empirical confirmation that the raised fields actually did conserve heat just as we had suspected they would. Although we had constructed a computer model of the thermal properties of raised fields based on our archaeological data, until we had restored the fields to full function, our conclusions about heat conservation remained in the realm of speculation.[2] We knew from our measurements of temperatures in the canals and field platforms that substantial heat was being absorbed during the day, and that this heat was radiating back out into the air or being drawn into the field platforms. Our measurements showed that at night, ambient temperatures in the raised fields rose two to three degrees centigrade on average. This proved solar heat was being conserved in the raised fields. But what we didn't know was if this solar-heating effect was of sufficient intensity and duration to combat the impact of a hard freeze. Now, we knew: The answer was a resounding yes!

The frost that year was an unmitigated disaster for the people of the high plateau. But, for us, it became the proverbial blessing in disguise. Within a matter of days, word had spread among surrounding communities that the crops on the raised fields had survived the hard freeze when most others on the hill slopes did not. People walked in from distant villages to see for themselves. We were ready. We took representatives of communities on guided tours of the fields, and invited them back to witness the harvest. By a random twist of fate, we had stumbled into a gold mine of positive publicity. The raised fields began to sell themselves to the farmers of the high plateau. After the harvest on Lakaya's fields that year, community interest in restoring raised fields jumped tenfold.

Six weeks after the terrible frosts of late February, we were back in Lakaya for the harvest. During the days of harvest on the raised fields, spirits were high, although throughout most of the altiplano the mood was overwhelmingly gloomy: most everyone else experienced catastrophic crop losses on their traditional fields. The bare statistics that we gathered in Lakaya tells the tale of two harvests. Losses on the dry-farmed, hill slope fields in Lakaya ranged from seventy to ninety percent of the crop; in many instances, the entire crop in individual farmer's plots was lost to the frost. In vivid contrast, frost damage on our raised fields averaged ten to twelve percent, and most of this was superficial. The frost affected the foliage of potato plants, but did not damage the edible tubers.

The difference in yields was even more astonishing. That year the traditional dry-farmed agricultural fields of Lakaya gave their cultivators an average return of 1.5 metric tons of potatoes per hectare (2.5 acres). Several individual farmers were wiped out completely: they were forced to plow their stunted, blackened plants back into the earth. But on the raised fields, the story was different.

I remember well the first day of harvest. Cosme, mattock in hand, led the extended Uruchi clan in digging out the now mature tubers. To repeated shouts of delight, they pulled potato after potato from the earth. Oswaldo and I got caught up in the collective excitement. I began to count the number of tubers from individual potato plants. Normally, farmers are happy to extract ten or twelve from a single plant. Repeatedly, I counted twenty, thirty, thirty-five. Even in the aftermath of the deadly frost, we were harvesting an unprecedented number of mature, glorious potatoes.

Everyone wore looks of total astonishment—even Oswaldo, who had so blithely predicted success. In the end, the potato yields on the raised fields averaged over fifteen metric tons per hectare, ten times the yield on the traditional, dry-farmed fields, and all without the use of fertilizers or pesticides. Some individual plots of land gave as much as twenty-seven metric tons of potatoes. All of the other crops we planted in Lakaya that first year performed just as well as the potatoes. Winter wheat, barley, oats, beans, onions, carrots, and even lettuce weathered the frost and yielded bumper crops. The amazed expressions on the faces of our raised-field farmers were priceless.

Apart from potatoes, we also achieved an astonishing harvest of information with our success in Lakaya. Now we had real data to incorporate into our estimates of the potential productivity of Tiahuanaco's ancient agricultural landscape. We now had the solution to the perennial question of how Tiahuanaco's magnificent cities were supported in such an apparently unpromising environment as the Andean high plateau.

The notion that Tiahuanaco could be nothing more than a particularly impressive ceremonial center was deeply embedded in the minds of countless foreign-born explorers and scholars of the region since the eighteenth century. In 1877, the indefatigable explorer and naturalist George Ephraim Squier published an epochal monograph on the Andes titled *Peru: Incidents of Travel and Explorations in the Land of the Incas.* In this monograph, Squier describes a brief sojourn in the ruins of Tiahuanaco in which he concluded that:

> We find nowhere in the vicinity [of Tiahuanaco] any decided traces of ancient habitations, such as abound elsewhere in Peru, in connection with most public edifices . . . This is not, prima facie, a region for nurturing or sustaining a large population and certainly not one wherein we should expect to find a capital. Tiahuanaco may have been a sacred spot or a shrine, the position of which was determined by accident, an augury, or a dream, but I can hardly believe that it was a seat of dominion.[3]

Squier's comments are fascinating. They represent one of the first expressions of the notion that Tiahuanaco's environmental setting was inherently inhospitable and unproductive and, therefore, ultimately responsible for the presumed lack of cities and civilization on the high plateau. Based on his superficial, impressionistic conclusions about the intractability of the environment, Squier concluded that the site itself never attained true urban proportions, or importance as "a seat of dominion." Squier's interpretation remains a strong theme in the interpretations of some contemporary archaeologists and historians.

We now know that these interpretations are entirely mistaken. Our experiments in restoring the raised fields have removed all doubt. The enormous landscape of raised fields developed by Tiahuanaco were unquestionably productive enough to support dense, concentrated human populations. Our experiments, in effect, have rewritten the Aymara's ancient history; a fundamental misunderstanding of that culture's civilization, expressed by Squier in the nineteenth century, is now corrected. The critical historical issue of how the ancient people of Tiahuanaco generated a sufficient food supply to support their cosmopolitan culture is now resolved.

But, even more, because of these experiments, we now also understand the underlying historical causes of the stark contrast between ancient abundance and modern impoverishment in the high plateaus around Tiahuanaco. With the disappearance of raised-field technology prior to the Spanish colonization of the Andean world, and the subsequent biological and cultural disaster of Indian contact with Europeans, the high plateau spiraled into unremitting decline. Today, it is a marginal environment—even though, in ecological terms, it is not inherently so. From rich, surplus-producing agricultural estates one thousand years ago, the altiplano has been reduced to a forbidding, frost- and drought-plagued landscape barely able to support subsistence farming at the most rudimentary levels. It is not terribly surprising that large-scale agricultural development (and agricultural developers) supported by international agencies have bypassed this once-rich environment for the more seductive tropical lands of the Amazonian floodplains. There, deforestation continues apace to support megadevelopment schemes employing familiar agricultural technology adopted from the Western world.

I wish that representatives of the international development community could have experienced the excitement of Lakaya's first harvest on its restored raised fields. Embedded notions about the altiplano's environmental and cultural marginality might have been exploded in an instant. If they had seen nearly one hundred people gathering in an unexpected harvest in the teeth of a killing frost, the possibilities for restoring the high plateau to productivity by reclaiming an ancient technology might seem more than romantic agrarian populism. If they talked to Cosme, mattock in hand, pulling potatoes from his fields, they might have understood that technical skill and ecological sophistication are not the monopoly of the modern world.

Underneath the surface of the indigenous world, and not always completely hidden or too deep, we can still tap enormous reservoirs of knowledge, fonts of priceless environmental wisdom, if we only approach that world with a genuine sense of openness and humility. If we could grasp time and reality as some of the Aymara do—if, for us, the reality of past and present was a seamless whole—we might be able to more fully appreciate the intimate connectedness of humans and their environment. We might see more clearly the long-term consequences of our actions on the fragile vessel we all inhabit. We might even discover new, unexpected paths to a sustainable future.

7

The Past Is Prologue

L IKE their ancestors, the Aymara perceive the world as a
complex skein of reciprocal relations. A dynamic balance between oneself and one's fellow humans and
between oneself and the natural world is the ideal. Work
invested in helping to raise someone's house or to harvest
their fields is exchanged for an equivalent value down the
line. Equal work for equal reward. And so it is with the living,
natural world. If you wish to reap a harvest from Pachamama,
from Lady Earth, you must feed her with the fruits of your
labor when she is depleted. If you wish for the fertilizing
rains from Lord Sky, you must make a proper pilgrimage to
offer sacrifice at the shrines high in the mountains.

Unlike Western concepts that humans must assert definitive control over their environment to assure their survival,
the Aymara and their ancestors developed a different operat-
ing principle: Human survival can be assured only by foster-
ing and sustaining a relationship of mutual respect and
exchange. The indigenous peoples of the Andes attribute to
the environment an animate character; the earth and the natural elements can be cajoled, bribed, and persuaded to help
sustain life. Life itself is an endless cycle of exchange punctu-

261

ated by personal effort and hard-won reward. In the world of the Aymara, one can never get something for nothing: to give one must receive, to receive one must give. This grasp of the intimate, interconnected natures of humans with each other and with their environment is not unique to the Aymara. The ethical imperative to preserve a kind of equivalent exchange of work and value in one's relationships can be found in other societies as well. But the Aymara, and the Andean peoples in general, have made the philosophy and practice of reciprocity the principal political and religious grounds of their social life. Reciprocity in perception, thought, and action structured the ancient Andean world, and, to a certain degree, still guides and transforms human relationships among the indigenous peoples of the Andes.

This is not to say that there is no inequality and injustice in their world, or that these social evils were only imposed by powerful outsiders from the time of the Spanish conquest until today. Injustice, inequality, cruelty, and greed seem universal in human society; they can emerge just as readily in a world where perfect reciprocity is the professed cultural ideal as in the dog-eat-dog world of perfect competition. Native politics in the court societies of the ancient Andes was as Machiavellian as that of Renaissance Europe. Intrigue, deception, nepotism, social climbing, accumulation of extraordinary wealth, savage warfare, domination—all were familiar elements in the lives of the ancient Andeans. After all, the direct ancestors of the Aymara, the people of Tiahuanaco, created one of the largest empires in the Western Hemisphere, and empires are never built on gentle persuasion alone.

The Aymara and their ancestors never lived in a Golden Age of Harmony with the earth. This is as much a myth as the notion that Western civilization is uniquely capable of environmental degradation on a large scale. Native American religious philosophy may emphasize and advocate harmony with the land, but this emphasis does not necessarily translate into real-life, on-the-ground effects. The equation of a

uniquely benign "Indian" philosophy with actions that conserved the environment, as if Native Americans were born
altruistic stewards of the land, was formulated by nineteenth-
century romantics, not by the Native Americans themselves.
This psychologically pleasing notion is nothing other than
what the cultural geographer William Denevan felicitously
called the "pristine myth." As Denevan comments:

> The Admiral [Columbus] himself spoke of a Terrestrial
> Paradise, beautiful and green and fertile, teeming with
> birds, with naked people living there whom he called
> Indians. But was the landscape encountered in the six-
> teenth century primarily pristine, virgin, a wilderness,
> nearly empty of people, or was it a humanized landscape,
> with the imprint of native Americans being dramatic and
> persistent? The former still seems to be the more com-
> mon view, but the latter may be more accurate.[1]

As Denevan acerbically remarks, Native American impact on
the natural environment was neither localized or ephemeral,

> nor were resources always used in a sound ecological
> way. The concern here is with the form and magnitude
> of environmental modification rather than with whether
> or not Indians lived in harmony with nature with sus-
> tainable systems of resource management. Sometimes
> they did; sometimes they didn't. What they did was to
> change their landscape nearly everywhere, not to the
> extent of post-Colonial Europeans but in important
> ways that merit attention.[2]

The advent of intensive agriculture and city life throughout the preindustrial world produced the technological and
demographic conditions that induced long-term, transformative changes in local physical environments. Irrigated agriculture, even when managed well, frequently resulted in hyper-
salinization of soils that caused serious problems for ancient
societies which relied on dependable agricultural production

for their economic well-being. The civilizations of southern Mesopotamia and the Indus Valley are perfect examples of societies that generated some of the conditions of their own decline, through intensification of irrigation systems to the point at which soil salinization became irreversible, permanently damaging the arable land that was the fundamental source of their food supply. The preindustrial Maya civilization of Central America radically altered their rain-forest environment through construction of massive agricultural systems and intense episodes of city building and urban renewal. The famous collapse of Maya civilization around A.D. 900 may be attributed, at least in part, to humanly induced alteration of a fragile tropical forest environment.[3]

Similarly, the ancestors of the contemporary Aymara Indians transformed their environment in significant ways, and in both positive and negative directions. They reshaped entire mountains by constructing massive, stepped agricultural terraces. They reclaimed vast swamplands by inventing new agricultural technologies to control and manipulate water at will. They deforested entire hillsides to power their craft-based industries.

The empire of Tiahuanaco disappeared one thousand years ago, but its descendants still till the same land and worship the same spirits of the earth and the sky. The Aymara share a glorious past, overshadowed by an uncertain future. They go about the business of their lives unrecognized outside of their homeland, well below the jaded threshold of world attention. Even in the sacred land of their ancestors, they mostly walk unnoticed.

If the Aymara villages of the Bolivian altiplano appear backward and inexorably locked into the agricultural cycle of the seasons, that is the tourist's view. Although desperately impoverished, inside these communities the Aymara people lead lives of great aspiration. They are eager for opportunities. Five hundred years of domination, ameliorated only in part by the social revolution of 1952, has left these villages in chronic poverty. Bolivia's fragile national economy has offered few genuine options for permanently improving their lot.

Neocolonialist attitudes still permeate the power structure of national society, and the shared perception of the Aymara among the elite is that of a marginal people inhabiting a marginal landscape. There is a serious problem of perception regarding both the environment and the indigenous communities inhabiting that environment, a kind of cognitive gap that intensifies and aggravates the already enormous social distance between Indian and non-Indian.

In Bolivia, Western-trained agronomists and other development specialists routinely perceive the altiplano as a marginal environment. They describe the altiplano as possessing "soil unfit for agriculture, suitable only for extensive and temporary grazing."[4] The overwhelming majority of large-scale agricultural development projects operate in tropical and subtropical environments far from the extensive arid plains of the high plateau. Even eliminating the abnormal geographic clustering of development projects in Bolivia in these tropical zones, induced by the international obsession with the coca-cocaine problem, it is clear that the common environmental perception of the Andean altiplano is one shaped by superficial understanding of its high local variability and underlying potentials. This distorted image has substantially and negatively affected economic investment in the altiplano.

Yet what these agronomists and development specialists are perceiving of the altiplano environment is, in fact, a historical artifact. Their vision is not deeply retrospective, but rather a shallow one, focusing on the present and the near past, perhaps at best the last three or four decades. They see a recent history of underutilization of the altiplano that they assume stems from inherent environmental limitations. They have not yet fully appreciated that the more relevant determinants of underutilization are social, historical, and economic in nature. Catastrophic demographic collapse, internal migration driven by national and international economic forces, and the loss of traditional cultural practices are the more germane factors explaining recent underutilization of the altiplano's natural resources. The environmental image constructed by the development specialists still remains uninformed by long-term historical and cultural perspectives on human use and realization of the altiplano ecosystem's potentials. As one French agronomer noted recently:

> Frequent assertions about the impossibility of improving agriculture on the Altiplano arise from the confusion between the physical and biological *potential* of the environment and its realization which is largely influenced by history and the functioning of societies. If tens of thousands of hectares of pre-Columbian ridge backs [raised fields] and terraces have been abandoned, is this because of climatic changes or because of a change in social organization and finalities . . . How, in fact, can a plain covered with the remains of ridge backs constructed for agriculture . . . be classed as "soil unfit for agriculture, suitable only for extensive and temporary grazing"? Either this provides an alibi to those who are profiting from the present situation, or one must generalize the case . . . of travelers who based all their conclusions on a sojourn on the Altiplano in the dry season.[5]

These acid comments rightly emphasize the need to understand the full-range of environmental potentials in the altiplano as these have been acted upon and developed in the ancient past.

At various historical conjunctures, the altiplano has been underutilized to varying degrees and for different reasons. Prior to 1500 B.C., the Lake Titicaca basin was environmentally unsuitable for large-scale, concentrated human populations. My research team's paleoenvironmental evidence shows that there was simply too little available water to support intensive farming. After the early sixteenth century European colonization, the altiplano was marginalized economically and organizationally; its current underutilization is the product of complex social forces, not natural or climatic ones. Between these two poles of pervasive underutilization, one environmentally and the other socially determined, the altiplano experienced episodes of intense natural resource development occasioned by the emergence and expansion of complex human societies such as Tiahuanaco.

But the project to restore raised fields to production demonstrates unequivocally that the altiplano is not inherently a marginal environment for agricultural development. We have discovered a simple fact: There is no environmental reason why the altiplano should not bloom again. With the proper technology, the high plateau—particularly the region around Lake Titicaca—has the potential for producing tremendous quantities of subsistence and cash crops. Bolivia currently imports a substantial proportion of its wheat, principally in the form of food aid programs supported by U.S. taxpayers. On the local scene, this aid frequently materializes as food-for-work projects—a system that binds Bolivia's native peoples into chronic forms of dependence. But even in the absence of an export economy, by our projections the altiplano with raised-field technology is capable of producing enough wheat to supply Bolivia's entire internal market. Again, this is the purely technological dimension; that is what the altiplano could produce, absent supervening social and economic forces such as internal market competition, foreign policy decisions, or other such external factors. In other words, from the perspective of production alone, we can envision an import substitution process that could provide employment and an assured income stream for small landholders in the rural reaches of the altiplano. Such a process might help slow the now staggering rates of internal migration within Bolivia from fields to cities and from the legitimate economy into the clandestine coca-cocaine economy. But, of course, it is precisely the supervening social and economic realities of contemporary altiplano life that remain at the core of the underdevelopment problem.

Most large-scale efforts mounted by international agencies to combat chronic poverty display a profound ignorance of local social realities. You cannot travel in the rural reaches of Bolivia and other Third World countries without passing through a depressing landscape of ill-conceived monuments to "big development" projects glittering in the sun: tractors in various stages of disrepair, dams no longer used, decaying pumping stations, contaminated watersheds, and fields silted over and suffering the effects of extreme salinization. Most of these projects were imposed upon the local populations, transported from a radically different social reality. The strategic choice by these international development agencies to focus on large-scale projects rather than on the individual needs of people and their villages have left the altiplano Aymara stranded in an increasingly impoverished landscape.

What we must understand is that in rural communities like that of the Aymara, agriculture remains a primary activity that not only provides the communities with food, but also provides its social life and perpetuates core cultural values. Understanding the social significance of such core values should be of deep concern to development specialists, not as a means of preserving the status quo (this, of course, would be a quixotic and undesirable goal in any event), but as a strategic instrument for designing and managing positive change in economic activities in a manner that will not destroy the unique qualities and individual strengths of these indigenous communities. Fifty years ago the great cultural geographer Carl Sauer questioned the efficacy of rapid technological modernization in indigenous societies, arguing instead that any program of change in rural communities should evolve gradually and incrementally build on the ground of traditional knowledge, both preserving local cultural diversity and drawing on local skills.

But that task is not easy. It requires persistence, and a willingness to explore and understand the complex web of local and cultural histories and the personal relationships that ground and motivate people. As Oswaldo and I discovered, this can be a risky proposition because, more than anything, it demands that one involve oneself in the messy realities of local politics. Still, after years of living on the high plateau, sharing food and life with the Aymara, I finally understood that the agricultural fields of communities such as Lakaya produce meaning, identity, and intense personal satisfaction as much as they produce potatoes. As they sustain the body, these fields of the Aymara nourish the spirit. Fields and spirit become one. Much of this I learned from participating in the ordinary life of the altiplano. My experiences of their ceremonies, festivals, and rituals inexorably shaped my perception of the Aymara vision of the world.

I last spoke with Cosme Uruchi in Lakaya on the Feast of All Saints' in November of 1990. Cosme had invited me to share a meal with his family in their compound of several small thatched and tin-roofed houses, as they celebrated the beginning of a new agricultural season. The Uruchi clan had expanded the area they cultivated in restored raised fields to nearly 25 acres. Now the cycle of planting had come round again.

The first two days of November are a poignant, sacred time in the high plateau. These are the ritually charged days of All Saints' and All Souls'. One day merges seamlessly into the other, as Indian families gather to welcome the souls of the dead who come to visit and to feast with the living. I was flattered but apprehensive about Cosme's invitation to share this intimate time with his family. Although inscribed in the Roman Catholic calendar, for the Aymara, the Feast of All Saints'/All Souls' holds an essential communal meaning and a psychological impact alien to the modern (if not to the ancient) incarnation of the Catholic Church. In one dimension, the Feast is a pagan festival of spring, commemorating the initiation of the yearly cycle of agricultural work, ritually marking the coming of the rains. At this time, too, the souls of the recent dead are dispatched on their journey from the netherworld to the world inhabited by the community of ancestors who watch over and protect the living. Ancestors become the emotional touchstone of these two remarkable days.

How can I evoke a sense of the almost painfully intimate connections that the Aymara feel for their dead? Skulls and bones are much in evidence, not as feared icons, but as revered essences of the departed—the long chain of remembered ancestors linking the living to the volatile spirits of the land and the sky. The French anthropologist Nathan Wachtel's meditation on his experience of All Saints'/All Souls' Day in the remote altiplano village of Chipaya eloquently captures elements of the emotional depth and urgency of the day:

> As All Saints' approaches, the waiting becomes particularly intense: the deceased come up more and more frequently in conversation; their souls are already gathered on the outskirts of the cemetery, waiting to visit. By noon on November 1, when the families deposit their offerings of food and drink on the tombs, you can feel a change occur: the souls are here, their presence almost palpable. The ritual has changed somewhat: in the past the bells rang continuously for more than twenty-four hours, so that the souls' visit took place against a backdrop of monotonous, repetitive music; now the bells sound only intermittently, briefly, like a call or salutation. The skulls of the founding ancestors are no longer transported to the church, but merely honored at the cemetery. The four skulls are lined up in the middle of the central row, facing south. The *alcaldes* and their wives kneel before them and pray, offering coca leaves and scattering generous offerings of alcohol. Their families form a circle around them. Cigarettes are affectionately lit for the ancestors to smoke. What a strange and intimate scene: the revered skulls with two or three burning cigarettes lodged in their nasal cavities. The cigarettes are smoked "by themselves," and this is seen as a good sign: when they burn easily to the end, the next year will be a good one, the harvest will be plentiful . . . The members of the family sit in a semicircle, passing cups of

270

liquor and remembering the deceased: stories and anec-
dotes are blended with tears and loud lamentations . . .
They sit with the souls all night, from the first to the second of November.[6]

Throughout the night of November 1 and into early
morning, I sat in flickering candlelight with the souls of the
Uruchi. Cosme was my guide, describing in graphic detail the
character and life of his ancestors. Every member of the family with memories of the dead contributed personal anec-
dotes, mostly, at first with great humor, recounting their
foibles and misadventures in life. In the course of the night,
as we drank and the litany of the dead come back to life continued, the family grew sentimental. Mirth became melancholy. Tears welled up in their eyes and streamed in glistening
rivulets down their cheeks. Liqour loosened their tongues.
Emotions ran raw, although, strangely enough, I didn't feel
threatened by the alcohol-induced hostility that always
seemed to hover ominously around such gatherings. Once
during the night, a drunkard, one of Cosme's nephews I
think, loudly attacked me, threatening to whip me on the
spot and demanding that I be thrown out into the night. He
was gently bundled up and taken out into the courtyard
where he fell into a stupor, rousing himself from time to time
to cry out angrily at the moon. Cosme asked for my forgive-
ness. Feeling like an intruder, I asked him for mine. But the
incident was not repeated.

I will never forget that night, and the long, mannered
sequence of libations we shared with the dead. Cosme had
taken me down an intimate path of memory, permitting me
to witness the souls of his ancestors. On the morning of All
Souls', I accompanied Cosme to the adobe-walled cemetery
high on the hill. There, on the bleak slope, we dispatched our
final ch'allas to the dead. They returned peacefully to their
own reality replete with our offerings. Passing through the
cemetery gate, a sudden peal of thunder broke our reverie,
shocking us back to the land of the living. Lightning irrupted

in the gray distance across the frozen peaks of the Cordillera. Roiling masses of thunderheads raced across the plains. A chill wind rose, swirling dust into our eyes. The ancestors had responded; the rains were coming.

On the shores of Lake Titicaca below, we could see the freshly turned brown earth of Lakaya's restored raised fields. The canals were not yet completely filled. Plumes of dry earth undulated across the fields, dancing to the horizon. I remarked to Cosme just how amazed I was that those newly planted fields, which appeared so barren now, would soon harbor a rich green overabundance of life. He said simply:

"Doctor, this will be a good year; all the signs are good, and we will have success with the suka kollus again. Next year we will expand them even more. We will have a better future here, don't you see?"

In those words, my own once-naive enthusiasm and faith echoed back to me. More than once I had pangs of doubt about our efforts to restore the raised fields. Did it stem from a quixotic denial of modern technologies? Was our intense commitment to an ancient technology, an ancient way of thought, nothing more than romanticism, as some critics so acidly claimed? Looking back at Cosme over the fields he and his family had restored to life, for the moment I dismissed all doubts from my mind.

I left Cosme to complete the festival of All Souls'. I had to leave for La Paz on the first leg of my trip back home to Chicago. I wanted to get an early start back to the city before drunks began lurching along the road. On the Day of All Souls', this would likely happen by noon. I intended to return to Lakaya for the harvest five months later, to celebrate again with Cosme and his family—both the living and the dead. I waved to Cosme as I backed out of his compound. He smiled and wished me God's speed on my journey. The last thing he said to me was, "We know you'll come back, Doctor. We know you always have."

And so I did. But Cosme never saw the harvest; that year his soul made the journey to the land of the ancestors. Oswaldo called to tell me of his death—from old age, I'm sure, although he still seemed so vital when I saw him last. We made plans for a small memorial service that would mix Aymara and Western styles of memory and grief. When I returned to Lakaya, I made a pilgrimage of my own to his grave site, marked by a small, already crumbling cement vault and a crudely painted wooden cross. I greeted Cosme and poured my offering of alcohol across the burial vault. Then, bending down, I laid a handful of shining green coca leaves beside his grave.

I am sure Cosme would have been pleased to learn that his prediction came true: it was a good harvest for the people of the altiplano, and an excellent one for Lakaya's raised fields. In almost all of the communities experimenting with raised fields that year, yields routinely passed eighteen metric tons of potatoes per hectare. In 1991, in the fourth year after our experiment with restoring raised fields began, Tiahuanaco's ancient agricultural technology once again became a permanent fixture of the landscape.

Since that first roller-coaster year in 1986, we have worked continuously with the people of Lakaya. Our program to rehabilitate raised-fields has expanded throughout the old heartland of the Tiahuanaco empire. Many other communities have begun their own raised-field restorations. Word of mouth and the visual impact of abundant harvests have done much to stimulate the adoption of the ancient technology. As I write these words, Oswaldo and I are working with over sixty communities in the high plateaus around Lake Titicaca. Several hundred Aymara farmers have adopted the agricultural techniques pioneered by their ancestors over two thousand years ago.

Much remains to be done. The difficult, often deeply frustrating struggle to develop new sources of income, to craft alternative ways of making a living in concert with the indigenous people of the high plateau, goes on. We have had constant setbacks and some success. But I retain a poignant, vivid memory that always revives my spirit:

I can still see Cosme, dressed in his striped, oxblood poncho, standing barefoot in a muddy and improbably green raised field with the wet cuffs of his twill pants rolled to his shins. He stares in amazement at row after unexpected row of leafy lettuce with heads as big as his own. In the background, the barren, salt-encrusted pastures of the high plateau stretch down to the shores of Lake Titicaca.

What is revealed in this image? I, at least, see the painful contrast of an ancient affluence set against a bitter landscape of modern poverty. But I also perceive the glimmerings of a once and future paradise.

Notes

Chapter 1: Into the Aymara World

1. Alfred Metreaux, *The History of the Incas* (New York: Pantheon Books, 1969), pp. 169–170.
2. Harry Tschopik Jr., "The Aymara," in *Handbook of South American Indians*, vol. 2, ed. J. Steward (Washington, D.C.: Bureau of American Ethnology 143, 1946), pp. 501–573.
3. Arthur Posnansky, *Tihuanacu: The Cradle of American Man*, vol. I-II (New York: J. J. Agustin Publishers, 1945), p. 33.
4. See, for instance, Adolf Bandelier, *The Islands of Titicaca and Koati* (New York: The Hispanic Society of America, 1910); Weston La Barre, *The Aymara Indians of the Lake Titicaca Plateau, Bolivia* (Washington, D.C.: Memoirs of the American Anthropological Association, no. 68, 1948); and Rigoberto Paredes, *Mitos, supersticiones y supervivencias populares de Bolivia* (La Paz, Bolivia: Arno Hermanos, 1936).
5. Stephen Toulmin, *Human Understanding: The Collective Use and Evolution of Concepts* (Princeton, N.J.: Princeton University Press, 1972), pp. 491, 501.
6. Toulmin, *Human Understanding*, p. 491.
7. Ibid.

Chapter 2: The Trembler on the Mountain

1. Robert Randall, "Los dos vasos: cosmovisión y politica de la embriaguez desde el incananato hasta la colonia," in *Borrachera y Memoria,* ed. Thierry Saignes (La Paz, Bolivia: Hisbol, 1993), p. 87.
2. Juan Antonio Manya, "Temible N'aqak?" in *Allpanchis,* vol. 1 (Cusco, Peru: Revista del Instituto de Pastoral Andina, 1969), p. 138.
3. Tschopik, "The Aymara," p. 567.
4. Thérèse Bouysse-Cassagne, *Lluvias y Cenizas: Dos Pachacuti en la Historia* (La Paz, Bolivia: Hisbol, 1988), pp. 92–98.
5. Luis Girault, *Rituales en las regiones Andinas de Bolivia y Peru* (La Paz, Bolivia: CERES, 1988), p. 307.

Chapter 3: Andean Genesis

1. Pedro de Cieza de León, *The Incas of Pedro de Cieza de León,* ed. V. von Hagen, trans. H. de Onis (Norman, Okla.: University of Oklahoma Press, 1959), pp. 283–284.

2. Pedro Sarmiento de Gamboa, *The Second Part of the General History Called Indica,* ed. C. Markham (London: The Hakluyt Society, 1948), pp. 198–201.

3. Antonio de la Calancha, *Crónica moralizada de la Ordén de San Agustín del Perú* (La Paz, Bolivia: Imprenta Artistica, 1939).

4. Juan de Betanzos, *Suma y Narración de los Incas,* ed. Maria del Carmen Martin Rubio (Madrid, Spain: Ediciones Atlas, 1987), pp. 11–15.

5. Crístobal de Molina, *Relación de las Fabulas y Ritos de los Incas* (Lima, Peru: San Marti y Cia, 1916).

6. Bernabé Cobo, "Del templo y edificios de Tihuanacu," in *Tihuanacu: antología de los principales escritos de los cronistas coloniales, americanistas e historiadores bolivianos,* ed. G. Otero (La Paz, Bolivia: Imprenta Artistica, 1939), p. 30.

7. Ludovico Bertonio, *Vocabulario de la Lengua Aymara* (La Paz, Bolivia: Edicion Ceres, 1984), p. 340.

8. Thierry Saignes, "En busca del poblamiento etnico de los Andes Bolivianos (Siglos XV y XVI)," *Avances de Investigacion* 3 (La Paz, Bolivia: Museo Nacional de Etnografía y Folklore, 1986).

9. Thérèse Bouysse-Cassagne, "Urco and Uma: Aymara Concepts of Space," in *Anthropological History of Andean Polities,* ed. J. Murra, N. Wachtel, and J. Revel (Cambridge, U.K.: Cambridge University Press, 1986), p. 209.

10. Tom Dillehay, *Monte Verde: A Late Pleistocene Settlement in Chile,* vol. 1 (Washington, D.C.: Smithsonian Institution Press, 1989).

11. I borrow this analogy from Michael Moseley, who uses it to make a similar point regarding the common heritage of the South American peoples in his book *The Inca and Their Ancestors* (London, U.K.: Thames and Hudson, 1992), p. 83.

12. See Jane Jacobs's, *The Economy of Cities* (New York: Vintage, 1970) for a discussion of the peculiar, vital economy of cities in the traditional world.

13. Nathan Wachtel, "Men of the Water: The Uru Problem (Sixteenth and Seventeenth Centuries)," in *Anthropological History of Andean Polities,* ed. J. Murra, N. Wachtel, and J. Revel (Cambridge, U.K.: Cambridge University Press, 1986), pp. 283–310.

14. See Sergio and Karen Chávez, "A Carved Stela from Taraco, Puno,

Peru and the Definition of an Early Style of Stone Sculpture from the Altiplano of Peru and Bolivia" (*Ñawpa Pacha* 13, 1975), pp. 45–83, for a detailed discussion of this stone sculpture. Karen Mohr Chavez defined the Yaya-Mama Religious Tradition and its association with pre-Tiahuanaco temples for the first time in her seminal article "The Significance of Chiripa in Lake Titicaca Basin Development," *Expedition,* Vol. 30, No. 3 (1988): pp. 17–26. In this article, she interprets the Yaya-Mama Religious Tradition as an important, unifying ideology in the Lake Titicaca basin linked to temples that functioned as both places of public worship and centers of commodity, and especially food storage.

15. Wendell Bennett, "Excavations in Bolivia," *Anthropological Papers of the American Museum of Natural History* 35 (New York: American Museum of Natural History, 1936): pp. 329–507.

16. Carlos Ponce Sanjinés, *Wankarani y Chiripa y su Relación con Tiwanaku* (La Paz, Bolivia: Academía Nacional de Ciencias, Publicación 25, 1970).

17. Paul Wheatley, *The Pivot of the Four Quarters: A Preliminary Enquiry into the Origins and Character of the Ancient Chinese City* (Chicago: Aldine, 1971). Wheatley cites René Berthelot's perspective in this magisterial analysis of the early Chinese city.

18. Arthur Wright, "The Cosmology of the Chinese City," in *The City in Late Imperial China,* ed. W. Skinner (Palo Alto, Calif.: Stanford University Press, 1977), p. 47.

19. Lewis Mumford, *The City in History: Its Origins, Its Transformations, and Its Prospects* (New York: Harcourt, Brace & World, Inc., 1961), p. 36.

20. Pedro de Mercado de Peñalosa, "Relacion de la Provincia de los Pacajes," in *Relaciones Geográficas de Indias, Peru,* tomo II (Madrid, Spain: Ministerio de Fomento, 1885).

21. Cieza de León, *The Incas of Pedro de Cieza de León,* p. 284.

Chapter 4: The Sacred City

1. Theodor Mommsen, *History of Rome,* 2nd ed., abr. (London: Wisdom, 1968), p. 6.

2. Cieza de León, *The Incas of Pedro de Cieza de León,* pp. 283–284.

3. Wendell Bennett, "Excavations at Tiahuanaco," *Anthropological Papers of the American Museum of Natural History* 34 (New York: American Museum of Natural History, 1934): pp. 359–494.

4. Cieza de León, *The Incas of Pedro de Cieza de León,* p. 283.

5. Johan Reinhard, "Chavin y Tiahuanaco," *Boletín de Lima* 50 (1987): pp. 29–52.

6. John Hyslop, *Inca Settlement Planning* (Austin: University of Texas Press, 1990).

7. Richard Townsend, *State and Cosmos in the Art of Tenochtitlan* (Washington, D.C.: Dumbarton Oaks Library and Research Collection, 1979); also see Wheatley, *The Pivot of the Four Quarters.*

8. John Rowe, "Urban Settlements in Ancient Peru," *Ñawpa Pacha* 1 (1963): pp. 1–27.

9. Hyslop, *Inca Settlement Planning;* also see Tom Zuidema, *Inca Civilization in Cuzco* (Austin: University of Texas Press, 1990).

10. Tom Zuidema (in press). "Llama Sacrifices and Computation: The Roots of the Inca Calendar in Huari-Tiahuanaco Culture," in *Archeoastronomy,* p. 16.

11. Zuidema, "Llama Sacrifices and Computation," p. 16.

12. Amy Oakland, *Tiwanaku Textile Style from the South Central Andes, Bolivia and North Chile* (Ph.D. diss., The University of Texas, 1987).

13. Bernabé Cobo (1653) cited in Geoffrey Conrad and Arthur Demarest, *Religion and Empire* (Cambridge, U.K.: Cambridge University Press, 1984), p. 114.

14. Bernabé Cobo, *History of the Inca Empire,* ed. and trans. R. Hamilton (Austin: The University of Texas Press, 1979), p. 125.

15. Arthur Posansky, *Tihuanacu: The Cradle of American Man* (New York: S.J. Augustin Publishers, 1945).

16. Tom Zuidema, "Llama Sacrifices and Computation," p. 16.

17. Georges Courty Créqui-Monfort, "Fouilles de la mission scientifique française à Tiahuanaco. Ses recherches archéologiques et ethnographiques en Bolivie, au Chili et dans la République Argentine," *Proceedings Internationaler Amerikanisten Kongress* 2 (1878) (Stuttgart, Germany): pp. 531–550.

18. Maurice Godelier, "Infrastructures, Societies, and History," *Current Anthropology* 19, 4 (1978): p 767.

Chapter 5: The World Turned Around

1. Michael I. Rostovtzeff, *Rome,* ed. E. Bickerman, trans. J. D. Duff (Oxford, U.K.: Oxford University Press, 1971), p. 318.

2. Ibid., p. 310.

3. See, for instance, Peter Garnsey's *Famine and Food Supply in the Graeco-Roman World* (Cambridge, U.K.: Cambridge University

Press, 1988) for a detailed consideration of the incidence of, and sociopolitical responses to, famine and food shortages in urban centers of the ancient Graeco-Roman world.

4. This passage is drawn from *The Chronicle of Joshua the Stylite* (Cambridge, U.K., 1882), cited in Garnsey, *Famine and Food Supply in the Graeco-Roman World*, pp. 3–5.

5. See Lonnie Thompson, L. Hastenrath, and B. Arnao, "Climate Ice Core Records from the Tropical Quelccaya Ice Cap," *Science* 203 (1979): pp. 1240–1243; L. Thompson, J. Bolzan, H. Brecher, P. Kruss, E. Moseley-Thompson, and K. Jezek, "Geophysical Investigations of the Tropical Quelccaya Ice Cap," *Journal of Glaciology* 28 (1982): pp. 57–68; L. Thompson, E. Moseley-Thompson, J. Bolzan, and B. Koci, "A 1500 Year Record of Tropical Precipitation Records in Ice Cores from the Quelccaya Ice Cap, Peru," *Science* 229 (1985): pp. 971–973; L. Thompson, M. Davis, E. Moseley-Thompson and K-b Liu, "Pre-Incan Agricultural Activity Recorded in Dust Layers in Two Tropical Ice Cores," *Nature* 336 (1988): pp. 763–765; and L. Thompson and E. Moseley-Thompson, "One-Half Millennium of Tropical Climate Variability as Recorded in the Stratigraphy of the Quelccaya Ice Cap, Peru," *Geophysical Union Monograph* 55 (1989).

6. The mathematically and technically inclined might wish to consult Thompson, et al., "A 1500 Year Record of Tropical Precipitation Records" for a full exposition of this mathematical model.

7. Scott Stine, "Extreme and Persistent Drought in California and Patagonia during Mediaeval Times," *Nature* 369 (1994): pp. 546–549.

8. H. H. Lamb, *Climate History and the Modern World* (London and New York: Methuen, 1982).

9. Bouysse-Cassagne, "Urco and Uma: Aymara Concepts of Space," p. 211.

10. B. Moses, *The Spanish Dependencies in South America* (New York: Harper and Brothers, 1914), p. 385.

Chapter 6: Restoration

1. Hans van den Berg, *La tierra no da así no más: los ritos agrícolas en la religión de los aymara-cristianos* (La Paz, Bolivia: Hisbol, 1990).

2. Alan Kolata and Charles Ortloff, "Thermal Analysis of Tiwanaku Raised Field Systems in the Lake Titicaca Basin of Bolivia," *Journal of Archaeological Science* 16 (1989): pp. 233–263.

3. George E. Squier. *Peru: Incidents of Travel and Exploration in the Land of the Incas* (New York: Harper Brothers, 1877), p. 30.

Chapter 7: The Past Is Prologue

1. William Denevan, "The Pristine Myth: The Landscape of the Americas in 1492," in *The Americas before and after 1492: Current Geographical Research, Annals of the Association of American Geographers* 82, no. 3 (1992): p. 369.
2. Denevan, The Pristine Myth: The Landscape of the Americas in 1492," p. 370.
3. Don Rice and Prudence Rice, "Lessons from the Maya," *Latin America Research Review* 19, no. 3 (1984): pp. 7–33.
4. Pierre Morlon, "Questions Related to Agriculture on the Peruvian Altiplano: Research Results and Hypotheses for Development, *Ecodevelopment News* 17 (1981): p. 27.
5. Morlon, "Questions Related to Agriculture on the Peruvian Altiplano," p. 27.
6. Nathan Wachtel, *Gods and Vampires: Return to Chipaya,* trans. Carol Volk (Chicago: University of Chicago Press, 1994), pp. 25–28.

Glossary

aptapi shared communal meal

achachilla mountain deity

Akapacha one of the three levels of Aymara cosmology, the world of humans

Alaxpacha one of the three levels of Aymara cosmology, the world of celestial deities/spirits/phenomena

awayo textile worn across the shoulders and back as a carrying cloth

cañawa high-protein chenopod grain adapted to high altitude, similar to quinoa

chicha fermented maize beer; also made with quinoa and cañawa

chiwchi miniature replicas of plants, animals, objects used in ritual *misa* (see below)

ch'alla ritual libation of chica, alcohol, or soft drinks

ch'uño Andean freeze-dried potatoes

ch'uwa ritual drinks of quinoa, cañawa, and other grains

curacas (or kurakas) native chiefs or lords of the Andes

haylli name for an Inca (quechua) battle song

ispallas spirits of plants, animals, animate creatures

jamp'atu toad; the toad is a symbolic mediator between earth and underworld

jilakata highest-ranking native political authority of the Aymara

juyraqowa aromatic herbaceous plant used in ritual *misa* (see below)

kharisiri (see also n'akaq and pistaco) "fat-stealer," legendary foreign vampire-like creature said to ambush, murder, and extract fat from Indians

khuchi pig

mallku native lord

Manqhapacha one of the three levels of Aymara cosmology, the underworld spirits and deities

281

misa "ritual table"; composite ritual offering that is assembled on paper and then burned. "Muxsa misa" is the type of misa called the "sweet offering."

misterios small rock candy emblems of Zodiac and other celestial phenomena used in ritual "misas" (see above)

mit'a Precolumbian Andean rotative labor tax; adopted by Spanish colonial authorities

nayra, nayrapacha eyes, the past; past time/place

Pachamama Lady Earth; female deity of the cultivated earth

Pachakuti "the world turned around," general Andean concept of world destruction and renewal

pollera colorful skirts worn by Aymara women

q'ara white-skinned foreigner

quinoa high-protein Andean grain adapted to high altitudes

qutu the Pleiades constellation

rayo lightning bolt

sajjra wiphina Aymara spirit of the frost envisioned as an old man with a long, white beard and "icy thunder bolts."

sank'ayu type of cactus used for predicting weather and crop production

suka kollu Aymara term for raised field

suka uma the canals between raised fields

taliri kind of Aymara shaman, specifically a shaman who places himself in a trance

tarwi an Andean leguminous plant adapted to high altitude

tiwi kind of fish whose motions are used to predict weather and crop production

tiwula fox; the howl of the tiwula is used to predict crop production

t'ola high-altitude shrub

waka object or place of spiritual power; often wakas become shrines

waychapanqara plant used to predict weather and crop production

yatiri Aymara shaman, diviner

Index

283